C000255764

Imperial White

Imperial White

Race, Diaspora, and the British Empire

Radhika Mohanram

University of Minnesota Press
Minneapolis / London

Chapter 4 was previously published as "White Water: Race and Oceans Down Under," *Journal of Colonialism and Colonial History* 4, no. 3 (2003); copyright The Johns Hopkins University Press; reprinted with permission of The Johns Hopkins University Press. Portions of chapter 5 previously appeared in *The Representation and Transformation of Literary Landscapes: Proceedings of the Fourth AISLI Conference*, edited by Francesco Cattani and Amanda Nadalini (Venice: Libreria Editrice Cafoscarina, 2006); reprinted with permission. Chapter 6 previously appeared in *European Journal of English Studies* 9, no. 3 (December 2005); published by Routledge / Taylor and Francis.

Copyright 2007 by the Regents of the University of Minnesota

All rights reserved. No part of this publication may be reproduced, stored in a retrieval system, or transmitted, in any form or by any means, electronic, mechanical, photocopying, recording, or otherwise, without the prior written permission of the publisher.

Published by the University of Minnesota Press
111 Third Avenue South, Suite 290
Minneapolis, MN 55401-2520
http://www.upress.umn.edu

Library of Congress Cataloging-in-Publication Data

Mohanram, Radhika.
    Imperial white : race, diaspora, and the British Empire / Radhika Mohanram.
    p.   cm.
    Includes bibliographical references and index.
    ISBN-13: 978-0-8166-4779-8 (acid-free paper)
    ISBN-10: 0-8166-4779-8 (acid-free paper)
    ISBN-13: 978-0-8166-4780-4 (pbk. : acid-free paper)
    ISBN-10: 0-8166-4780-1 (pbk. : acid-free paper)
    1. Whites—Race identity—Great Britain—History—19th century. 2. Whites—Race identity—Great Britain—Colonies—History—19th century. 3. Ethnicity—Great Britain—History—19th century. 4. Ethnicity—Great Britain—Colonies—History—19th century. 5. Sex role—Great Britain—History—19th century. 6. Sex role—Great Britain—Colonies—History—19th century.
7. Great Britain—Colonies—Race relations. I. Title.
    DA125.A1M64 2007
    305.82'10171241—dc22
                                  2007018904

Printed in the United States of America on acid-free paper

The University of Minnesota is an equal-opportunity educator and employer.

12 11 10 09 08 07   10 9 8 7 6 5 4 3 2 1

This book is for Luisa and Guido

Contents

Acknowledgments

I would like to thank the School of English, Communication, and Philosophy at Cardiff University, Wales, for granting me a sabbatical to help finish the manuscript. I am grateful to the Arts and Humanities Research Council in the United Kingdom for granting me an AHRC-funded research leave in the fall of 2004. With these two study leaves I had an entire year for sustained thinking and for completing most of this work. I would also like to thank the University of Waikato, New Zealand, which over the years has continued to support my scholarship in all sorts of ways.

I am very grateful to the University of Minnesota Press, especially Carrie Mullen, Richard Morrison, Adam Brunner, Heather Burns, Nancy Sauro, and Michele Hodgson for believing in my project and for the continued support that the Press has shown me.

A number of friends and colleagues in Australia, Greece, India, Italy, New Zealand, the United Kingdom, and the United States have read chapters or participated in conversations for sounding out ideas. I am extremely grateful to all of you for entertaining my often undeveloped ideas and for giving me feedback, asking the right questions, and making suggestions: Bill Ashcroft, Kate Belsey, Elleke Boehmer, Simon Burrows, Ralph Crane, Liz DeLoughrey, Ruth Evans, Devleena Ghosh, Helen Gilbert, Hilary Haines, Graham Huggan, Stephen Knight, Cristina

Lombardi-Diop, Maureen Lynch, Lyn McCredden, Padmini Mongia, Meenakshi Mukherjee, Makarand Paranjpe, Luisa Pèrcopo, Sarah Shieff, Angela Smith, William Spurlin, Jackie Stacey, Terry Threadgold, Helen Tiffin, Cynthia vanden Driesen, Chris Weedon, Janet Wilson, and Effie Yiannopoulou. I also want to show my gratitude to the best neighbors, Morgen Hall and Rob Kennedy, for sharing their studies and desks with me when mine were out of commission.

I particularly want to acknowledge and thank my mother, Susheela. As usual, a month before the deadline to submit this manuscript, she materialized at our home and cooked inspiring meals to keep me intellectually sharp for the duration. Does she intuit my deadlines, or do I schedule them for when I know she will visit me?

Introduction:
Postcolonial, Non-Victorian Nonwhite

Of course, my writing ultimately has its autobiographical moments. One of my favorite movies of all time, Andrew Niccol's 1997 sci-fi *Gattaca,* promises that in the posthuman, "not too distant future," racial discriminations become unknown, a forgotten part of a long-past history, an inexplicable curiosity of a bygone age. In the globalized, posthuman future, men and women of all races work together. If race, class, gender, and sexuality do not function with quite the same resonance as we know them, other discriminations rush to fill the vacuum left behind in Gattaca. In the world depicted, discrimination is "down to a science": prenatal genetic intervention ensures that every child has "the best possible start in life." Those discriminated against are born of natural childbirth. In this upside-down world, where natural means genetically engineered, and those born through natural childbirth are called "invalids" and condemned to a lifetime of labor as servants (cleaning, facilitating, and being invisible), the individuated identity of Enlightenment philosophy is mediated through science: there are concert pianists with twelve fingers, the absence of myopia, and, above all, the annihilation of agency. Genetically predetermined fate is everything.

Can discrimination be "down to a science"? Surely, this is familiar to us; the calipers, cephalometers, craniometers, craniophores, and craniostats that measured and defined racial anatomy of the nineteenth century haven't faded completely from memory yet. In the world we live in post–9/11, the memory of the London bombings still raw, there is an intensification in the surveillance of and the meanings assigned to skin tones, eyes, genitals, hair, and other somatic markers of race in the discursive realm, within representation, as well as in the intervention of the state that is on the constant lookout for terrorists in the quotidian. In the name of whiteness, even superpower (and not-so-superpower) states such as the United States, the United Kingdom, and Australia have intensified their surveillance over their darker/Islamic citizens. In the name of acting upon the white man's burden, Iraq has been liberated. In the name of white fear, Islamic-looking people have been killed by mobs in places as far apart as New Zealand, Texas, and even the Stockwell tube station in London. In the name of maintaining whiteness, keeping Europe as white as possible, immigration and asylum policies are constantly being tightened. Yes, it is not a safe world in New Labour's Britain, even for someone like me, in my middle years, female, and of Hindu Indian origin, having spent my adult years in the West. Despite the fact I just do not in any way fit within the profile of terrorist, I still grin uneasily at the mounted police as I walk my dog past them in the park: I am waiting for the Althusserian "Hey, you!" Is it just my paranoia or do I have some reason to be edgy? If a Brazilian can be mistaken for an Asian terrorist in the Stockwell tube station, and then shot in the head seven times in a crowded train, am I justified in being slightly nervous?

How does whiteness signify to nonwhites who see it as a privileged signifier? How does the discourse of race converge with the politics of racism under its signification? Toni Morrison's Baby Suggs in *Beloved* exclaims, "There is no bad luck in the world but white folks."[1] For bell hooks, whiteness bespoke terror. Crossing from the black part of town to the white side of town near which her grandparents lived, she states: "I remember the fear, being scared to walk to Baba's, or grandmother's house, because we would have to pass that terrifying whiteness—those white faces on the porches staring us down with hate. Even when empty or vacant those porches seemed to say *danger,* you do not belong here, you are not safe."[2] Nonwhite academic voices rarely seem to interrogate whiteness, as if the terror that it evokes puts the brakes on any further analysis. Of the few works are Toni Morrison's *Playing in the Dark: Whiteness in the Literary Imagination,* a work that examines conceits, tropes, and metaphors and argues that blackness is the organizing principle, even in American fiction that has no black characters,[3] and Kalpana Seshadri-Crooks's *Desiring Whiteness,* a work that develops a psychoanalytic theory of the specificity of the symbolic structure of race in its similarity and distinction from other types of differences, such as those of class, gender, nationality, and sexuality.[4] There have not been many other book-length analyses of this topic by theorists or literary or cultural critics of color. Or, perhaps, one can counter this claim by saying that all literary and cultural critics of color in the West are writing about whiteness, even when they are writing about blackness.

Critics of color seldom write about whiteness as a topic, because they feel that they would unwittingly reinscribe its dominance and privilege to the detriment of other political, racial, and social identities. Thus, in writing about whiteness, they recenter rather than decenter it. Further, writing about whiteness reinscribes colonialism in that it forces the critic of color to situate herself as Other in order to write about hegemonic whiteness. It also elevates whiteness and sustains it into a bodily and social ideal. Unlike the agenda of the white colleague who, on writing about whiteness, is participating in the project of making visible the invisible and the unmarked, the critic of color is differently located. As Sara Ahmed puts it pithily: "Whiteness is only invisible for those who inhabit it. For those who don't it is hard not to see whiteness. . . . Writing about whiteness as a non-white person . . . is not writing about something that is 'outside' the structure of my ordinary experience."[5]

My interest in the topic of whiteness began after several bruising encounters with some white feminists in the early 1990s in the United States and of what I then perceived as their single-minded brutality toward black feminists, not within theoretical discourses or in their writings— they were too sophisticated for that—but in their everyday interactions. After one such encounter, which had tremendous repercussions for me at that time, I, morosely but reciprocally racist, exclaimed to a close (white, lesbian, feminist) friend, "God, how I hate white women." I was stunned to see tears welling in her eyes, even as she was silent. The moment passed. Her response cannot be explained away with any knee-jerk responses. No, I didn't feel manipulated into refocusing on her pain rather than mine. Yes, notwithstanding her feminism, she was also a racialized subject. Yes, in the racialized world of the United States, with its close calibrations of race, class, and gendered and sexual identity, she was higher than I on the food chain. Yet weren't there other ways of forming relationships? In the economy of emotions, dislocated from the social hierarchy of modernity, we were just two friends who loved each other as friends and as human beings. Just as black people have been demanding to be perceived in their heterogeneity, must we not accord at least a little thought to white heterogeneity? Don't we see and accept our friends in their complexities?

This personal instance planted in me the germ of the idea that has resulted in this book, in which, for the most part, I read whiteness from within a postcolonial frame, heterogenize it, and trace the contours of white thinking within academic and theoretical discourse. This work is a postcolonial examination of nineteenth-century Britain with a focus on its whiteness and suggests that British (imperial) culture not only shaped the colonies, but that the imperial rule of colonies shifted— and gave new meanings to—British embodiment. In concentrating on British whiteness in its cultural and historical specificity, I apply the methods of American whiteness studies scholarship onto the historical materiality of nineteenth-century British imperial culture. I also examine white diaspora, a phenomenon of the nineteenth century and a subject that often passes unmentioned within diaspora studies. In so doing, I heterogenize whiteness and racialize the relationship between the metropole and the peripheral colonies. I also examine if whiteness, like theory, can travel and, by being particularly attentive to current scholarship on gender, sexuality, race, and class, provide a rereading—and rethinking—of British imperial whiteness.

My foci initially seem not that revelatory; after all, who doesn't know that academic discourse is white? Further, the notion of individuated identity within Enlightenment thought itself ensures and bestows a heterogeneity to whiteness. In fact, this strategy of heterogenizing whiteness has elicited sharp criticism from Robyn Wiegman, who, in the well-cited "Whiteness Studies and the Paradox of Particularity," points out that "marked as the difference within whiteness, the anti-racist white subject becomes particular by asserting a political difference from its racial 'self.'"[6] Wiegman castigates whiteness studies writers on two counts. First, notwithstanding the political agenda to dismantle the hegemony of whiteness, the focus on labor history by historians such as David Roediger, Noel Ignatiev, and Theodore Allen[7] has resulted in, among other things, the recovery of "contemporary whiteness from the transcendent universalism that has been understood as its mode of productive power by providing a prewhite particularity, which gets reproduced as prewhite injury and minoritization."[8] Thus, there is a textual elision from a focus on race to that of classed or ethnic difference, and far from attesting to the complexity of racial formations, it instead re-positions whites as victims. Second, related to this elision, this strategy of heterogenizing through particularity has resulted in the usurpation of the position of racial minorities by minoritized whites (and thus an occlusion of actual racial minorities) and the writing of whiteness to be now occupying the space of the margins as well.

Wiegman's assessment of practitioners of American whiteness stud-ies is thought-provoking. I think she correctly indicates that the status of whites in present-day America powerfully influences the reading of the past. The United States, with its increasing rate of unemployment and the erosion of its economic dominance (a feature of the whole of the twentieth century) in the face of rising Asian and European econo-mies, the loss of its moral authority in the face of the Iraq war under the leadership of George W. Bush, alongside the effects of globalization and changing demographics that suggest that by the year 2050, the num-ber of U.S. whites will be overtaken by the country's nonwhite popu-lation, is at a crossroads. That status forces the United States (and other Western European nations in similar situations) to rethink its racializa-tion and the policies and practices that cohere around it. It is these shift-ing demographics and the effects of global capital that will eventually bring down white hegemony and the universalization of whiteness. The Gattaca-ization of the world will come to pass. Other discriminations will rush in to fill the vacuum left by the vacating hierarchy of races.

However, Wiegman's assessment is problematic in its own way. Just as she castigates whiteness studies scholars for the unwitting effects of their pursuit of particularity—that is, the encroachment and usurpa-tion of the margins from blacks in their scholarship—her essay too un-wittingly causes the effect of speaking for the marginalized, thus sealing the complete silencing and writing out of the racialized Other in white-ness studies. Notwithstanding that it is our physical presence that in-forms and gives meaning to white embodiment, within whiteness stud-ies there is a complete occlusion of the black subject. Notwithstanding that white embodiment could have come into inscription only within a modernity that classified people into racial hierarchies, black subjects are just absent in these works. Notwithstanding that Eurocentrism was a racialized knowledge and negotiated class and gender relations, in-forming them with the hierarchies of race, actual black bodies are miss-ing from the analysis of whiteness studies. So, in the works of Noel

Ignatiev and David Roediger, the ethnicized and minoritized whites are examined in their relationship to other whites and not to other non-white groups. Black subjects are peripheral to these analyses, but absolutely central to the *comprehension* of them. Underpinning their works is the understanding that whites can become whites only by not being blacks. Blackness functions as the residual effect, the spoor of this upward mobility within modernity. So notwithstanding Wiegman's critique of whiteness studies scholars, it is inevitable that, if the framework must preclude any focus on blacks, then ethnicized whites and working-class whites will usurp the marginal spaces normally allocated to and occupied by black subjects. Wiegman's analysis replicates the occlusions of whiteness studies scholars in that she does not proceed to pinpoint the silences in the text, though she leads up to them, and in so doing produces the effect of speaking for the racialized subjects as if we are unable to speak for ourselves.

And this tight, exclusive framework of whiteness studies is problematic for me. How do you break the back of white dominance, surely the main agenda of whiteness studies scholars, if you cannot even bear to include blacks within the parameters of the framework? This gap is particularly glaring in a recent interview of Mike Hill, one of the pioneers of whiteness studies in the United States whose writings have influenced my own scholarship. Upon being asked, "How would you understand some of the connections between whiteness and the discourse of ownership, possession and belonging, and how this connects to the denial of the sovereignty of First Nations people?" all that Hill can say is, "I've done only a little research in the area of Indigenous people *per se*. . . . To the First Nations sovereignty issue, more appropriate people than I should be invited to speak."[9] I wanted him to reread Gayatri Chakravorty Spivak's words, "Why not develop a certain degree of rage against the history that has written such an abject script for you that you are silenced?"[10] "Try to unlearn your privilege."[11] Hill's response is a little baffling, especially given the passion and eloquence with which he had responded to all the previous questions. Why does his analysis of whiteness have nothing much to do with indigenous issues? After all, the United States is a settler colony, and indigenous loss in the United States is directly related to settler gains. Or is the colonial history of the United States not important to contemporary U.S. whiteness studies, which instead use the civil rights movement as their starting point, or even, to a certain extent, the history of slavery? Indeed, the colonization of America coincides historically with the emergence of the categorization of races. The production of the white colonial in America is contingent upon both the usurpation of indigenous land and the racialization of Native Americans, African Americans, or any of the other racial minorities who participated in the history and the making of that nation. In short, why is it that ethnic studies scholarship has to be nuanced by its relationship to the study of whiteness but the reverse doesn't hold true?

I am not suggesting that American whiteness studies have little to offer me. In fact, the reverse is true in that everywhere in this book you will see the influence of historians like Theodore Allen and David Roediger and their superb and intriguing reading of the archives, which I, too, though not trained as a historian, try to emulate here. In recent years I have particularly felt the importance of excavating the sedimentation of history, which, to put in a cliché, helps you understand the present. I also feel that the glamour of theoretical frameworks seduces you into a dehistoricization of the present, as if the latter sprang fully formed out of Jove's head and as if postmodern and poststructuralist thoughts themselves are not underpinned by the history, the material and intellectual conditions that produced them. Rather, I think, there are disciplinary differences between the whiteness studies labor historians and this work. While they are firmly located in history, specifically labor history, my own training and writing have been in literary and cultural studies with an emphasis on postcolonial and feminist thought. My starting point is different, then, with black feminists and postcolonial and cultural theorists: Gayatri Spivak, bell hooks, Edward Said, and Frantz Fanon, as well as Sigmund Freud and Michel Foucault.

Furthermore, pivotal works like those by Roediger, Ignatiev, and Allen have tended to prioritize class to the detriment of race in their analysis, even though their works use the category of race to valorize class, as if the two categories were mutually exclusive. Whiteness becomes a metaphor for class mobility. Everywhere in their scholarship you can see the tight imbrication of race and class; yet this imbrication is not sustained or maintained in that there is a superseding of class mobility over race. Even though the political intent of showing the upward mobility of poor, white bodies is to underscore and to question the cultural fabrication of race, the fact remains that there is no such solution for black bodies, pinned by the materiality of their blackness in a world that insists on racialization. Even completely assimilated, we will remain black as long as the category of race is given any emphasis.

In Allen's monumental, double-volume *Invention of the White Race,* it is not until the second volume that he juxtaposes and includes, briefly, the status of Native Americans and African Americans alongside that of the Irish Americans in the racializing of America. In Ignatiev's work, even in the chapter on anti-Negro rioting, he focuses on the whitening of the immigrant Irish in the United States through the riots rather than on the African Americans who were victimized in the riots. Ignatiev's work also focuses on the working class and the Irish. The Irish become an acceptable form of blackness in the structural erasure of actual black embodiment in these texts. How would Roediger's focus have shifted had he done contrapuntal readings of the ascendancy of the whites that paralleled the lowering of African and Native Americans? Would each event have echoed the other? And if there were clear connections between the two, how would it have refocused the agenda of whiteness studies—a divesting of white hegemony? Would it focus entirely on white ethnicity or white marginality, or would it of necessity demand an analysis of the trajectories of power? Furthermore, how would their framework that excludes black embodiment resonate now in the post–9/11 world, in which the Western democracies are waging a war on terror, and all terrorists are nonwhite and the upholders of democracies are white for the most part?

In some contrast to the proliferation of whiteness studies scholarship in the United States, British scholars have been reticent about this area of research. If the starting point for the American scholars has been slavery and the Civil War, for us in Britain it is colonialism (and slavery only to a lesser extent) and its impact on contemporary multiculturalism. The United Kingdom prefers not to examine too closely its role in the slave trade, notwithstanding that it was the largest slave-trading nation and that major slave ports like Bristol and Liverpool became immensely wealthy through this business. Nor will we dwell too long on the role Britain played in developing its sugar colonies and the transportation of slaves in the Middle Passage. Britain, instead, mostly prefers to concentrate on its role of having banned the slave trade from 1807 on. With three-quarters of the people living in the world today having been affected by colonialism, it has become the less shameful and more acceptable past of the late-eighteenth to mid-twentieth centuries in Britain. British whiteness studies scholars are few and they inevitably (with one exception) maintain focus on social and cultural history and colonial legacies: Vron Ware, Catherine Hall, Richard Dyer, Robert Young, and Paul Gilroy. Genealogically, the study of whiteness in the United Kingdom is associated with white feminism in works like Vron Ware's *Beyond the Pale* and, more recently, in her work *Out of Whiteness*.[12] Included in this group is Catherine Hall's *Civilising Subjects*, in which she does a historical excavation of the role of the missionaries in the West Indies.[13] Ware and Hall's researches emphasize the contrapuntal relationship between Empire and England that shaped the white woman's identity. For them, racial and cultural differences in Britain are often played out through the figure of the white woman. Richard Dyer's very readable work *White* is unusual in that it does not focus completely on British social or racial history, but rather on the cultural representation of whiteness by whites within Western culture. His generalized treatment of whiteness, unmarked by geography, gender, and ethnicity or by the history of colonialism, makes it a homogenizing characteristic that brought diverse nationalities together. Notwithstanding his inclusion of gender and class analysis, Dyer's white bodies ultimately don't seem very nuanced. If the subversive purpose of whiteness studies is "to reveal *within* the very integuments of 'whiteness' the agonistic elements that make it the unsettled, disturbed form of authority that it is—the incommensurable 'differences' that it must surmount; the histories of trauma and terror that it must perpetrate and from which it must protect itself; the amnesia it imposes on itself; the violence it inflicts in the process of becoming, a transparent and transcendent force of authority,"[14] then Dyer's work does not quite achieve these ends. Reinscribing the histories of trauma and terror is left for Gilroy to do.[15]

The impetus for this work also comes from the fact that a number of contemporary scholars of the Victorian period, while acknowledging the presence of Britain's colonies, nevertheless sever the link between the imperial center and its colonies. Thus, a schism occurs in scholarship on the nineteenth century in that those works on Britain's imperial past that deal strictly with colonial matters on the one hand, and those that deal with domestic politics on the other, restrict themselves to an insular version of Britain with no mention of its colonies. Rather, the works explore Britain's relationship to continental Europe, as if much of their interaction with their European neighbors had not been played out in the colonies or were not over colonial holdings. Often the contrapuntal and rich relationship between domestic issues and imperial rule, between political and social crises in the colonies and its impact on metropolitan notions of the self, are left unexplored by cultural theorists and social historians of nineteenth-century Britain.

Imperial White critically examines the racial construction of Britain as white in nineteenth-century imperial culture. Is whiteness the norm, the template from which people of color are aberrations, or is whiteness a race as well? If the latter, what are its determinants? Are all white people white in similar ways? These questions are the starting points of my analysis of nineteenth-century metropolitan and colonial whiteness. In the nineteenth century, Britain was at its most expansive in terms of Empire; furthermore, it also saw the end of slavery. I focus on the nineteenth century for three reasons: First, given the ubiquity of Empire in the everyday life of nineteenth-century Britain, its engagement with the colonies produced radical shifts in its comprehension of Britishness. For instance, the dietary habits of the British changed in that era, as did tastes in clothing, fabric, decoration, choices in color, and the art influenced by orientalism. Thus, the construction of the British subject is constituted by the notion of difference and the Other. Second, the mind–body split of the Cartesian framework that informed the nineteenth-century construction of subjectivity was reproduced within comprehensions of race, in that blackness was metonymically linked to the body and whiteness to the disembodied mind: Whiteness conferred an invisibility. Within this context, it would be vital to redraw the contours of the occluded white body. Finally, the close structural relationship between gender, class, and race becomes visible by locating this work within nineteenth-century cultural history since our contemporary comprehensions of these terms originate in that era.

Taking into consideration that this century saw a proliferation of theories on racial difference, this work asks questions such as: How was the whiteness that was incorporated into Britishness in the nineteenth century connected to and constructed by the presence of Empire? How were nineteenth-century comprehensions of class distinctions marked by race science? What is the connection between class (in Britain) and race (in the colonies) or vice versa? How was whiteness incorporated into the newly configured masculinity in the mid-nineteenth century? What was the status of white femininity? Were women white? Does heterosexuality have a color? Does domestic whiteness differ from colonial whiteness? How do race and whiteness signify within psychoanalytic discourse? I explore these questions by examining literary texts, legislations, social history, and newspaper accounts of the age to provide a historically and geographically nuanced study of nineteenth-century British imperial whiteness.

Imperial White also critically examines the white diaspora that occurred in the nineteenth century. There has been a tendency to concentrate on black subjects within diaspora studies, a field that examines the effects of mass movements (either through slavery or indenture), immigration, and the displacement of people from their nations and lands. The white diasporic subject has quite often been ignored in this field of study. Such an occlusion has also resulted in the white subject's right to movement, a naturalization of their bodies, with a simultaneous marking and an excess of scrutiny of black bodies. Yet there were large movements of Europeans to non-European spaces in the years between 1820 and 1914. Fully fifty-five million Europeans (one-fifth of the population of Europe in 1820) moved to the colonies in this period. The British comprised a large proportion of this population. In fact, one can posit that notions of Britishness were shaped by its growing domination not only in Europe but the whole world. Britain's territories stretched from Canada and the Caribbean in the Western Hemisphere to India, Australia, and a good proportion of the African continent. Fully three-quarter million British women formed a surplus in the 1871 census of Britain, as three-quarter million British men were overseas in the running of the Empire. In 1947, when India attained its independence, 350,000 British men and women departed for "home." Indeed, the nineteenth century saw the spreading of whiteness all over the globe, in what Alfred Crosby calls "a Caucasian tsunami."[16] Therefore, the analysis of nineteenth-century British cultural history must take into account that Britishness was already globalized and cosmopolitan, marked by both the domestic and the imperial. This work uses the premise of interconnection to explore how the meaning of race shifts and travels in the nineteenth century within Britain and in its relationship to the colonies.

This project is divided into two parts, consisting of three chapters each, to examine whiteness in its heterogeneity. The first section examines the changing meanings of masculinity, femininity, and sexuality, respectively. I speculate that a changing awareness of themselves as white contributed to shifts in the practices and meanings of gender and sexuality among the British in the nineteenth century. I also track how the determinant of class shaped these three terms. The second section is set in three different British colonies, Australia, New Zealand, and India, to examine if whiteness can travel, if it resembles itself when it functions as an immigrant, when it is dislocated from its own autochthonous space when encountering racially different indigenous groups. This section also deals with the shape-shifting nature of whiteness, its disparate significations, and the relationship between race and class.

Equally important, a substantial number of chapters read racial formations and the unmarked comprehensions of race within theoretical texts, especially in those by Freud and Foucault. I chose these two theorists because of their influence in the academy, especially among scholars of literary and cultural studies within matters of gender, sexuality, and representation. Freud's theories, as they are read in the Anglo world, resonate with Victorian sensibility in matters of race, gender, and sexuality. Sander Gilman has suggested that Freud's theoretical framework is marked by a blackness, a metonym of Freud's Jewishness.[17] However, I think that Freud's theories are all marked by a European sensibility and a valorizing of the "civilized" and an understanding of it within the context of colonialism and the advances of anthropology. I do contrapuntal readings in all the chapters to show the interconnections between white and black embodiment. The notion of unmarked presupposes that the focus on black embodiment (or no embodiment, even) is just a cover-up, a cloaking device, for whiteness and white thinking. By providing a counterpoint, the implications of racialization become completely visible. My preference for contrapuntal readings reveals how deeply ensconced I am within postcolonial thought and how influential Said's work has been for me. It is Spivak's eclectic code-switching between Marxism, psychoanalysis, deconstruction, and feminist thought, I think, that exposes critical theory as being infused with racial thinking. Spivak's postcolonial work sets high standards for whiteness studies.

The first chapter on white masculinity redraws the contours of white British imperial bodies in the mid-nineteenth century. This chapter reads the seamless narrative that is produced when you juxtapose two events that took place in disconnected spaces and among separate races: the Sepoy Mutiny of 1857 in India and the 1857 publication of Thomas Hughes's *Tom Brown's School Days*. The first event, often termed in India as the first war of independence, was a mutiny of Indian soldiers against their British officers that lasted a year. The second event inaugurated the genre of schoolboy fiction. Though the two events are unrelated, my juxtaposition produces the faint map of the mid-nineteenth-century reconstruction of masculinity as one formed in response to the imperial needs of the nation. Notions of the liberal male were underpinned by the representation of the colonized Other as effete, excessive, unrestrained, and untrustworthy. Faced with its colonial Other in India (and later in Morant Bay in the West Indies in 1865), British masculinity forged itself as white, a racialization and masculinization promoted by schoolboy fiction.

The second chapter focuses on the racialization of white women in the nineteenth century. The questions dealt with in this chapter are: Can women accede to whiteness, given that most of the signifiers of whiteness did not pertain to them? If British masculinity was now always already white, how could you read white femininity? Were white women raced differently than white men? How did class significations work to embody women? Having suggested that signifiers such as youth, athleticism, the muscular body, and health all were metonymically linked to whiteness, I speculate in this chapter on the effects of such a signification on the meaning of white British women's embodiment. Richard Dyer's work suggests that white women epitomized a distilled form of whiteness that led to their overvaluation. I, however, approach this topic differently. By examining the material evidence of British women's lives, I suggest that their whiteness was liminal, almost temporary. Indeed, the overvaluation of white women is directly connected to their undervalued status. How would Dyer's analysis stand up to the Contagious Diseases Acts? This juxtaposition of the CD Acts next to bourgeois definitions of femininity provides an alternate meaning to white women's bodies, suggesting that they become white through a process of osmosis in their relationships with white men rather than from being intrinsically white in themselves. Indeed, an examination of the material lives of working-class women reveals the ambiguous whiteness of women. Finally, I provide a reading of Freud's "Femininity," one of the most interesting and influential theoretical texts on white women, which, though written in the early twentieth century, is predicated on an understanding of nineteenth-century women. I focus on the material politics and history that adhere to this text and show that presumptions about race are mapped onto Freud's analysis of women's bodies, which, like black bodies, were perceived as being degenerate.

Having analyzed masculinity and femininity within the framework of whiteness, and having suggested that blackness signifies a degeneracy,

I next analyze sexuality. Does heterosexuality have a color? This chapter consists of three sections. In the first part, I make a sustained analysis of the question "Does difference, predicated on the body, have a history?" I read the history of anatomical sciences, which first defined the marked body (both of race and gender) as different in the eighteenth and nineteenth centuries. In the second part of chapter 3 I analyze the unwritten text from within the context of the marked body and the history of colonialism in Foucault's landmark work, *The History of Sexuality,* a text that has revolutionized gender and sexuality studies in the academy. If the history of colonialism is reinscribed into the history of Victorian sexuality, then how can we read Foucault? In the third section of the chapter, I ask: How does the factoring in of race shift the way we read the legislations over sexuality in the Victorian Age? I look in particular at the Labouchère Amendment, a legislation passed against homosexuals in the late Victorian period, and at the Contagious Diseases Acts, both of which together have mapped the discourse of degeneracy and black behavior onto homosexuals and prostitutes. One can thus speculate that heterosexuality itself, in theoretical texts and in legislations, is raced as proper, white behavior.

Chapters 1–3 are set in the metropole and examine in great detail how nineteenth-century notions of masculinity, femininity, and sexuality incorporate notions of race and class within them. None of these terms can be extricated from the others without all of them falling apart as well. In part II, "In the South," I analyze the different significations of whiteness in the colonies. By crossing waters, the relationship between race and class becomes more—and differently—visible than they do in the metropole. These chapters explore how the concept of whiteness travels. I examine how whiteness in the colonies effaces some of the significations that occur in the metropole while creating new ones. In traveling to the colonies, white bodies experience their whiteness as marked in ways they did not at home. The dialogue generated between the two parts of the book is important, and it will show, among other things, that the price of the naturalization and universalism of white bodies is the senses of terror and loneliness that are experienced by the white subjects in the diaspora.

In chapter 4, I cross the Pacific and into the antipodes where upside-down is the right side up and birds with beaks live in the water. Nineteenth-century Australia is obsessed with seeking and finding the inland sea, and I start by asking the question "Is there a cultural meaning to water?" Gaston Bachelard's monumental *Water and Dreams* emphasizes a Freudian "oceanic feeling" of the sublime, the deep, and the indefinite. This chapter examines the trope of oceanic/water and its connection to colonialism. Within the context of the scarcity of water, the use and availability of water suggests the racializing of the individual in two ways. First, in the eighteenth and nineteenth centuries the "oceanic feeling" gave way to the ocean as being central to mercantilism, trade, and commerce. The energy of oceans, floods, and torrents became a trope for the vital and threatening power of Britain's imperial identity. Second, the trope of water is closely linked to the context of hygiene. While Norbert Elias perceives the disguising of bodily smells as part of the civilizing process, I contend that bodily smells were linked to the availability of plentiful water and the racializing of bodies. The nineteenth century tied soapsuds and the domestic use of water to make hierarchical and racial distinctions between humans. Bodily smells signified the savage in the colonies and the poor working classes at home. Water has become the detergent of smell from the nineteenth century onward. In the final section, I unpack the significance of the pursuit of water in Australian explorer journals like those of Major Thomas Mitchell, Edward John Eyre, Matthew Flinders, and Charles Sturt. Why did they pursue the theory of the inland sea in colonial Australia? How does the settler colony use the trope of water in its desire to dispossess aboriginals of their land? The inland sea becomes a trope for racial purity, white hegemony, and colonial power.

In chapter 5 I move to New Zealand and examine the wages of whiteness in the antipodes. New Zealand history complicates any simple comprehensions of race. The signing of the Treaty of Waitangi in 1840 by a number of New Zealand Maori chiefs and the British Crown inaugurated the formation of this new colony. This treaty gave equal partnership and status to Maori and white settlers alike, thus preventing, to a large extent, the anthropological discourse of development that was usually applied to indigenous people. In addition to the legal status of the treaty, the demographics of New Zealand in the 1840s—Maori outnumbering the settlers—often left the latter at the mercy and goodwill of the former. To be white in New Zealand thus bespoke a vulnerability. The concept of whiteness reveals itself to have shifting significations, meaning different things at different historical moments and geographical spaces.

Against the backdrop of the treaty I read two aspects of whiteness in New Zealand, benevolence and melancholia. How are metropolitan responsibilities linked to conquered territories? How is distant suffering within global networks of exchange and exploitation significant in the construction of whiteness? The first half of the chapter attempts to use Freud's framework of the melancholic and to map race onto melancholia. In the second half I trace the gendering of melancholia in pioneer women's texts.

In the final chapter, set in India, I read a work that is considered a cornerstone in describing British Indian embodiment: Rudyard Kipling's *Kim.* By looking at the ambiguities that cohere around Irish embodiment, I problematize yet another aspect of whiteness: its racism toward its own color. Can the intersection of Irishness and poverty still confer a whiteness in colonies of domination? Why is an Irish protagonist used as a hinge figure to join and separate the racial divide between the British and the Indians?

My work thus unwittingly follows a heterosexual model of the nuclear family: men, women, sexuality, and the Irish white child's body. The aim of this work is to deploy a postcolonial framework in which to read British cultural and social history and the phenomenon of the naturalization of white embodiment in a century that relentlessly focused and analyzed the marked body within the context of race science, which treated bodies as empirical objects. I weave historical, cultural, theoretical, and literary texts together in an effort to historicize the ways in which British expansion contributed to local and diverse productions of whiteness in the colonies, which, paradoxically, became interpolated into metropolitan discourses as universal. Ultimately, this work uses a postcolonial feminist analysis of whiteness to explore how masculinity, femininity, and sexuality were central to the maintenance of colonialism and to the shaping of black and white lives in particular historical and territorial contexts.

PART I

In the Metropole

CHAPTER 1

White Masculinity:
Playing at Rugby and the Sepoy Mutiny

May 1857 marks the narrative opening for this chapter, a date that is central to modern Indian history as it records the beginning of the Sepoy Mutiny in Meerut, India, or the Indian Mutiny, or the Great Revolt, or the First War of National Independence, as it is variously called. For one year and one month, Indian soldiers and the British fought for control over India and the subsequent unfolding/narrative of colonial history. This event inaugurated the future shape of the British Empire: it spelled the end of the East India Company's hold over India and marked its formal takeover by the British Crown. The central features of this event were the sieges of the British in Delhi, the restoration of the Emperor Bahadur Shah II to the throne, the siege at Lucknow, and the central Indian campaign by Tantia Topi and the Rani of Jhansi in 1858. In the cooler climes of Britain, 1857 also saw the publication of Thomas Hughes's *Tom Brown's School Days,* an adventure story about a British public-school boy that went into five editions in the same year. Twenty-eight thousand copies of this work had been sold by 1862, and it was the preferred reading of schoolboys even in 1908, fifty-one years later, having foreseen the birth of a whole new genre in writing: the adventure novel for schoolboys.[1] The two incidents are clearly not connected. Not only are they separated geographically, but one belongs to the world of adults and is about the "atrocities" committed by Indians on the British in India, especially their women,[2] while the other is a fictional account of life at Rugby, the famous public school run by Dr. Thomas Arnold.

Yet a connection between the two bears some teasing out, because as Jeffrey Weeks notes in *Sex, Politics, and Society,* "From the 1860s, there was a new cult of masculinity in the public schools. . . . The model of the early public school was the monastry *[sic].* The model of the later public school was definitely military."[3] Again, David Newsome suggests that the comprehension of masculinity underwent a metamorphosis in the second half of the nineteenth century: "To the early Victorian it represented a concern with a successful transition from Christian immaturity to maturity, demonstrated by earnestness, selflessness and integrity; to the late Victorian it stood for neo-Spartan virility as exemplified by stoicism, hardiness and endurance."[4] But why does the trope of the monastery get superseded by that of the military in the imagination of the 1860s in Britain? Why this shift from Christianity to neo-Spartan virility? How does this superimposition affect the construction of masculinity in the Victorian Age? Herbert Sussman contextualizes the new masculine poetics within the industrial age. Norman Vance locates the midcentury shift by drawing a picture of a hermetically sealed Britain under siege, battered by the changes it was undergoing: the reform bills of 1832 and 1857, the Chartist movement, the Napoleanic wars, the threat of French invasion in 1853, the Crimean War, and the Indian Mutiny of 1857.[5] Underlying these analyses is the presumption of Britain as enclosure, as pure identity, which has governed understandings of outside and inside, or international and national, within the political context and influenced a large number of studies of the Victorian Age in Britain. Even recent works in Victorian studies tend to analyze Britain as a place hermetically sealed, separate, distinct, and uninfluenced by outside events or other places in the constructions of its social life.[6]

Yet by midcentury, Victorian Britain was already cosmopolitan, in contact with numerous places and cultures. The span of the Victorian Age, from 1837 to 1901, was marked by tremendous changes in the day-to-day life of the British. The British Empire spanned territories from Canada and the Caribbean to parts of Africa, India, and what we now refer to as Australia and New Zealand. Its trade monopoly had not only shifted the British economy and class system, but also indelibly changed its tastes and aesthetics. As mentioned earlier, in the century between 1820 and 1920, the bulk of which fell within the years of Victoria's reign,

55 million Europeans (one-fifth of the population in Europe in 1820) moved to the colonies.[7] The 55 million were overrepresented by the British. But the white diaspora was also gendered: in the 1871 census in Britain there was a surplus of 718,566 women of marriageable age in Britain and an equal surplus of British men in the New World.[8] Further, by the mid-1800s more than 35 percent of women in their child-bearing years, between ages twenty and forty-four, were single. These statistics had a tremendous impact on identity politics in Britain; the asymmetry of gender representation resituated British women differently. For instance, in New Zealand women got the vote in 1893, three decades before they were granted suffrage in Britain. Further, the rationalization of imperialism is closely intertwined with the ideology of masculinity in mid-Victorian Britain.

In this chapter I will analyze the national and the international, the public and the private, and gender and sexuality via the trope of British masculinity. I hasten to add that my focus is not on the rewriting of history, nor on the literary analysis of a text, nor even about gender studies, but rather how the texts from the various arenas and disciplines intersected in the rewriting of British masculinity as white in the mid-nineteenth century. Further, I will trace the contours of the nodal year 1857 and the constructions of gender and sexuality that accrete to it. In short, I suggest that the curriculum at Rugby and the events in British India in 1857 are mutually interconnected. In this analysis, I will locate the year 1857 within its cultural context by reading the significance of this year contrapuntally—the way it signifies in India and its significa-tion in Britain.

Around 1857: India and Britain

I suggest that 1857 becomes a watershed year that functioned to cre-ate a new sense of white male subjectivity and culminated in a par-ticular construction of Britishness. First, the events that led to the crisis of 1857 in India: In brief, the East India Company gained a foothold in India in 1613 when it received permission from the Mughal rulers to establish a trading station. It maintained its own army, initially for the purpose of fighting against France, which also had its trading posts in India, and eventually for the sake of gaining monopoly in India. In 1765, Robert Clive secured for the company the revenue management of Bengal. Soon it extended its power by using its army to enter into alliances with local princes, which depleted their sovereignty over their own states. Britain, alarmed by the company's acquisition of power, in 1773 passed a Regulating Act and made it accountable to the Crown. In 1784, the India Act was passed, which brought the company completely under the control of the British government. In 1786, Lord Cornwallis was appointed governor–general in India, answerable to the president of the Board of Control in London. Cornwallis started the process of Europeanizing the civil service in India.

In May 1857, a number of sepoys (Indian soldiers) rose in revolt because of a rumor that the cartridges for their new Enfield rifles were greased with beef and pork fat. Beef was taboo for the Hindu soldier and pork for the Muslim, and the insistence of the British officers that they unwrap the cartridges by ripping them open with their teeth was perceived as yet another instance of the British trying to make them lose their religions. The soldiers rose in revolt and soon built a following of disaffected groups who wanted to overthrow the British yoke. Quickly, the mutiny spread to other parts of India under British control, and the latter fought for more than a year to suppress the sepoys, during which time terrible atrocities were committed by both sides. As a result of the mutiny, Queen Victoria abolished the East India Company and brought India directly under British rule in 1858. In *Ideologies of the Raj,* Thomas Metcalf underscores Victoria's insistence on religious toleration and "abstinence from interference with the customs or beliefs of the Indian people."[9]

I want to draw attention to the discourse of religious tolerance because most accounts of the mutiny highlight the use of greased cartridges as the cause of the revolt. Here, Christianity becomes associated with Western modernity, and accounts of the mutiny are premised on the intertwining of the light shed by Christianity with that of British Enlightenment. For instance, the noted historian Percival Spear's analysis suggests the inevitable clash when people embodying modernity interact with those of an old belief system. He states, "Tension was inevitable if the new world of the West was to mingle with the old."[10] Spear adds that the use of the greased cartridges was a genuine mistake, and upon realizing it, "cartridges were withdrawn, explanations were offered but the flashpoint had been reached" (141). In the most respected version of the mutiny written for lay audiences, Christopher Hibbert suggests that rumors abounded that the British were out to Christianize the Indians, and that "the widows of British soldiers killed in the Crimean War were being shipped out to India where the principal *zemindars* [landowners] would be compelled to marry them, thus ensuring that their estates would fall into Christian hands."[11] Charles Ball's 1859 account of the Indian Mutiny too glosses over possible reasons for the uprising and locates the crisis in "a suspicion of meditated interference with the inviolable immunities of [the soldiers'] faith and the privileges of their *caste.*"[12]

In these and other accounts there is a clear demarcation between the British and the Indian soldier, and the latter is constructed as superstitious, irrational, giving validity to rumor. By implication, the British are rational and place their emphasis on facts that are irrefutable. In her interpretation of mutiny history, Jenny Sharpe suggests, "By attributing the origins of rebellion to the fear of technology, colonial explanations represent the Mutiny as a war between religious fanaticism and Reason."[13] While I agree with Sharpe's suggestion that the discursive production of the Indian as superstitious was to highlight the Enlightenment reasoning of the British, I want to go a step further and suggest that the fixation on the greased-cartridges explanation within colonial historiography subordinates other possible reasons for the mutiny.

In fact, Indian historiography on the mutiny records a whole host of other reasons for the uprising that are surprisingly glossed over.[14] First, under Lord Wellesley (1798–1805), the Marquess of Hastings (1813–1823), and Lord Dalhousie (1848–1856), an aggressive policy of British domination was pursued by offering military assistance to native rulers and gaining influence over and privileges from them. Thus, influence was obtained over the dominions of Hyderabad, Oudh, and Peshwa by Lord Wellesley; war was declared against those dominions that opposed the British. The second reason was the institution of the Doctrine of Lapse by Lord Dalhousie. This doctrine decreed that rulers of independent states that were under the influence of the British could not adopt sons if they had no natural heirs, as was customary. These states were to lapse to the British instead. Thus, the British incorporated a number of semiautonomous states like Satara, Nagpur, and Jhansi. Lord Dalhousie also annexed a number of states on the grounds of misrule by the native kings/princes. In short, by the end of Lord Dalhousie's governor–generalship, just before the mutiny, the map of British India had almost reached its fullest form.

But discontent was not due to political conditions alone. The growing influence of the East India Company meant monopolies were established that disadvantaged their Indian competitors. The company's
political–military power resulted in its goods not being subject to local
tariffs or taxes. Thus, the British could undersell their goods in local
markets.[15] The company men amassed vast fortunes at the expense of
Indians. Furthermore, agrarian policies instituted by the British shifted
the balance of power in traditional Indian hierarchies in India. For instance, the Permanent Settlement introduced by Lord Cornwallis required the compulsory sale of lands of zemindars (landowners) who
defaulted on their payments.[16] In addition, all classes of Indian people
were affected by the changes in the administrative system and practices
they were unfamiliar with. Furthermore, the Charter of 1813 permitted the unrestricted entry of Christian missionaries to India. In their
zeal to promote Christianity, these missionaries reviled Hinduism and
Islam, leading Indians to believe that the British wanted all of India to
be Christianized.

Though colonial historiography records all these and myriad other
reasons for the growing unrest in the Indian population, they are
glossed over in favor of foregrounding the *spontaneity* of the 1857 mutiny. In fact, there had been a number of isolated mutinies and resis-
tances regarding pay by both British and Indian soldiers *before* 1857.
Again, the sepoys, or Indian soldiers, were disaffected by the presence
of an increased number of English subalterns in the army, for it meant
that they had no real authority in the military anymore. Power dif-
ferentials in the military were based on racial differences. As T. R. E.
Holmes notes, the native soldier "knew that he could never attain the
pay of an English subaltern, and the rank that he may attain after some
thirty years of faithful service, would not protect him from the inso-
lent dictation of an ensign fresh from England."[17] Not only did this
translate into a lack of recognition of the ability of the Indian soldier,
it had direct consequences on his finances. This general disaffection led
to various mutinies, including those at Vellore in 1806; at Barrackpur
in 1824; at Assam in 1825; in 1838 at Hyderabad and Secunderabad; in
1843 at Jabalpur by the Sixth Madras Cavalry; in 1844 at Sindh; in 1849
in the Punjab; and in 1850 at Govindgarh.[18] In fact, the earliest mutiny
by native troops occurred in 1764. In short, the 1857 Sepoy Mutiny was
neither spontaneous nor caused due to religious reasons alone, but was

rather the culmination of a series of mutinies that indicated a general disaffection at the presence of the British army in India.

LIBERAL

By constructing the Sepoy Mutiny as spontaneous and occluding these other reasons, a certain discursive construction of the British in India is implied: benign yet brave, rational, and bearing no ill will to the Indians in its aftermath. It is this particular construction of the British that is tied to the other event I cite at the beginning of this chapter, that which also occurred in 1857: the publication of *Tom Brown's School Days*. But before I examine this reconstructed masculinity, I need to read 1857 as it signified in Britain because both geographical locations are important. I do not argue that the mutiny was caused by events in Britain, but rather that events in each place changed its signification in the other and braid the two places tightly together.

From the early 1800s onward, the Evangelical movement and the Utilitarians in Britain had set the nation on the path of liberalism. While one was religious and the other secular, the trajectories of these movements were intertwined. The two movements underscored individualism, one born free of the bondage of both the priest and the aristocracy. The evangelical emphasized a salvation that came after an illumination of consciousness; the liberal believed in the rational working of law, education, and free trade that would transform the individual.[19] Further, they both believed that human nature was the same everywhere. The intertwined discourses were at the heart of the rise of the middle class, increase in free trade, and the establishment of the Liberal Party in the 1860s during William Gladstone's time, as well as the institution of colonial policies in India. This new intertwined ideology of liberalism and evangelism brought about a whole host of legislative enactments in Britain, such as the Reform Bill in 1832, which was perceived as the ultimate measure of reform; the second Reform Bill in 1867, which granted universal male suffrage in Britain; the New Poor Law in 1834; and the repeal of the Corn Laws in 1845, introduced by the conservative ministry.[20] Thomas Metcalf points out that the liberal movement itself was not partisan but rather heterogenous and diverse in Britain and included aristocratic Whigs, Tory Peelites, Radicals, and Benthamite Utilitarians among its members.[21]

Colonial historiography tends to read a continuum between the growing liberal movement in Britain and the reform in India as the desire of the civilized British to shed the light of the Enlightenment in savage spaces. Indeed, India became a "laboratory for the creation of the liberal administrative state" precisely because the uniformity of reform could be advocated in India and not in Britain, where the liberal movement was heterogenous until the 1860s.[22] However, from the 1830s onward there was a standardizing of state-sponsored education, the codifying of laws, and open competitive examinations for its bureaucracy (Indian Civil Service), where merit rather than birth determined membership in the civil service in India. Furthermore, the perception that India would benefit from British liberalism was established as early as 1818, when James Mill, in *The History of British India*, explained the "hideous state of society" as caused by the aristocrats and the priestly caste in India. It is within this context of liberalism that Macaulay's *Minutes* on Indian education (later Lord Macaulay) argued for the English language as the medium of instruction in schools and colleges to create a class who could act as "interpreters between us and the millions we govern; a class of persons Indian in blood and colour, but English in taste, in opinions, in morals, and in intellect."[23]

COLONIAL

Britain clearly wanted to construct India in its own image, as is evident in Lord Macaulay's speech on July 10, 1833. Furthermore, constructing India in its own image obviously made economic sense as well:

> On the most selfish view of the case, far better for us that the people of India were well-governed and independent of us, than ill-governed and subject to us; that they were ruled by their kings, but wearing our broadcloth, and working with our cutlery, than they were performing their salaams to English collectors and English magistrates, but were too ignorant to value, or too poor to buy English manufactures. To trade with civilized men is infinitely more profitable than to govern savages.[24]

Another way to explore the liberal British desire to remake the Indian in his own image is through the concept of metaphor. Metaphors have an assimilative property about them that permits "the use of [an] expression in other than its proper or normal sense, in some context that allows the improper or abnormal sense to be detected and appropriately transformed."[25] Within this context, an English education and the English language were meant to transform and make the Indian like the

British. But, as David Lloyd points out in "Race under Representation," metaphors do not assert complete identity between the two elements. He suggests that "metaphor is not merely the oscillation between sameness and difference, but the process of subordinating difference to identity."[26] However, the process of assimilation of the different elements contained within metaphors also demands the suppression of difference and constantly underscores that no subordinate element can be completely assimilated. The second element will always remain unequal, different. This principle of metaphorization underlies the liberal discourse in India. John Stuart Mill, the proponent of liberal values, was himself uneasily aware of the lack of equality extended to Indians and realized the essentially despotic nature of British rule in India. He stated:

> The only choice the case admits is a choice of despotisms. . . . There are, as we have already seen, conditions of society in which a vigorous despotism is in itself the best mode of government for training the people in what is specifically wanting to render them capable of a higher civilization.[27]

In "Sly Civility," Homi Bhabha comments on liberal discourse in the colonies and suggests that British authority in India was predicated on understanding that it was civility's supplement and democracy's despotic double. In this essay and in "Of Mimicry and Man," Bhabha points to liberalism functioning within an economy of metonymy (rather than metaphor) in the colonies. He suggests that it is the metonymical principle that makes the mimicking Indian menacing because of its "prodigious and strategic production of conflictual, fantastic, discriminatory 'identity effects' in the play of power, that is elusive because it hides no essence, no 'itself.'" The Indian is menacing precisely because he is hollow with no substance, a mimic man of liberal thought, but not a product of the evolution of its history.[28]

The 1857 mutiny suggests that the consequence of a liberal education was not the enlightenment of Indians, but rather the production of a menacing aspect of them, in that they also demanded autonomy for themselves. Bhabha's assertion that there is a presence of ambivalence that underpins mimicking and repetition becomes significant, in that (though English in taste, opinions, morals, and intellect) the representation of Indians also made them a grotesquely displaced image of the British, which in their very difference suggested them to be in excess of the economy of identity. Thus, the Indian who was supposed to be the replica of the British would always be a hybrid, "a problematic of colonial representation . . . that reverse[d] the effects of colonial disavowal, so that the other 'denied' knowledges enter[ed] upon the dominant discourse and estrange[d] the basis of its authority."[29] In short, the desired effect of liberal education—to create an India in its own image—gave rise to unforeseen, uncontrolled, uncontrollable forms of representation.

Such an effect of liberal discourse and its manifestations in the colonies is almost predictable, not merely because of the difference of cultural contexts, but because of its underpinnings of racial difference. As Emmanuel Chukwudi Eze has pointed out, Enlightenment philosophy and scientific reason of the eighteenth century, which shaped political events and thinking in the nineteenth century, had a highly ambiguous relationship to racial diversity.[30] It is a commonplace to suggest that, within Enlightenment scientific thought, nature was conceptualized within a hierarchical system. Plants, animals, and humans were taxonomized according to a classificatory schema that was formulated by Europeans, naturalizing and unmarking its bias toward them. British liberal democratic discourse, with its origins in the Enlightenment movement and its emphasis on re-creating the Indian in its own image, inevitably carried out this hierarchization of race, thus simultaneously undercutting its own liberal philosophy that all men are born equal.

In *Soldier Heroes,* Graham Dawson draws on the traditions of adventure and chivalry and shows how the notion of Empire and the dangers it posed constructed modern concepts of heroes in Britain.[31] Dawson analyzes British masculinity in particular, but I want to show how it is intertwined with the production of Indian masculinity as well. The 1857 mutiny could be read within both the principles of metaphor and that of metonymy. If the former principles are to be used in an understanding of this event, then the Indian's inability to assimilate himself completely because of the residue left behind by his darkened body, because of his embodiment, puts him in a hierarchical relation with the British. He needed to be governed; he needed to assume a subordinate position in the army; he needed to be Christianized. In fact, his visible difference would prevent him from ever being conferred with a liberal subjectivity. He was a British man who could never be fully realized. If, however, the principle of metonymy were to operate in understanding mimicry, then the Indian becomes menacing; his duplicity demanded his suppression; his lack of substance demanded his governance; his unspeakable rites required his Christianization. Both narratives/tropes conclude in the same way: the Indian is incomplete, unrealizable. The schema of liberal manhood, that which would give the Indian man shape, form, and ability to think and reason, never quite achieved its goal. As a copy of the original, the Indian was in a hierarchical relation to the British. Furthermore, the logic of copies determines that the purity of the original can never be achieved; inevitably, corruption creeps in and the copy always already carries a debasement and a contamination within it. The liberal man of Britain was reproduced as an unreliable, deceptive, menacing man, a darker double in the colonies. The liberal framework came undone at the site of its application.

In short, the menacing aspect of the unachieved Indian was realized in the 1857 mutiny, wherein his unpredictability was unleashed on the British for a year and a month. Plans for an English education failed at two levels: First, the British construction, imposition, and repetition of liberal democratic thought had to emphasize one aspect of it—the intrinsic superiority of the British. Second, far from remaking the Indian as a liberal, Macaulay's plans for an English education in India also failed eventually because it instead created a monstrous double who seemed to prefer his own version of liberal thought—that all men are created equal—and demanded the recognition of this version by demanding and achieving independence.

1857: *TOM BROWN'S SCHOOL DAYS*

The year 1857 can be read as a series of discontinuous events in discontinuous spaces that yet interrelate, give meaning to, and implicate each other. As mentioned earlier, not only was it the year of the Sepoy Mutiny in India but also, with the publication of Thomas Hughes's *Tom Brown's School Days*,[32] it inaugurated a new literary genre in Britain written specifically to amuse and edify the young, namely schoolboy fiction. Fictions written for children had existed before this event, but were few in number: John Newbery's 1744 work *A Little Pretty Pocket Book*, Maria Edgeworth's fiction, and Thomas Day's *Sandford and Merton*. These works functioned mainly to teach facts and moral lessons. Hughes's 1857 novel was the first fictional account of the real world of middle-class boys in a real English public school. The novel deals with the protagonist Tom Brown from a family of rural gentry and his schooldays at Rugby during the time that Dr. Thomas Arnold was its headmaster. Though this work is set entirely in Rugby and deals with the day-to-day life of public-school boys, it became the precursor to adventure series such as the *Boy's Own Paper (BOP)*. *BOP* amalgamated the genre of schoolboy fiction such as *Tom Brown* with that of what is popularly known as Robinsonades, stories modeled on Daniel Defoe's *Robinson Crusoe*. Among various Robinsonades were R. L. Stevenson's *Treasure Island,* R. M. Ballantyne's *Coral Island,* and Captain Marryat's *Midshipman Easy*. (The American writer Herman Melville's *Typee* and *Moby Dick* can be categorized within this genre.) While not written specifically for children, they all dealt with voyages, desert islands, or shipwrecks.[33]

The popularity of these works in Victorian Britain can be traced to rising literacy rates in Europe in general. Coupled with this rise was an increase in prosperity, which enabled the Victorian British public to buy books and magazines. Indeed, as D. Vincent records in *Literacy and Popular Culture in England, 1750–1914,* by 1839, 67 percent of British men and 51 percent of British women were literate. By the end of the century, the numbers increased to include more than 90 percent of men and 75 percent of women.[34] The 1840s also saw the growing popularity of the *Penny Magazine* and the *London Illustrated News*. Reproduction technologies (in publishing), such as color lithography and color printing from wood, made books and magazines more attractive, visually appealing, and relatively cheap because of mass production.[35] Tracing the history and manifestations of the adventure story or "ripping yarns," written specifically for men and boys in the latter half of the nineteenth century, Robert Dixon indicates in *Writing the Colonial Adventure* that they were published in response to two distinct features in the writing of fiction. First, ripping yarns deflected attention from the schools of realism and naturalism, which dominated the market at that time and which were characterized by brooding and unmanly plot features that seemed to require excessive knowledge of a woman's nature. Rider Haggard, for instance, insisted on the "unmanly" qualities of naturalistic writers like Emile Zola. Second, women writers composed more than 40 percent of the marketplace by the 1870s, which resulted in the feminizing of the genre of the romance. Stevenson, Haggard, and Arthur Conan Doyle, writing at the interface of the Robinsonade and the schoolboy fiction, wrested this genre back to masculinity and a predominantly male audience.[36]

Thomas Hughes's novel does not have much of a plot in comparison to other examples in the various genres it spawned. It first locates Tom

Brown with his family in rural Berkshire, devoted to their "clanship" and the rural way of life, never leaving the county except once in five years. The opening chapters describe their way of life and Tom's companions: Charity Lamb, his nursemaid; Benjy, a servant of the family; and Toby, the terrier. In keeping with family tradition, from this idyllic country life Tom is sent to Rugby, which is then under the stewardship of Dr. Thomas Arnold. At Rugby, Tom is popular with his peers, negotiates his way through the bullying and fagging from fifth- and sixth-form boys, and does reasonably well scholastically, but even better at sports such as football and cricket. Among his friends are East, who by the end of the novel leaves for India to join his regiment, and George Arthur, the pale, sickly boy who Tom protects initially, but who eventually forces Tom to consider the values of being honest, straightforward, and a Christian as taught by Dr. Arnold. Tom eventually graduates from Rugby and enters Oxford. The novel ends with his manly mourning upon hearing of Dr. Arnold's death. Tom does not have the adventures of the young boys of *BOP*. However, this work records a number of aspects of mid-Victorian life that all converged to produce a reconstructed British masculinity at midcentury. The discourses deployed in the novel deal with the rise of the middle class, the importance of public schools, the importance of athletics, and the construction of a muscular Christianity.

This midcentury discursive shift in masculinity can be contextualized within the political scene in Britain. In *Athleticism in the Victorian and Edwardian Public Schools,* J. A. Mangan suggests that the Industrial Revolution, coupled with the subduing of the Chartist movement and the repeal of the Corn Laws in 1845, which sent feudal/landed society hierarchies into decline, allowed for the emergence and rise of a new middle class.[37] The free-trade policy in Britain led, in its turn, to economic prosperity. The passage of these laws, along with the New Poor Law, led to the liberal imagination of the nation. The middle class also gained ground with army reforms after the Crimean War and Universities Acts in 1854 and 1856 that abolished religious entry requirements and restrictions to Oxford and Cambridge.[38] In 1855, the formation of the Administrative Reform Association led to open competition for state administrative positions in Britain, a reform that mirrored the 1853 reform for competition in the Indian Civil Service. Thus, the formation of a new middle class with a liberal, nationalistic sensibility can be traced to this new male within the proliferation of public schools in

Britain, especially under the early influence of Dr. Thomas Arnold of Rugby. Mangan suggests, "He was in accord with the mood of his time: a reformation of manners which characterised mid-Victorian middle-class society. . . . His ambition, as he proclaimed it, was the creation of Christian gentlemen, and he pursued it with obsessional intensity."[39]

Indeed, the public schools catering to a middle-class clientele underscored the centrality of a moral upbringing in the making of the British public-school boy. In a scene in *Tom Brown's School Days,* Tom, notwithstanding the ridicule that he would face at the hands of his peers, follows the example set by George Arthur: he falls on his knees and starts praying as he had promised to do to his mother before leaving home. The authorial comment that follows states: "It was no light act of courage in those days, my dear boys, for a little fellow to say his prayers publicly, even at Rugby."[40] Soon his act is emulated by almost all the other boys in his form. Yet his newfound piety is not detrimental to the development of his masculinity, for Dr. Arnold's definition of manliness was "first, religious and moral principle; second, gentlemanly conduct; third, intellectual ability."[41]

This intersection of masculinity and Christian piety manifested itself as muscular Christianity and was subscribed to, in particular, by Charles Kingsley and Thomas Hughes. In *Tom Brown at Oxford,* the sequel to the one set at Rugby, Hughes defines this term:

> So far as I know, the least of the muscular Christians has hold of the old chivalrous and Christian belief that a man's body is given to him to be trained and brought into subjection and then used for the protection of the weak, the advancement of all righteous causes and the subduing of the earth which God has given to the children of men.[42]

The connection between muscular Christianity and imperialism ("subduing of the earth which God has given to the children of men") becomes visible at this juncture. Muscular Christianity soon became associated with all the public schools and was espoused by Hely Almond of Loretto, William Raymond of Lancing Hill, and C. J. Vaughan of Harrow, to name just a few of the headmasters.

There is one more factor that converges with this rise of the middle class, the proliferation of public schools, and the construction of muscular Christianity in mid-Victorian Britain: namely, the emphasis on athletic programs in public schools. For the first time, at midcentury, schools invested heavily in gymnasiums and hired physical-education instructors. Before these years, schools had emphasized only scholastics. The sole emphasis on scholastics had resulted in schoolboys frequently exploring and roaming the countryside, getting into trouble, killing animals and birds, and maiming and stoning dogs and horses in their free time.[43] With athletics starting to play a large role in the curriculum, a certain construction of the maturing schoolboy was evoked: to act rather than merely to think, to be healthy in body, to conform—in short, to be a team player. This swing of the pendulum from emphasis on scholastics to athletics resulted in its opposite, in an increased metonymical linking between the intellectual and questionable masculinity. Harold Nicholson sums up this link: "It was taught on all sides that manliness and self-control were the highest aims of English boyhood: he was taught that all but the most material forms of intelligence were slightly effeminate: he learnt as they all learnt, to rely on action rather than ideas."[44] Further, notions of British manhood were inscribed in their boyhood. Hughes opined that Rugby schoolboys had "a genial and hearty freshness and youthfulness of character. They lose nothing of the boy that is worth keeping, but build up the man upon it."[45]

Indeed, all the significations of manliness and effeminacy are present in the contrast that Tom Brown and George Arthur provide in *Tom Brown's School Days*. Whereas Tom is robust, healthy, and brown, George Arthur is pale and sickly; furthermore, the latter falls seriously ill and has to take a whole term off school to recover. However, by the end of the novel, after having spent several years in school with its plain, wholesome, and plentiful food and exercise, George Arthur reappears and participates in Tom's last cricket match: "His figure, though slight, is well knit and active, and replaced by silent, quaint fun with which his face twinkles all over." If any doubts exist about George Arthur's masculinity, they are partially soothed when he scores three runs despite the expert bowling and fielding.

In Bruce Haley's reading of Hughes's novel, the masculinization of George Arthur is fundamental to muscular Christianity because the foundation of true manliness is youthful pluck and vigor. Haley reads *Tom Brown's School Days* within the larger framework of the Victorian obsession with health and their perception of a healthy, well-knit body as encasing a well-formed mind. Haley draws a nightmarish picture of Britain. For instance, the Industrial Revolution led to black spittle among miners, grinder's rot among potters, and deteriorating vision and asthma among dressmakers, to name just a few of the occupational maladies.[46] Further, Britain was subject to contagions. Between 1831 and 1833, there were two flu epidemics and a cholera epidemic that claimed fifty-two thousand lives; between 1836 and 1842 there were flu, typhoid, smallpox, and scarlet fever epidemics; between 1837 and 1841, sixty-four thousand lives were claimed by typhus alone; scarlet fever, which raged in 1840, caused twenty thousand deaths; when Ireland was struck by the potato famine, it was also struck by typhus; when the Irish moved to Liverpool and Glasgow to seek work, so did the typhus move with them and accounted for thirty thousand deaths; between 1838 and 1840, measles and whooping cough accounted for fifty thousand deaths; further, fully one-quarter of all the deaths in this period were caused by tuberculosis.

It was not just contagions that caused diseases in Britain. Hygiene was poor as well, and Haley re-creates a filthy, fetid Britain for his readers:

> Sewers had flat bottoms, and because drains were made of stone, seepage was considerable. . . . For middle-class homes in the manufacturing towns, elevated sites were carefully chosen, with the result that sewage filtered or flowed down into the lower areas where the laboring populations dwelt. . . . In Leeds the Aire River, fouled by the town's refuse, flooded periodically, sending noxious waters into the ground floors and basements of low-lying houses.[47]

Haley contextualizes the Victorian obsession with health against the backdrop of the routine, periodic fecal floods in Britain. Even Parliament had to carry on business in 1858–1859 when the Thames flooded by covering windows with disinfectant-soaked cloths. Within such a context, the determination to have a healthy body—to prevent disease rather than merely to cure it—is totally understandable. Notable thinkers of the Victorian Age—George Henry Lewes, Thomas Carlyle, Charles Darwin, George Eliot, Lord Tennyson, George Meredith, and John Ruskin, among others—all were obsessed with illness and health. Thus, in Haley's reckoning, health for the Victorians was necessary for a wholeness; the mind and a virtuous existence was impossible without good health. Furthermore, if the body was in optimum condition, it could maximize its use of its environment.[48]

CONTRAPUNTAL READING

I began this chapter by discussing the Sepoy Mutiny of 1857 within the context of the implementation of liberal ideals and goals in India. I have

also examined the renewed sense of masculinity and shifting subjectivation marked by a bourgeois sensibility, manly piety, and concerns over
health. But how are these two events connected? So far, they seem entirely and arbitrarily held together by the signifier 1857. At this juncture,
I will explore the two locations contrapuntally, a term popularized in
postcolonial discourse by Edward Said, who in *Culture and Imperialism*
suggests that

> we must read the great canonical texts, and perhaps also the entire ar-
> chive of modern and pre-modern European and American culture, with
> an effort to draw out, extend, give emphasis, give voice to what is silent
> or marginally present or ideologically represented in such works.
>
> In practical terms, "contrapuntal reading," as I have called it, means
> reading a text with an understanding of what is involved when an author
> shows, for instance, that a colonial sugar plantation is seen as important
> in the process of maintaining a particular style of life in England.[49]

How do we arrive at a contrapuntal reading that links these two
seemingly unrelated events in two different places? How do they throw
light on each other? A contrapuntal reading strategy makes visible the
ripples that disturb and interrupt a linear flow of history. If we read the
Sepoy Mutiny as being both the conditions and the effects of the shifts
in masculinity that mark *Tom Brown's School Days,* then we can see
that the cultural histories of India and Britain are woven as an intricate
pattern. Each event functions as the mutual limitation of the other. For
me the link between them becomes visible when I ask, "Where is the
manly British body in 1857?" It is indeed peculiar that an ideology that
underscored muscularity and the well-knit, well-formed manly body
does *not* cause an eroticizing of the body, but instead causes a simultaneous *vanishing* of the material white, sexual, male body. I suggest that
the nineteenth-century manly British body, its sexuality and passion,
became visible in a *scientia sexualis*.[50] Unable to speak of its own erotics,
it manifested itself only through notions of hygiene, the biological, the
medicalization of the body, the racial, the animal. In fact, the pleasure
of the manly Victorian British body was reenacted through discourses
of the Other body. It is within racial science (and in discourses on the
woman's body) that the spirit of the Enlightenment becomes visible,
that the Sepoy Mutiny converges with *Tom Brown's School Days.*

Indeed, such a link had been portended if we were to lay out a narrative that includes the works of Francis Barker, Peter Stallybrass and

Allon White, Thomas Laqueur, and George Mosse, to name just a few. In *The Tremulous Private Body,* a work that deals with the history of the body and subjection, Francis Barker reads Descartes to suggest the construction of the bourgeois subject with an ability to read itself as Other as being historically located within a capitalistic and an Enlightenment framework. This splitting of the subject is along the lines of subject and object and is played out in the drama of mind and body. Barker explains that the splitting of the subject gives rise to its consciousness, which is vital to its sense of freedom and individuation and results in its attempt to control its inner self. Together, both frameworks allowed for a bourgeois modernity, which permitted a "depassionat[ing]" of the body, which in turn dropped out of public view in the created division between the public and the private.[51] This construction of the conscious self drained the body of its chaos and grotesquerie. The body had become the vessel for the soul and was thus contained and controlled by the conscious. However, Barker points out, the body continues to be problematic, and only outlawing the body can purchase individuation.

What, then, became of the body that stubbornly refused to go away? For Peter Stallybrass and Allon White, the body is at the center of Enlightenment discourse in that it is linked to poverty and class. In *The Politics and Poetics of Transgression,* they examine embodiment and disembodiment as represented in classical statuary in the Renaissance via the works of Mikhail Bakhtin. They point out that in the Renaissance, two forms of iconography functioned as binary opposites: the classical body and the grotesque body.[52] Whereas the former was always literally placed on a pedestal, the latter was always a part of a mob scene that suggested their commonness. The lack of orifices in the classical statue was in opposition to the grotesque body, which was embodied with open mouth, large stomach, and genitalia. If the former suggests a closed body and a growing disembodiment with an emphasis on the self-sufficient individual and a representation of mind rather than body, the latter is doubly gross because of its embodiment. Stallybrass and White conclude that the body cannot be thought outside of "a social topography," the meaning of the body being the meaning attributed to the social/cultural landscape in which it comes into being.[53]

The splitting of the body according to class differences, or according to notions of the public and private, marked medical discourses on the body as well. For Thomas Laqueur, the Enlightenment had also led to the notion of the two-sexed body. Whereas previously all human bodies within medical discourse were described as having only one template, by the early eighteenth century the two sexes and their differences had been discovered. Bodies were no longer seen as variations of each other, but as being irreconcilably different.[54]

The depassioning of the manly British body needs to be read within this context of the mind/body split, a common enough premise in discourses on gender. However, I suggest that this split was reenacted on racial lines as well. Within the contexts described by Barker et al. in answer to the question as to what happened to the white, manly British body, one more reference needs to be made. *In Nationalism and Sexuality,* George Mosse links healthiness and the healthy body with the development of respectability, an attitude that is historically associated with the rise of the middle class in England and Germany. Mosse suggests that both countries have a shared moral heritage (Protestantism), both had similar attitudes toward the French Revolution, and both underscored responsibility as "a means of controlling the passions, thereby encouraging ideals of human beauty, friendship, and love that supposedly transcended sexuality."[55] In Mosse's work, any foregrounding of the male body is aligned with homosexuality, a practice that was particularly taboo within the militaristic framework that Britain was moving toward in the second half of the nineteenth century. Yet homoeroticism/homosociality existed and abounded primarily because of the education of middle-class male children in public schools, followed by Oxford or Cambridge. For Jeffrey Richards, Victorian public schools and society were saturated with the ethos of chivalry as in ancient Greece and manifested itself as a code of behavior and qualities such as bravery, loyalty, courtesy, modesty, and purity.[56] Mosse furthermore suggests that manliness was also deemed to be void of sexuality and the passions of the body were to be controlled.[57]

I suggest that the discourse of Enlightenment, which demanded the mind/body split and the split between the public and private, was superimposed in the nineteenth century by the discourses of nationalism and race science. Indeed, there is a disembodying, a neutralizing and making bland of mid-Victorian masculinity despite its overinvestment in muscularity, athleticism, and youth. One can safely conclude that a liberal, democratic, bourgeois, white individual had come into ascendancy, eclipsing in power the aristocratic group that had preceded him in the last century. Within this framework, embodiment or the emphasis on the body signified chaos, disease, the grotesque, the orificial, the penetrable, sexual, physical, appetitious, the Other—in fact, not unlike the representations of the Indian male around 1857 within the bourgeois mid-Victorian British imagination. It had to be controlled. It is these significations that link *Tom Brown* to the Sepoy Mutiny.

But what happened to the white male body? If the white body dematerializes, where does the materiality of the body get expressed? I suggest that the vanishing British muscular body remanifests itself through a process of displacement within discourses of the black body and, in particular, in race science. If we read the dominant ideology of bourgeois Britain and its desire for disembodiment, then the cultural injunction against the body is compensated by the overinvestment in the embodiment of the black, the indigenous, or the native in race science. Indeed, it can be said to contain traces of the yearning for the body-in-disembodiment, the lost manly British body. Nineteenth-century discourses of race science functioned as a screen, a formation that was produced as a compromise wrought by the repressed white bourgeois body and its desire to maintain the cultural injunction of excising the body.

Collette Guillamin hints at this suggestion of the proliferation of race science caused by the expunging of the British body as well. She locates a discursive shift in the eighteenth century when the system of marks on the body changed in status from being a symbol to "a sign of a specific nature."[58] For Guillamin, prior to the eighteenth century, marks on the body such as tattoos and brands indicated relationships of power in which the dominating group inscribed the bodies that were subject to them. Other marks such as the beard and clothing indicated the social status of the person wearing them. However, from the eighteenth century, the marking of bodies was read as natural. Guillamin states: "The taxonomies were transformed into classification systems based on a morphological mark, in which the latter is *presumed to precede* the classification."[59] Thus, systems of power were *naturalized* so that those who were in power had unmarked bodies and those who were not were marked in some way, mostly through race or gender.

This discursive shift in the eighteenth century was amplified in the nineteenth century with its increased investment in race science. For instance, phrenology, the (pseudo)science that correlated people's mental abilities and the shape of their heads, became popular in the first half of the nineteenth century. This science led to the comparison of anatomies, and what originally started as a study of differences among individual humans quickly became a study of group differences.

By 1869 skull measurements became a shorthand method of reading social, cultural, and historical meaning about the individual and the national. Again, monogenism was popularized by James Pritchard and Sir William Lawrence, who both argued for a commonality of origin among humans. Both used analogical reasoning to determine that just as the same animal species can be found in different color varieties, so can humans. Robert Knox's influential work *The Races of Man* was published in 1850. In 1859, Charles Darwin published his *The Origin of Species* and in 1871 *The Descent of Man*. Together Darwin's works argued that species were not fixed, but were constantly evolving because of their tendency to select those traits that were favorable for survival. Thus, humans and animals had a common ancestry and were further linked through their capacities for reasoning, imagining, curiosity, and inventiveness. Furthermore, just as animals were less evolved than humans, some humans were less evolved than others.

I highlight very few of the race scientists of the nineteenth century. I have not referred to the works of Spencer, Gobineau, Humboldt, Lamarck, Agassiz, Ritter, Niebuhr, or Matthew Arnold.[60] The point I wish to make is that the proliferation of knowledges constructed around the marked body in the nineteenth century prove Foucault's characterization of the repressive hypothesis in the arena of embodiment as well. In *The History of Sexuality,* Foucault points out that, according to the repressive hypothesis to gain mastery over something, it was first "necessary to subjugate it at the level of language, control its free circulation in speech, expunge it from the things that were said, and extinguish the words that rendered it too visibly present."[61] If bourgeois sensibility required the expunging of its body, there was no such prohibition on the overrepresention of the black body. In fact, the excess of racial discourses produced in the nineteenth century can be read as a hysteria brought about by a certain form of subjectivation, which demanded the repression of the body, the very ground, the constitutive condition of that subjectivation.

What, then, does the black body signify to race science? And what does race science signify to bourgeois subjectivation? I suggest that race science does not express some predetermined essence, but in fact *fabricates* the very corporeality of blackness. Race science authorizes, binds, coheres, maps, and brings meaning to the markings on the black body. As such, race science is enmeshed within the web of power and is hardly neutral. Judith Butler, who has extensively examined the notion of the performative, especially within the context of gender and heterosexual injunctions, cites Louis Althusser's notion of interpellation to explain the function of the performative.[62] In Althusser's text, the police calls out a "Hey you!" to the subject walking down the street, and the subject who turns back is interpellated within "the juridical and social formation of the subject."[63] Race science hails the black native into a juridical and social subject, but one whose terms are set within the legal and social framework of Britain or Europe. In short, the black subject performs the social, cultural injunctions mapped upon his body and in so doing valorizes the "discoveries" of race science. Thus, the performativity of the black body is linked to Bhabha's notion of mimicry in that the social, juridical injunctions of a liberal Western framework cannot completely predict the materiality of an Other culture, its bodies, meanings, and mappings. In such a reading, Macaulay and Mills's liberal/evangelical framework are all aspects of race science. As such, the black body constructed by race science functions as a screen for a materiality it cannot know or articulate. The limitations, constructions, and lack within race science are always exposed in the *unpredictability of blackness*. In the end, though, the lost body of the bourgeois British is displaced onto blackness by race science. These very discourses reveal yet another construction of disembodiment, which becomes visible every time blackness does not perform the way it is meant to do, as during the Sepoy Mutiny of 1857. Race science constructs a form of materiality that is a partial representation of the materiality it hopes to get within its purview.

If the blackness of nineteenth-century discourse on race is a personification of the disembodied body, a catachresis, what then is whiteness? It too is performative, performing the juridical and social formations of the white subject. It too is underpinned by discourses of capitalism, colonialism, and liberalism. In fact, these very discourses of the nation construct a whiteness for maximum efficiency, one that will not be riddled with dissensions between classes, regionalisms, and sexualities. All these divisive differences that would locate the subject within an individuality and individual expressions of themselves would be uneconomical within a colonial situation where whites had to cohere as a group to homogenize blacks and rule them. Athleticism and muscular Christianity, far from locating the adolescent male body (for whom adventure fiction was written) as erotic, subsumes them under representations of whiteness, which has the burden and duty of ruling the unruly blacks in the colonies. Whiteness itself performs the social, cultural, and juridical injunctions of capitalism and colonialism. There is no articulable, material body anywhere at all.

I have attempted to rematerialize and rehistoricize the British body in the mid-nineteenth century. The reading of the Sepoy Mutiny as spontaneous becomes problematic when the historical data in which it is anchored is examined. I have tried to read the signification of 1857 in Britain and the meanings layered in the shift in masculinity and to sew the two faces of 1857 and see what contrapuntal meanings emerge when they are juxtaposed together. Finally, I have suggested that race science, be it within biology, anthropology/ethnology, political studies, geography, or any of the disciplines that are premised on the binarity of races, passed themselves as being neutral and descriptive when in fact they were prescriptive and shaped and formed bodies.

In all of this I have not undertaken to locate the woman's body or how she figures within the context of midcentury Victorian masculinity. I will just briefly say that within such a linking of whiteness with masculinity, and within the context of the expanding Empire as well as the siege, the embodiment of women—their weakness, their sexual availability, their penetrable bodies—becomes a liability for establishing the supremacy and invulnerability of whiteness. They had to be contained as the Angel in the House.[64] If whiteness was reincoded within a militaristic masculinity, then white women were not white in themselves but could be linked to whiteness only as a supplement. Their whiteness was retroactively conferred upon them due to their heterosexual relationships with white men, not because they were white. In short, they could not perform whiteness as this term was already incorporated within masculinity; they could only ever mime it. Their bodies, marked by gender, emulated and exceeded midcentury whiteness. It is white-in-difference.

What, then, was midcentury whiteness? It contained markers of muscularity, maleness, youth, the bourgeoise, athleticism, health, disembodiment, and homosociality. What it was not was the marked body, be it through race or gender, intellectual, homosexual or heterosexual, or visible. In the nineteenth century, whiteness became invisible, universalized in discourse and present, literally, in every part of the globe.

CHAPTER 2

The Whiteness of Women:
In Theory and under Lock and Key

The focus of the previous chapter was on the changing meaning of British masculinity in the mid-nineteenth century, changes brought about by events that occurred in the far reaches of Empire as much as those in Britain, which tightly braided masculinity with a whiteness. In this chapter I will examine the racialization of white British women in the nineteenth century. If men were racialized because of political events overseas, how would women, traditionally located in the private realm, be racialized? Would they be exempt from the discourse of hierarchy that pervades racial thinking?

Look at the following statistics and their implications for gender relationships in the Victorian Age. There was a surplus of 718,566 women over men in the 1871 census in Britain. In 1861, there was a male excess of 14,602 in the ten-to-fourteen-year age group; but by the twenty-to-twenty-four-year and twenty-five-to-twenty-nine-year age group, there was a female excess of 209,663 in England and Wales.[1] Further, men and women started marrying later than before, and in the early 1900s the average age of marriage was twenty-seven years for men and twenty-five years for women. In the late Victorian period, the population boomed in Britain, showing an increase from thirty-one million in 1871 to forty-five million in 1911, almost a 45 percent increase in forty years. The 1871 census calculated that 1,173 babies were born in Britain every day and predicted that 468, or 39 percent, of them would immigrate overseas. In the late Victorian and Edwardian periods, six million Britons immigrated to the New World or to the colonies. Added to these were other changing demographic features: the rapid urbanization of Britain (by World War I, only 8 percent of the British were employed in agriculture, as opposed to 27 percent in Germany and 38 percent in France);[2] the century-long rise of the middle class into the predominant political force that it has become; and an expanded Empire, which spanned Canada and the Caribbean to parts of Africa and Asia, the whole of the Indian subcontinent, Australia, and New Zealand. Not only was there a burgeoning middle class, but there was also a rapidly expanding working class in the wake of the Industrial Revolution. Women were seen as delicate and located within the home in the Victorian domestic ideology. However, the reality was different. Between 1851 and 1881 the number of female domestic servants (women working away from their homes) increased 33 percent.[3] There was a disproportionate increase of women in places like London, Surrey, and coastal holiday resorts.[4] In short, millions of working-class women participated in heavy manual labor.

The level of flux and change in the day-to-day lives of the nineteenth-century British was immense indeed. It is well known that there was a reconfiguration of notions of class and gender in Britain during the nineteenth century. What does such a sizeable surplus of marriageable women do to the construction of gender and heterosexuality? What implications did Britain's baby boom between 1871 and 1911 have for the notion of the family, employment, economy, and class? If Britain was becoming a nation of urban people, how did gender relations reconfigure themselves to accommodate this drift? If it was going through a diaspora of its people, how was Britishness being reconstructed? How could the slippage between the woman as Angel in the House and woman as manual laborer be reconciled within the dominant ideology? I will explore these questions by examining the embodiment of British women because I think the answers were written on her body. Women's relationship to the nation is problematic because notions of nationness and nationalism are predicated on women's exclusion from the polity.[5] In fact, women are not so much excluded as they are considered requisite for the production of the meaning of the nation, as they are located as *the very ground* upon which the meaning of the nation itself rests. But in providing it with a meaning, she is also simultaneously left out of the very meaning she constitutes in the sense that she has fewer rights and enjoys fewer equalities than do her male counterparts. How, then, are British women of the nineteenth century and their bodies constructed within the whiteness and imperialism it signified, especially when the former term had notions of masculinity inscribed within it?

The whiteness of British women was central to definitions of British-ness in the nineteenth century for a couple of reasons. First, beyond its contact with the Other in foreign spaces, Britain was subject to a large traffic from foreigners. Over three million non-British entered Britain in the late Victorian period. Four hundred thousand people of non-British origin settled in Britain in that period. By the time the cen-sus was taken again in 1911, there were four thousand Asians, twelve thousand people of African origin, and nine thousand West Indians living in Britain.[6] Indeed, one can hazard that Britishness was starting to get complicated and race had become central to its significations. Second, the nineteenth century saw a massive amount of research done on race and racialized bodies, which produced new emergent meanings of racial differences. This was the age that saw works of British racial and social scientists such as Edward Freeman, who popularized notions of Anglo-Saxon superiority; Robert Knox's work, *Races of Man* (1850), was central to the formation of comprehensions of Britishness. In the 1860s James Hunt, founding president of the Anthropological Society of London and admirer of James Knox, insisted that racial classifica-tion could not be transcended; again, racial theorists adopted Charles Darwin's notions of "natural selection" and Herbert Spencer's "survival of the fittest." Finally, Sir Francis Galton, the founder of eugenics and a cousin of Charles Darwin, published his influential work *Hereditary Genius* in 1869, which divided humans into races with stereotypes.

In this chapter I will particularly investigate the discursive con-structions of the whiteness of British women. I will consider how race, class, gender, and sexuality interact and configure in the production of nineteenth-century British women, not in the colonies but in Britain. How would our comprehensions of class, gender, and sexuality shift if examined via the master signifier of whiteness rather than through class or gender? I will concentrate on the whiteness of women precisely because it is so problematic and because it makes visible the constructed nature of class, race, and sexuality. The whiteness of women reveals the *grammar* of these configurations and the way they interact with each other to produce a white identity. I will first explore the relationship between whiteness and class, and then between whiteness and sexuality, through the body of the woman. Finally, I will do a reading of Sigmund Freud's "Femininity" because, though neither a British text nor one that properly belongs to the nineteenth century, it is saturated with all those elements that were central to nineteenth-century definitions of womanhood. This text, to my mind, informs our comprehension of nineteenth-century femininity, which was central to second-wave feminist activity in the late 1960s and the 1970s.

WHITE AND CLASS

Can bodies embody class? Certainly poverty and wealth are visibly written on the body. As innumerable scholars have pointed out, the human body underwent a fundamental shift in meaning in the West with late eighteenth-century Enlightenment. For instance, Thomas Laqueur painstakingly traces this shift in bodily meaning and locates it within the emergent discourse of human liberty and equality during the Enlightenment period, the logic and rationality of which could not preclude equality for women and their bodies.[7] Laqueur points out that "political theorists beginning with Hobbes had argued that there is no basis in nature for any specific source of authority—of a king over his people, of slaveholder over slave, nor, it followed, of man over women."[8] This political shift in meaning influenced a shift in thinking about women's bodies so that, far from being perceived as hierarchically inferior to male bodies, they were now perceived as being different. Further, as Jeffrey Weeks, Catherine Hall, and Ann Stoler all have indicated, nineteenth-century industrialization and the rise of the middle class also profoundly influenced the representation of women.[9] Even the rationality of science was not exempt from being marked by historical and cultural shifts in the constitution and representation of materiality. It is within the context of the Enlightenment and the articulating of liberal democracy that the political constructed what was purported to be natural.[10] The story of citizenship in a liberal democracy shaped the history of embodiment to a great extent. Both were mutually interconnected. To this I will also reiterate the obvious: that the Enlightenment was fundamentally not just a philosophical and political movement about rationality and science and against the mysticism of religion, but also about *class formations,* in that it underwrote the ascendancy of the middle class and the hegemonic loss of the aristocracy. As such, issues of class, embodiment, and citizenship will mark any discourse on scientific thinking and the nature of rationality itself.

It is with these preliminary qualifiers that I turn to the urtext of whiteness studies in the United Kingdom, Richard Dyer's *White*. In this work, Dyer locates white women as being whiter than white men, as being the distillation of white attributes such as morality, ideals, the angelic, the spiritual, and the ethereal. Specifically looking at visual representations of white women in art, film, and photography, Dyer traces a continuum in the iconography of all white women, regardless of national or class origin. Dyer suggests that the representation of white women as angels reached its extreme at three specific moments in the nineteenth century: the Sepoy Mutiny of 1857, the Jamaican Revolt of 1865, and the American Civil War, all of which were felt to threaten white hegemony.[11] Further, in this text he indicates a hierarchy of white skins that intersect with gender and class formations: not only are all men marked by a tanned skin, but tanned skin itself becomes a marker of membership to the working class. Thus, we can see that the white skin of white women was possible only for those belonging to the bourgeoisie. Within this context, men's tanned skins did not necessarily locate them as belonging to a particular class; it was their earning capacity more than the hues of their skin that gave them memberships to different classes.

Is white femininity outside the ambit of class? If class distinction (i.e., variations of hue) comes into visibility only via masculine forms (earning capacity), does it affect the discursive construction of femininity and womanhood, traditionally located within the home? There is a certain unchanging quality attributed to femininity within the Victorian domestic ideology. Catherine Hall locates the origins of bourgeois femininity in Britain within the transitions that the country faced between 1780 to 1832, when it shifted from a society dominated by aristocrats to one dominated by industrial capitalists and a growing middle class.[12] According to Hall, before the late eighteenth century, women contributed to the economic benefit of the family. When the Evangelicals' perception of morality started dominating in the late eighteenth century, they set the standards of behavior for the whole class. Perceiving the aristocrats to be morally lax, and fearing a revolution similar to the one in France, the Evangelicals valorized family life and ideals to bring stability to life at a time when everything else was in flux: the economic and social order, notions of citizenship, and definitions of a nation that was starting to emerge as an imperial power. In this redefinition of morality, women were relocated within the home to signify constancy.[13] Furthermore, the dominance of the Evangelicals among the bourgeoisie influenced the very class-consciousness and gender formations within that group.

The emergent middle-class definition of femininity in the Victorian era was part of a larger shift in the recontextualizing of the family. For instance, the term "family" (as in the nuclear family and as applying to parents and children only) was used for the first time in Britain in 1829 and a little earlier in France.[14] Further, the late eighteenth century saw a shift toward a close emotional bonding between members of the immediate family that began to exclude neighbors and kin.[15] Lawrence Stone points out that there was also an emerging sense of a strong individual autonomy that could be linked to the switch to romantic, sexual love as the basis for marriage as opposed to the arranged marriages of previous centuries that gave importance to lineage. Obviously, the ascendancy of the middle class led to changing familial, sexual, and gender constructions. As Jeffrey Weeks points out, these changing constructions are closely linked to the separation of work and home and the growing realization that the individual was central to the economy.[16]

But if economy meant a national rather than a familial economy, what about the women then? Leaving aside Victorian definitions and practices of family and sexuality for the moment, I want to dwell on the fact that middle-class comprehensions of femininity are *definitive* to representations of Victorian femininity. In fact, so central are the class markers of Victorian femininity that they have become unmarked, invisible, and yet fundamental to their very comprehension. The Victorian woman, especially in Britain, was perceived as central to the family; she was located as passive, in the home, in the private realm, "the Angel in the House."[17] She was dependent on men and submissive to them, gentle, self-sacrificing, capable of self-renunciation. Her primary role was that of wife and mother. She was spiritual and took care of this dimension of the family. She was paradoxically both womanly yet childlike. In John Ruskin's words:

> The perfect loveliness of a woman's countenance can only consist in the majestic peace, which is found in the memory of happy and useful years . . . and from the joining of this with that yet more majestic childishness, which is still full of change and promise. . . . There is no old age where there is still that promise—it is eternal youth.[18]

My enumeration of these traits of the Victorian woman is a commonplace, especially within feminist analysis. The Victorian woman's dependence on men arose out of the ascendance of the middle class, which located nonworking women at home and made them financially dependent. Further, her location in the private realm, for reasons of being in charge of the spiritual needs of the family, was part of the cult of domesticity that reconciled the tensions between the moral values of Christianity and the economic burgeoning of Western Europe within industrial capitalism.

It is this unitary definition of woman as wife and mistress of the home that also dislocates her from class distinctions. While bourgeois ideology maintained and reinscribed the distinction between active and passive, public and private, the world and the home, it did not include class difference within its meanings. I emphasize the bourgeois woman's representation as curiously unmarked by class status because it seems so unrelated to the definition attributed to her male counterpart. In the classic definition of the bourgeoisie, Eric Hobsbawm states it to mean "a body of persons of power and influence, independent of the power and influence of traditional birth and status. To belong to it a man had to be 'someone'; *a person who counted as an individual, because of his wealth, his capacity to command other men*, or otherwise to influence them."[19] Social standing and wealth are central for Hobsbawm, as is the bourgeois male's ability to command other men (presumably of the lower class). He was distinguished from the aristocracy in that he earned his right to command and did not inherit it. The lower-class male, in turn, took on an object status, his sole function being to enhance the agency of the bourgeois male. The woman, on the other hand, perceived as being outside class markers, was located on a passive ground whose sole function was to provide class distinctions among men. Thus, she brought about a mythical unity to the various classes of men who were united through her classlessness, her evenness, her transcending of distinctions. Further, their connection to an unchanging, pure form of Britishness cohered them into a nation, a people reinterpellated with common identities, values, aspirations, and culture, notwithstanding differences in class origin, regions, and backgrounds.

What, then, was invested in such a location of woman within domestic ideology, within the realm of the private, within the home, when the reality was something different, given that vast numbers of women did *not* comply with the dominant ideology and worked outside their home for a living? This lack of compliance was not limited to working-class women alone. As James Hammerton points out, thousands of middle-class women who were unmarried and could not continue to live in genteel poverty immigrated to the colonies.[20]

Such a categorization of woman also located them outside of temporality, outside of history. If woman became a metaphor for the essence of Britishness, then her unchanging nature, through the process of displacement, became a metaphor for the unchanging nature of Britishness itself. I suggest that women's redefinition as being unchanging functioned to naturalize and essentialize a neo-Britishness, thus obscuring the constructed nature of history, politics, and society, as well as femininity. Further, the unmarking of the class status of women within the domestic ideology ultimately can be seen as the unmarking of the whiteness of the British itself. The logic functioned thus: women naturally belonged to the private; they were white. Notions of whiteness got linked to the bourgeoisie. Working-class people were darker; they belonged to the public sphere. Thus, a link was made between comprehensions of race and class.

Such a construction of woman also located her outside of classifications and outside of social or political distinctions. This refusal to insert women into the classifications reserved for men was a curious fact, given that the Victorians were renowned for their proliferation of classifying systems. For instance, animals, humans, and plants underwent a plethora of classifying and reclassifying in the Victorian Age. In Pierre Bourdieu's words, classifications and distinctions function "below the level of consciousness and language, beyond the reach of introspective scrutiny or control by the will."[21] Bourdieu insists on the relationship between knowledge, classifications, and ideology and points out that structures of classifications are "practices of agents who respond to invitations or threats of a world they have helped produce."[22] In *The Order of Things,* Michel Foucault locates this predilection to classify within the Enlightenment and the need to create order out of what was perceived as chaos. He states, "By virtue of structure, the great proliferation of beings occupying the surface of the globe is able to enter both into the sequence of a descriptive language and into the field of mathesis that would also be a general science of order."[23] Furthermore, Harriet Ritvo suggests in *The Animal Estate* that before the Enlightenment "people perceived themselves to be at the mercy of natural forces."[24] Ritvo adds that by the end of the Victorian Age, due to the advances made in science and engineering, nature was felt to be under human control and more manageable. Classificatory systems were part of this project to wrest control of what were perceived as uncontrollable natural forces. It is now common to suggest that classificatory systems of plants, animals, and so on, far from being objective and scientific, in fact revealed hierarchical relationships of class, nationality, race, and species and even between people themselves. Ritvo gives an example of this when she asks, "[Why] were the whippets raced by miners perceived as different from the greyhounds raced by more genteel sportsmen in 19th century England?"[25]

In this age of classifications, why then were women perceived to be outside of them? Indeed, such a location of being outside of classifications itself was a form of categorization meant to produce a particular form of meaning. I want to suggest that domestic ideology's categorization of women as unchanging and always the same effectively covered over the marks of her boundary status and of her role of being the reproducer of the ethnic/racial group. Her sexuality became a matter of tremendous concern for men, a matter to be policed because she could dilute the ethnic/racial group. In this recognition of her boundary status and a simultaneous covering up or denial of it by locating her at the center—the very core—of Britishness, a hysteria becomes visible. What made the British woman the innermost, the purest, was precisely that *she was also the boundary,* the space of dilution, making the outer into an inner. At the very moment the British woman played the role of the essential and constitutive of Britishness, she undermined it by showing her potential/ability to contaminate it.[26] Thus, contamination was at the very heart, the very core of white Britishness. Yes, the British woman's body and her whiteness were utterly problematic, so vexing and unreliable. She was not patriotic. Her whiteness could so easily be muddied; her body was so flimsy it could easily produce and lapse into a blackness as well. It is this boundary status of the woman's body that problematizes race (white) and class (middle class) as both natural *and* constructed.

What I have suggested is that Victorian domestic ideology was marked not only by gender divisions, but also by class and racial boundaries. Feminist critiques of the domestic ideology have valorized the split between men and women only within tropes of inside/outside, private/public, and home/world. I am suggesting instead that the simultaneous (symbolic) overvaluation of the woman and the (social) undervaluation of her implicates the interior domestic space in matters beyond that of the woman's position. Indeed, to insist on seeing just gender divisions between the public and private split would be to reinscribe Lockean thinking, which, as Carole Pateman has pointed out, is problematic. While on one hand Locke insisted that natural differences between men are irrelevant to political equality, on the other hand he claimed that natural differences between men and women validate the subjection of women by men.[27]

I have not underscored the gender inequity that is spatialized in Victorian society, but rather have seen the place of the private as the space of interdiction, the forbidden come into view, because it is the space where race, class, and gender injunctions coalesce, imbricate, and overlap and are bound together. The confining of women within an ascriptive domestic space is a confining of the formation and specificity of the middle class and of whiteness, of class and race. It is an attempt to construct space that is free of the incursions of history. For only in so doing can the *naturalizing* of gender, race, and class constructions occur. Gender thus becomes a metaphor for class or for race; domestic ideology is a substitute signifier of white hegemony, of middle-class dominance; it becomes the code for rereading the underpinning of British imperialism. In short, gender is mapped onto race, is mapped onto class. The naturalizing—this is the way it has always been—must be asserted for all three to function seamlessly and invisibly together. As Homi Bhabha says, "The recesses of the domestic space become sites for history's intricate invasions. In that displacement, the borders between world and home become confused; and, uncannily forcing upon us a vision that is divided as it is disorienting."[28]

If the interdicted incursions of history are reinscribed into the domestic space, what can we see besides whiteness and middle-classness and imperialism? We can see that the supremacy of race (read: white), class (read: middle class), and gender (read: man) is possible only through the interdiction; it is dependent upon it. Further, the manliness of men who interacted in both the public, masculine world and the private, feminine world becomes suspect in that they are as much a part of the private sphere as they are of the public space; the whiteness of white people becomes muddied in that they literally rub shoulders with literally blackened, working-class people; the middle-classness of middle-class men becomes contaminated because of their daily incursions into working-class spaces.

THE CONTAGIOUS DISEASES ACTS

Things fall apart when working-class women are brought into the equation of the gender division of public and private. The carefully constructed binaries crumble when we start reinfusing the lives of millions of working-class women into the domestic ideology. I have set the analysis of this section at a certain historical moment of the Victorian Age: 1864, when the first of the three Contagious Diseases Acts were passed. Briefly summarized, there was a rise in the incidence of venereal disease in the British military. From 1823 to the 1860s, venereal diseases accounted for more than 33 percent of all sick cases in the army stationed in Britain. Hospitals were bulging with gonorrhea and syphilis admissions. But the rate was far greater in the colonies. While in 1864 venereal disease struck 290.7 per 1,000 troops based in Britain,[29] the official rate of venereal disease among British soldiers in Bengal was 522.3 per 1,000 between 1889 and 1892.[30] These numbers were alarming because the diseases spread to the civilian population in Britain. The extent of the spread of venereal disease among the civilians could not be accurately ascertained, because the only statistics maintained were death rates caused by syphilis, not by all parasyphilitic diseases. In the first half of 1846 alone, infants below one year of age accounted for thirty of fifty-six reported syphilis deaths.[31] The public response to this medical dilemma was to blame prostitutes as being the source for the increase in venereal disease. As a result, lock hospitals were built in Britain to house venereal-diseased patients, particularly poor prostitutes. The lock hospitals were a curious echo of the private realm in which bourgeois women were kept confined to within domestic ideology. The lock hospital at Southwark originated at the site of a medieval house for lepers, who had been kept constrained.[32] The lock hospitals of the Victorian Age worked on the same principles of separating and often confining the patients, who were female and predominantly of working-class origin. However, their middle-class male clients, who also spread venereal disease, were not so confined.

In the early 1860s, the incidence of venereal disease in Britain shot up dramatically when the troops returned from India after quelling the Sepoy Mutiny. The Contagious Diseases Acts of 1864, 1866, and 1869 were originally intended to contain venereal diseases in garrison towns and ports where troops were stationed. The acts functioned to identify women who were common prostitutes, and the police were authorized

to make sure that these women were subjected to fortnightly gynecological examinations. If found to have gonorrhea or syphilis, they would
then be confined to lock hospitals. The 1866 extension of the Contagious
Diseases Act functioned to include more districts, which could forcibly subject suspected prostitutes to gynecological examinations. By the
1869 extension, these acts were in operation in eighteen districts. In the
wake of these acts, there was a growing realization of their encroachment of civil liberties and its singling out and targeting of working-class
women. Eventually, by the efforts of the Ladies National Association,
working-class men, and individual leaders such as Josephine Butler, an
alliance of feminists and radicals was forged and the acts were repealed
in 1886.

That the acts targeted working-class women is evident if we examine
the class composition of prostitutes who were often poor daughters of
poor parents. According to Abraham Flexner, they were the "unskilled
daughters of the unskilled classes."[33] A number of these women started
their work lives in low-paid jobs such as domestic servant or charring
and laundering, eventually becoming prostitutes to be able to eat. Alternatively, these women had been orphaned at an early age.[34] The demographics of working-class women who were prostitutes vary. The year
1861 saw the highest police estimates of known prostitutes: 29,572 in
England and Wales, 7,124 in London alone.[35] However, there were a
number of "dollymops" who were prostitutes by night and milliners or
dressmakers by day. *Westminster Review* fixed the national total estimate
between 50,000 and 368,000 prostitutes in the 1830s and 1840s, though
police estimates suggested that there were fewer than 30,000 prostitutes
working nationally in the 1850s.[36] The Contagious Diseases Acts were
passed to control prostitutes, but not their male customers. While vene-
reologists advocated the repressive regime of lock hospitals for women,
they did not focus as much attention on the men as source and agent
for the spread of venereal diseases, especially within the middle class.

On another continent, on the other side of the world, prostitutes
in India were treated in similar ways. Disease-free Indian prostitutes
whom the soldiers frequented in seventy-five cantonments where the
Indian army was stationed had a designated red-light area behind regimental lines between 1855 and 1888. These prostitutes were also subjected to checkups and placed in lock hospitals and treated if found
to have sexually communicable diseases. The only injunction placed

on the Indian prostitute working behind regimental lines was that she could not be seen consorting with Indian customers as she was meant to save herself for white British soldiers.[37]

STATISTICS AND SURVEILLANCE

There are several ways of analyzing the Contagious Diseases Acts and its repercussions. Feminist historians have tended to read it from within a narrative of liberal ideology, wherein transgressed women's rights are set right by women's rights advocates like Josephine Butler. Further, the repeal of the Contagious Diseases Acts is seen within a narrative of a growing momentum toward women's suffrage and equal rights in the twentieth century. I will shift my focus to another aspect: the trope of surveillance that inheres to the gendered division between the public/private dichotomy, because it is within the context of this trope that the relationship between class and race becomes visible.

The notion of respectability underpins any comprehension of the public/private dichotomy. As George Mosse points out, the rise of the middle class is enmeshed with the production of respectability, which had elements of "frugality, devotion to duty, and restraint of the passions."[38] These aspirations allowed the dominating middle class to set themselves apart from the aristocracy as well as the working class; the latter in particular was perceived as being sexually immoral. This description of sexual immorality was limited to prostitutes but also included most members of the working class, even those who did adopt the bourgeois value of respectability. Central to this value was the notion that the presence of women in public spaces signaled their membership in the ranks of prostitution and the vices. The nineteenth-century historian Peter Gaskell indicated the breakdown in family life caused by machines and factory work: "Recklessness, improvidence and unnecessary poverty, starvation, drunkenness, parental cruelty and carelessness, filial disobedience, neglect of conjugal rights, absence of maternal love, destruction of brotherly and sisterly affection, are too often its constituents."[39] Working-class women with jobs outside the domestic space and especially in factories were deemed immoral because of the "promiscuous mingling of sexes."[40] Further, the rising illegitimate birth rate was blamed on working women. Indeed, the increased number of female domestic servants increased opportunities for sexual liaisons not only cross-class, but also within the working class itself. In short, working-class women's sexuality and working lives were interpreted by bourgeois domestic ideology as lacking devotion to familial duty.

The Victorian obsession with maintaining statistics concerned with sexuality and sexual deviance is directly related to bourgeois respectability, a thesis that Michel Foucault has so brilliantly explored in *The History of Sexuality*. For Foucault, in newly emergent Western industrialized nations with a growing bourgeoisie there was a definite shift in attitudes to sexuality in that it became intertwined within a power/knowledge regime. Any aspect of life related to sexuality—birth rates, fertility, contagious diseases—all got enmeshed within this regime, and *scientia sexualis,* which insisted on the "truth of sex," became the order of the day. Within such a framework, sex got transformed into a discourse and was expressed within a ritualized confession, be it to a physician, a psychiatrist, a sexologist, or a statistician.[41] Indeed, as Françoise Barret-Ducrocq records in *Love in the Time of Victoria,* the Foundling Hospital, which took in illegitimate children, made it mandatory for unmarried mothers to confess "to show that her good faith had been betrayed, that she had given way to carnal passion only after a promise of marriage or against her will; that she therefore had no other children; and that her conduct had always been irreproachable in every other respect."[42]

For Foucault, the embourgeoisement of the nineteenth century resulted in the treating of sex as harboring a fundamental secret, and the power/knowledge regime demanded the "pleasure of analysis" of sexuality. To this I want to add that central to bourgeois respectability was the trope of surveillance in that working-class women's lives were subject to the scrutiny of middle-class values. Indeed, the separation between public and private was not only that between the sexes but also that of the classes, for the middle class with its ability to locate itself as the norm also escaped the eyes of surveillance itself. It was not their sexual habits but those of the working class that were studied at great length by social scientists. To that extent, all members of the middle class (regardless of their sex) belonged to the private realm, as public spaces in the Victorian era were always being surveyed.[43] It is precisely this difference between seeing and being seen and knowing and being known that distinguishes the classed trope of private and public, or the middle and working classes, or the sexual and the respectable.

And it is within the context of surveillance, the truth about sexuality, and the power/knowledge division of the public and private that we must read William Acton's categorization and enumeration of symptoms of venereal disease among twenty-four female patients admitted to St. Bartholomew's Hospital on November 26, 1840. The list is exhaustive and begins: "1. Bubo. Sore at the entrance to vagina. 2. Sores. 3. Condylomata. 4. Itch, gonorrhea, excoriation. 5. Suppurating bubo. Gonorrhea." The list goes on and on and on, and concludes with the twenty-fourth female patient, who is described as having not one but two buboes and condylomata.[44] In direct contrast to Acton's careful maintenance of records of Victorian prostitutes, Robert Hyam describes middle-class men in the Empire who mention their venereal disease casually, concentrating instead on their sexual exploits.[45] In short, the power/knowledge regime is not only classed but also gendered. It is at a peculiar intersection of class and race.

BLACK AND CLASS

Previously I cited Richard Dyer, who likened the whiteness of women to the whiteness and sexual innocence of the Virgin Mother and connected it to notions of the pure and the private. I now want to ask the obvious: How do we read the poor women, the working-class women, the prostitutes within this framework? What color were they, since the Victorian Age discursively constructed them as neither sexually innocent nor belonging to the realm of the private, a feature so central to the definitive definitions of Victorian femininity? To reread femininity and recontextualize the relationship between black and class, I need to make a slight detour and explore the field of biological sciences in brief. The word "biology," which gave shape to that particular science, was coined no earlier than 1802.[46] I think the female anatomy in the nineteenth century demarcated—and scrambled—notions of black and white, middle and working class.

It is well established that the Enlightenment attempted to define man's place in nature. Frequent contact with the racial Other from the seventeenth century onward had resulted in scientific inquiry about racial/biological origins in the eighteenth and nineteenth centuries. These inquiries bifurcated into two paths. First, the genealogy of languages was explored to arrive at some "truth" about race and racial mixture. Barthold Niebuhr, John Kemble, Hippolyte Taine, and Jules Michelet all explored race and language as determined by geography and the environment. Second, comparative anatomy and natural history, ethnology, and anthropology were developed to provide answers to the quest to find out about racial origins. Jean-Baptiste Lamarck, Etienne St. Hilaire, and Paul Broca, among others, worked within the latter field.[47]

In Europe, geographical exploration in the seventeenth through the nineteenth centuries had resulted in colonization and human exploitation, and the racial theories that developed were marked by a peculiar amalgam of economics, justification of human exploitation, and science masquerading as being objective, rational, and enlightened. The nineteenth century saw two distinct phases that related geography to race: monogenism and polygenism. In the early part of the century, monogenists believed in the common origin of all humankind to form one species. They argued that geographical and environmental differences transformed the one species into distinct racial varieties. In Britain, James Pritchard and William Lawrence popularized monogenism. Comparing humans of different races alongside animals of the same species, Lawrence argued that the racial variations among humans were no different than the varieties among animals.[48]

By midcentury, polygenism, which established the multiple origins of humans in multiple locations, became popular. Such a theory insisted that varying geographical environments produced differing physical, mental, and moral attributes, and that racial differences proved that human beings could be categorized into distinctive species. This latter view gave rise to the anxious question: What happened to races when they were out of their proper places, especially within the context of the emancipation of slaves after the Civil War in the United States?[49] The major issue of the day was the place occupied by the African American within the nation. Political inequality was thus redeployed as racial/ anatomical inferiority. Further, the physical and "moral" deterioration of whites in tropical places seemed to suggest that everyone should stay in their natural environment. However, the extensive nature of European colonialism also produced other racial/anatomical sciences such as phrenology, leading to the justification of the colonial enterprise since this science proved that the white European body was deemed as the most developed and as having achieved the highest form of being. Phrenology, initially, was not a race science. Developed in 1795 by the Austrian anatomist Johann Gall, phrenology was based on the premise that the brain was an organ of the mind and the mind was a composite of distinct individual faculties. Further, since the brain was housed in the head, the shape of the skull could reveal the abilities and capabilities of the person.[50] Head measurements were correlated to various behaviors. Not surprisingly, this science was used to develop racial biology and to essentialize racial types. Soon new "technologies of measurements," such as the calipers, cephalometers, craniometers, craniophores, craniostats, and so on, were developed.[51] Comparisons of anatomy resulted in maintaining and interpreting statistics on brain weights and skull capacities. The smaller head of the Negro was interpreted as revealing intellectual inferiority. Lower races, especially Africans, were revealed to have protuberant jaws—like apes—and long heads, both of which proved their inferiority. Anatomy, indeed, was destiny, and the lower races indicated that they were yet to achieve a European anatomy.

I draw attention to biological/racial sciences because it was within this context that we could see that a woman's body, unlike the male bourgeois body, was not white unto itself. Anatomical sciences, initially developed to prove the disparity between races, were also used to prove the disparity between the sexes. For instance, like people of lower races, white women too had low brain weights. Like Africans, they too were long-headed with narrow skulls and were discovered to have protruding jaws.[52] As was observed in people of lower races, the white woman's nose was flatter, her forehead misshapen, her earlobes attached—she was atavistic.[53] The white European prostitute (like the madwoman) was related through her facial features and her enlarged genitals to the Asian and African woman. Like people of lower races she was lazy; she was corpulent. As Pauline Tarnowsky suggests within the context of the nineteenth-century prostitute in Russia, physical blemishes on the prostitute such as the absence of her earlobe and her thick hair were all stigmata, signifiers of her degeneration and her sexuality. As prostitutes aged, their

> strong jaws and cheek-bones and their masculine aspect [previously] hidden by adipose tissue, emerge, salient angles stand out, and the face grows virile, uglier than a man's . . . and the countenance, once attractive, exhibits the full degenerate type which early grace had concealed.[54]

Her mannish cheekbones revealed her as not quite feminine. Her inability to conform to accepted modes of femininity also tied the prostitute to the working-class woman.

In "Black Bodies, White Bodies," Sander Gilman makes the connection between the black woman with the enormous buttocks—the

Hottentot Venus—and the Victorian British prostitute. Gilman suggests that the Victorian obsession with the physiognomy of Sarah Bartmann, the Hottentot Venus, resulted in the autopsy of her body at her death with special attention paid to her genitalia and buttocks. Her genitalia became a synecdoche and a code for her bodily difference, and her figure converged with that of the British prostitute; both embodied excessive sexuality as well as disease. The corpulent prostitute and the big-buttocked Hottentot Venus mirrored each other, and the diseased genitals of the prostitute became a metaphor for the pollution that the blacks signified. Gilman concludes, "It is thus the inherent fear of the difference in the anatomy of the Other which lies behind the synthesis of images. The Other's pathology is revealed in anatomy."[55]

Within this context, the virulence against prostitutes (and, by extension, the poor women who did not conform to the ideals of the Angel in the House) that the Contagious Diseases Acts contained is meaningful. In its isolation of the prostitutes and not their male clients, and in the convergence of the meaning of black sexuality and (fallen) white women's sexuality, the Contagious Diseases Acts covered over and became a way of expressing the fears and anxieties of white identity. If there was not much difference between the lowest form of humans, such as the Hottentot woman who was reputed to copulate even with orangutans, and the white prostitutes in Europe, what was one to conclude about racial difference, polygenism, and the intrinsic superiority of white civilization and embodiment? What did it make of white middle-class men?

Biological science was dominated by analogical thinking, which tended to see a physiological similarity between the black body and the white woman's body. In seeing them as metaphors for each other, biologists and anthropologists, among others, paid "attention to details hitherto unnoticed, to emphasize aspects of human experience otherwise treated as unimportant, to make new features into 'signs' signifying inferiority."[56] The dominance of analogical thinking created new kinds of knowledge, in that it organized scientists' understanding of causality. In so doing, analogical thinking also suppressed information about humans: information and statistics that did not support the scientists' theses were ignored or deemed unimportant. Analogical thinking that linked the black woman and the prostitute's bodies, locating both of them as inferior, in the end also metonymically linked *all* women's bodies to them; all women were biologically inferior. Thus, white women were *not* white unto themselves. White women were, in fact, not that separate from being *black*.

To bring this point to a conclusion, I want to add one more idea by using the notion of troping. Hayden White points out that tropes or metaphors "generate figures of speech or thought by their variation from what is 'normally' expected, and by the associations they establish between concepts normally felt not to be related."[57] In short, tropes allow for the seeing of the like in the unalike. Further, by troping there is a signal-switching that allows not only for new meanings to come into being, but also for the old line of thought to come to a halt, to fall out of view. Further, in a reversal of Freud's "The Uncanny," troping is also the understanding of a thought or idea through which the unfamiliar is rendered familiar and the unclassifiable becomes nonthreatening. Hayden White points out that the mimetic text that faithfully records reality needs to be read as also simultaneously troping, covering over, veering away from, and repressing, since language and processes of thought proceed through troping.

If we are to use White's notion of troping, how can we think about the discourses of class and race, which converge on the prostitute's body? What is the uncanny moment that must be made nonthreatening? What ideas must be repressed to veer attention via the troping? Why is the black woman's body, and not the black man's, used to conflate the distinct signifiers, that is, woman, black, and poor? If the trope is a linguistic equivalent of the psychological mechanism of defense, what must be defended? And from whom?

It is easy enough to talk about the relationship between class and race in the colonies. Class relationships in colonial spaces could not manifest themselves in the same way they did in Europe because, as Theodore Allen implies, there needs to be the right proportion of the laboring class, the petty bourgeois, and the bourgeoisie for that to happen.[58] In the colonies, in the New World, with the disproportion between blacks and whites, the latter could be easily outnumbered or go into decline. Within the materiality of the threat of the racial Other, it would not have made sense for whites to divide themselves completely because of class differences. The poor whites needed to be incorporated within the signifier "white" to swell the numbers and keep the blacks in their place. Thus, one could say that whiteness was not just about racial differences, but also about the covering over of class differences in the threat of black violence. Class gets troped by race and racing puts the brakes on pursuing the discourse on class.

I do not, however, mean that the discourse of class precedes that of race. Indeed, the discourse of class difference emerges particularly around the Enlightenment, with its philosophy of equal rights and ownership of property, and is almost contemporaneous with the discourse of racial difference. I say "almost" because racial discourse preceded class discourse in the works of Comte de Buffon and Johann Friedrich Blumenbach. However, the eighteenth and nineteenth centuries oversaw the burgeoning of the laboring class as well as an increase in colonized, black Others. Furthermore, internal elements within whiteness were also threatening if we consider that the French Revolution was a classed revolt. Europe saw 1830 and 1848 as the great years of revolution of the masses. In Britain, the Chartist movement between 1838 and 1848 saw the collection of three million signatures demanding universal (read: male) suffrage. In short, the bourgeoisie, which came into ascendancy only in the nineteenth century, was already having their position threatened by the laboring class. The troping of class and race worked here too in that class mobility was perceived as equivalent to miscegenation. The laboring class, like the blacks, was dirty, unhygienic, unwashed, illiterate, sexually perverted, inferior. They were a double metaphor for blackness, in that their dirty labor made them literally black every day. And in so blackening them, they also became less threatening within the discourse of progress and improvement. They too became the white man's burden, ultimately unequal to the bourgeoisie. All of these anxieties become visible on the prostitute's body, the fallen woman's body; in fact, the woman's body.

What I have suggested thus far is that notions of whiteness in the dominant representations of Victorian femininity cohere around heterosexuality, which, in turn, is hinged on clear demarcations between deviance and decency, public and private. In the desire of dominant discourse to essentialize whiteness and make a biological fact of its superiority, women's bodies were perceived as vulnerable to contamination. The chink in the white armor was the multitudinous presence of prostitutes all over Britain. Their diseases, their deviance, their degeneration, their very embodiment associated them with blackness, with animality. Thus, the woman's body scrambled the boundary between white and black. The interchangeability between the tropes of blackness and the laboring class that were inscribed on the prostitute's body also revealed that whiteness was particularly marked by bourgeois values and required membership within the bourgeoisie.

Within such a context, the misogyny and the virulence maintained against prostitutes in medical treatment and in lock hospitals can be seen as a desire to relocate all women, including those of the middle class, literally within the space of the private. As such, the prostitute and the middle-class woman, and by extension the laboring class and the black woman, all mirrored each other; there was collusion between their modes of representation. Elaine Showalter implies exactly such a mirroring when she points out that middle-class men in search of a wife were also urged for signs of inward, invisible faults, for the stigmata that marked the fallen woman.[59] If women were to be kept hidden, be it as the Angel in the House or as the prostitute in the lock hospital, then we must conclude that what was to be kept hidden was their liminal status. White women were chameleons who turned black quite routinely and in so doing eroded the invincibility and purity of whiteness. Whiteness was always already black as well. The invulnerability and superiority of whiteness was under siege, under threat, questionable. It was revealed to be a political and imperial, rather than a biological, construct. And this message was written on the white woman's body.

Rereading Freud's "Femininity"

In this section I will read Freud's text on "Femininity" because it is such an influential text for second- and third-wave feminists in its critique of the comprehension of femininity as having been essentialized within gender theory. Published in 1933 (or, to be more precise, on December 6, 1932, a month ahead of the official publication date), "Femininity" was the fifth piece in Freud's *New Introductory Lectures on Psychoanalysis*. But the new lectures were misnamed in that they were never lectured: Freud had undergone an operation for mouth cancer, which "had made speaking in public impossible for him."[60] Muted in speech but as prolific a writer as ever, Freud included in this collection his final and definitive version of his theorizing on femininity, a theme he had rehearsed previously in 1925 in "Some Psychical Consequences of the Anatomical Distinctions between the Sexes" and again in 1931 in "Female Sexuality."

Freud's theorizing on sexuality (especially that of women and children) is closely braided with his development of the field of psychoanalysis itself. Both originated in 1885–86 when Freud went to Paris to study the treatment of hysteria in children with Jean Martin Charcot. Later Freud continued this field of work with Josef Breuer and jointly published *Studies in Hysteria* in 1895. Freud's relationship with Breuer, which is well documented, resulted in his development of the science of psychoanalysis, with the publication of *The Interpretation of Dreams* (1900) and *Three Essays on the Theory of Sexuality* (1905). It was when he failed to analyze his patient Dora's hysteria that he realized the fragmentary nature of woman's sexuality. Indeed, many of Freud's texts considered central to the field of cultural and literary studies, such as "The Uncanny," "The Unconscious," "Repression," and "On Narcissism," are based on his theorizing of women and their sexuality.

For Freud, the narratives of maturation and sexuality for girls and boys follow complex paths, both using the Oedipus myth as a template. In fact, the importance of the Oedipus myth had been realized by Freud as early as October 15, 1897, when he wrote to his friend Wilhelm Fliess that "we can understand the riveting power of Oedipus Rex." He added, "The Greek legend seizes on a compulsion which *everyone* recognizes because he feels his existence within himself."[61] In his earliest versions, Freud applied the Oedipus myth to read both genders. However, by 1923, when he wrote "The Infantile Genital Organization," he started questioning his use of one model for both sexes, especially when factoring in the child's relationship with the mother. In 1925, when he wrote "Some Psychical Consequences," the earliest of his three papers on the theory of femininity, Freud merely advanced the notion of the emotional equivalence of the young boy and girl: both form attachments to their mother. By the time he wrote "Female Sexuality," he speculated on the consequences of the young girl's attachment to her mother; she also had an additional task (when compared to her male counterpart) to change her love-object from her mother to her father.

In "Femininity," Freud amplified most fully the process through which the girl accedes into femininity and heterosexuality and finally becomes a woman. In this essay, he elaborates on the Oedipus myth to suggest that, at a certain moment in their history of maturation, both the boy and the girl recognize the centrality of the father to the trajectory of their desire. This moment also inaugurated their comprehension of anatomical differences. The mother's body and its always already castrated condition become proof of the power of the father, his might signified by his penis. While the boy conceded to the supremacy of the father and his castrating ability, internalized his superego, and controlled his desire for his mother, the girl followed a different path to maturation. She transferred her affections from her mother to her father. In short, while the boy is always already inserted into a narrative of heterosexuality, the girl has to learn it. To complete this narrative, Freud indicates that an effect of the girl's castrated condition was her inability to internalize the superego, resulting in her lack of sense of the law and justice and lack of conscience. Freud insisted that her lack of a penis results in her being passive, a position the girl occupies forever.

Freud's text and views on femininity garnered lively debates among the psychoanalytic community in the 1920s and 1930s and among feminists between the 1970s and 1990s. In the first set of debates between Freud and his colleagues such as Karen Horney, Karl Abraham, and Helene Deutsch, much concern was expended on the significance of the mother to femininity, the centrality of the castration complex, and the notion of passivity. So, for instance, femininity became a product of penis envy, coupled with the loss of the maternal body, the inability to disidentify with the mother, and a predilection for masochism and narcissism. In these debates, unlike the Cartesian dictum that severed the link between the mind and the body, women's bodies were perceived to affect their minds.

In the second series of debates, feminists such as Nancy Chodorow, Juliet Mitchell, Jacqueline Rose, Julia Kristeva, and Luce Irigaray, to name just a few, analyzed the centrality of Freud's framework to the notion of identity.[62] The work of Jacques Lacan heavily influenced this cluster of debates, and the significance of repression became central to the construction of femininity. There was a focus on the acquisition of language as a compensation for the loss of the maternal body in these debates. But in crucial ways, the second series of debates merely reiterated the first; femininity continued to be read within a framework of lack.

While the second series of debates cohering around the notion of identity define and elaborate the second wave of feminism and re-examine the issue of gender, they are problematic in that they *dislocate* discourses of the body, femininity, and gender from the *history* in which they were produced. Indeed, much feminist theory, influenced by psychoanalysis—a discourse that insists on the *constructed* nature of subjects—has tended to posit the female body as an essence while simultaneously insisting on the constructed nature of femininity as an effect of the misogyny that has produced it. In their insistence on the constructed nature of femininity, second-wave feminists have in fact reproduced femininity and female sexuality, especially within the nuclear family configuration, as "ontologically stable," coherent, and in an "unbroken continuum"[63] by repeating and using as a premise the arguments of Freud and Lacan.

However, it is my contention that Freud, born in Europe in the mid-Victorian period, was not so revolutionary as to remain uninfluenced by Victorian constructions of femininity. In fact, his theories on women's sexuality seem to elaborate precisely nineteenth-century notions of the woman and the body. As Sander Gilman points out, Darwin influenced Freud in that he saw the world within the framework of biology.[64] Though written in the first few decades of the twentieth century, Freud's text is saturated with the occluded discourses of racial formations, their relationship to gender formations, class formations, the rise of the bourgeoisie, and a certain production of sexuality, all of which were markers of the nineteenth century. In fact, rereading "Femininity" within the context of the nineteenth century makes us realize the reproduction of these occlusions in most of the feminist debates of the late twentieth century, so that notions of femininity rematerialize again as dislocated from race and class concerns. I will retrace the material conditions of the nineteenth-century European woman by using Freud's "Femininity" as a template. Indeed, nineteenth-century productions of women via discourses of children, race, class, and human, the distinction between the public/private split, and scientific constructions of the material body, though invisible, structure our understanding of Freud's "Femininity." And it is some of these occluded discourses that I wish to bring back into visibility. For the sake of brevity, I will rehistoricize only two instances of "Femininity" that contribute to our understanding of whiteness in the nineteenth century.

Oedipus and History

Can we historicize Oedipus or, more precisely, recontextualize the Sophocles myth? I want to unpack the trope of Oedipus from the nineteenth-century backdrop in which it is produced. When Freud referred to Oedipus in his 1897 letter to Fliess, he interpreted this complex as *a human condition* by linking Oedipus with Hamlet. This continuum from the late sixteenth century, when *Hamlet* was written, into the late nineteenth century via the trope of Oedipus, supposedly naturalizes this neurosis to normality. However, such a linking becomes problematic when we remember that the notion of the Greeks as the ancestor for Western Europeans was very much a particular construct of the late eighteenth century. In other words, there is no "natural" link between Greek mythology and the European subjectivity that Freud seems to be invoking.

One can historically locate Greek revival to the eighteenth and early nineteenth centuries, a phenomenon that accompanied the rise of the bourgeoisie and modern nationalism, especially within the context of liberal democracy. In *Black Athena,* Martin Bernal suggests the continuum between ancient Greece and Western Europe as a fiction constructed in the age of imperialism.[65] For Bernal, the conquest of Greece by the Egyptians and Phoenicians, previously accepted as historical facts, became untenable in the nineteenth century because Greece was now being reconstructed as the cradle of Europe. Bernal adds that cold places like Switzerland, Northern Germany, and Scotland, with their clean air, harsh terrain and climate, and snowy mountains, were particularly linked to the Western European body. The discipline, health, tautness, and uprightness of European embodiment were perceived as qualities having originated in Greece within an Aryan/Caucasian mythology.[66]

The Greek revival, occasioned in the late eighteenth century by German thinkers like J. J. Winckelmann, Goethe, Lessing, and A. W. Schlegel, who were rediscovering art forms like sculpting, architecture, and drama, transformed Greece into a metaphor for the pure form of ancient European life.[67] Northern Europe, especially Germany and Britain, which were in the middle of the Industrial Revolution as well as a transformation into modern nation-states, saw themselves as having descended from the Greeks. For George Mosse, Winckelmann's *History of Ancient Art* influenced future generations of Europeans to perceive its muscular images of men as "the symbols of masculinity, the nation, and its youth."[68] This revival of Greek sculpture also relocated masculinity and men as serene and devoid of sensuousness. Winckelmann underscored this interpretation in particular when he saw the statue in Rome of Laocoon being strangled by snakes. The self-restraint on Laocoon's face was perceived as central to masculine beauty and represented noble simplicity and calm grandeur, the transcendence of the individual and his passions. Winckelmann remarked, "The quiet and repose of the body reveals the lofty and harmonious spirit of he who braves the greatest dangers for the sake of justice, who provides for his country's defence and brings peace to his subjects."[69] The austere virility associated with the Doric order played a large part in this interpretation.[70] For Winckelmann, Greek art transformed the individual into universal validity. Mosse points out that the Greek revival was co-opted by nationalism and that "the nation protected the ideal of beauty from the lower passions of man and helped transform it into a symbol of self-control and purity."[71]

While Greek art and architecture emphasized calmness and self-restraint, the tragedies emphasized something else: the torrent of violent feelings and dark passions. The revival of Greek tragedies was initiated by Schlegel's lectures on drama in 1808 (translated into English in 1815). However, Schlegel's interpretation of Greek tragedies was in keeping with that of Winckelmann's perception of calmness: "It is only before the groupes of Niobe or Laocoon that we first enter into the spirit . . . of Sophocles."[72] In his preface to *Merope,* Matthew Arnold explained the antithesis by pointing out that the torrent of emotions resulted in a sense of acquiescence and repose, by which he meant the reposefulness that the spectator felt after the catharsis of emotions.[73]

While the muted suffering in Laocoon's face embodied the link between rising nationalistic sentiments in eighteenth-to-nineteenth-century Western and Northern Europe and the refashioning of masculinity, women were excluded from the meaning and forms of representation that the Greek revival brought to Europe. Instead, they were represented through notions of the medieval. Britannia, Germania, and Marianne in France were all figures of women who represented the preindustrial, standing for morality and chastity, virtues that the Greeklike men had obviously to protect. The figure of Germania was perceived as having "a classical quality" outside of time and place, in contrast to John Bull, who wore modern Victorian clothing.[74]

I need to make one more reference to this cluster that coheres around the Greek revival: that of the rise of the bourgeoisie. It is a historical commonplace to link the political and economic gains made by the middle class with the Industrial Revolution, which consequently resulted in changes in the economic, cultural, and social fabric in Western Europe. This rise also led to the promotion of bourgeois values all across Western Europe with an emphasis on hard work, the self-restraint of emotions and sexual behavior, and rising national sentiments.[75] One could argue that celebration of self-restraint in the late eighteenth and nineteenth centuries constituted, while being constituted by, the Greek revival.

I suggest that Freud's choice of narrative to theorize gender constructions in the West is neither "obvious" nor "natural," but rather saturated with the implications of Greek revival, its connection to nationalism in Western Europe, industrialization, the reconfiguration of masculinity, and the rise of the middle class. Greek masculinity, iconography, and Greece itself all were coded as light, youth, radiance, and calm in late eighteenth- and nineteenth-century Europe. Within this context, the Oedipal framework, with its reference to a Greek hero and a Greek legend, *excises* women and femininity from participating in it, a fact that is replicated in Freud, where women function as a lack. His choice of Oedipus as the template for the heteromaturation process was saturated with the meanings of the Greek revival. Indeed, the pitfalls that befall women in their path to maturation in "Femininity" are numerous. For instance, she could become masochistic, could develop penis envy, sexual inhibitions, neurosis, or a masculinity complex; further, she is not able to develop a superego, and by age thirty becomes unchangeable and psychically rigid. Alternatively, she could develop into a normal, normative femininity, which in this text suspiciously resembles the neurotic woman as well. The point I wish to make is that Freud's very choice of framework and narrative precluded locating women as being different. Instead, the unitary, unifying narrative of Oedipus is equitably applied to both the young boy and girl, and she is consequently read as a lack. Notwithstanding the fact that Oedipus's own story is a *failed* narrative, and one of violence that threatens mutilation/castration upon its subjects while forcing them to follow normative gender constructions, its very Greekness codes it as male, light/white, and calm. Further, all these various factors produced an idealized body, one that was male, muscular, and tanned, yet white and fit, to which the nations of Western Europe aspired. In this context, women were once more left out of the loop of perfect bodily forms. In the end, Western women of the nineteenth century were not calm, but constructed as neurotic and hysteric. Nor did they have the perfect bodily form; that belonged to the men. Freud's "Femininity" contains only one form of activity for a woman: nursing her baby. Her imperfect passive body cannot have any more agency.

THE DEGENERATE WOMAN

The trope of Oedipus indicates that whiteness was always already masculine, signifying rationality, mind, and the perfect male body. What was femininity then? If femininity was excised from Greek forms, to what discourses was it linked? In *Freud, Race, and Gender,* Sander Gilman suggests that the psychoanalytic discourse on femininity by Freud be read through the lens of race.[76] Gilman fleshes out an anti-Semitic Vienna in which Freud grew up and lived and describes the gathering forces of the Holocaust, which served as the backdrop for Freud's theorizing on femininity. For Gilman, Freud's work should be perceived as reproducing a metaphorical structure in that the framework of race structured his notion of femininity: when Freud wrote about the woman's body, he was really writing about the Jewish man's body. Like her flawed, castrated body, the Jewish man too had a flawed, circumcised body, that which marked him as being an outsider, an Other. In Gilman's reading, Freud's psychoanalytic discourse thus becomes Jewish discourse, and the difference between the gentile male and the Jewish male's embodiments is rewritten as masculinity and femininity, respectively.

The metaphorical relationship between the circumcised Jewish male and the (unraced) woman in Freud's text hinges on the visual, the ability to look and to be seen. As such, the trope of Oedipus and the unmutilated penis of the perfect male form construct the flawed bodies of the castrated woman and the circumcised man. Indeed, in being structured in opposition to perfection, both the woman and the Jew are written as black. Gilman's reading of Freud's theorizing on the woman's body fits seamlessly with the reading of white femininity I have given thus far. But I want to ask the following questions of Gilman's text: Where have all the women gone? In the end, are women only the mutilated or incomplete forms of men?

Next, I will pursue the one-sexed model of perfect forms instituted by Freud and its relationship to whiteness and race. The origins of the one-sexed model lie in the Old World. The definitive text on the human body that influenced Western philosophers and physicians from the second century A.D. to the Enlightenment was that written by the anatomist Galen of Pergamum.[77] For Galen, men and women had the same reproductive organs, only reversed. So the vaginal passage corresponded with the penis, the ovaries with the testicles, the fallopian tubes with the spermatic ducts, and so on. Accordingly, the woman was the man reversed, in that while for him his genitalia remained external, for her they turned in and extended inward. The woman's body was colder, less well formed than a man's, and therefore needed the man for reproduction. Being so inverted and in having her organs at the wrong place, she was a less perfect man. This particular model is similar to the one espoused by Aristotle, for whom biological distinctions could be hierarchized and ranked. The woman represented materiality, and the man had the power to fashion that materiality into humans within the context of reproduction. Thus, woman as an unformed man was located as physically and mentally inferior, which notion also underpinned medieval comprehensions of gender and the body. For Laqueur, "anatomy—modern sex—could . . . be construed as metaphor, another name for the 'reality' of woman's lesser perfection."[78] Ultimately, the one-sex model was "an exercise in preserving the Father, he who stands not only for order but for the very existence of civilization itself."[79] Thus, the comprehension and insistence of a one-sexed body was political and social rather than just about old-fashioned prejudices or misogyny.

The Enlightenment, with its refusal to accept "natural" authority of the king over subject or man over woman, finally reshifted biological sciences so women would be perceived as being different from men. With the Enlightenment, a woman's body and her reproductive organs started getting their own nomenclatures, which also permitted it to be perceived as different and not within a teleology where male (white) bodies spelled perfection. It is a poststructuralist commonplace to point out that the concept of difference cannot be comprehended unless it falls within the parameters of, and is an elaboration of, the same. Indeed, any representation of the same cannot come into inscription without locating the different as the constitutive outside. In short, the notion of difference becomes the unspeakable condition of representation itself. It is not surprising, then, that within such a reading, woman as difference, her body as difference, cannot even come into inscription. That her very body appears only in catachresis is visible when we ask the following of post-Enlightenment analyses of her body: What is the political investment in the concept of difference? Do the equal rights espoused by the Enlightenment equate to an *acceptance* of difference, interpreted differently from being part of the same? Can the woman's body, deemed as difference, be perceived as being outside a preconceived teleology? How are we to regard the embodiment of women in a two-sexed model, especially when the model is based on comprehensions of Enlightenment philosophy and identity politics, which themselves are premised on a Cartesian split that valorizes mind over body? In other words, there is a fundamental problem between the *aspirations* of a two-sexed model and its actual *practice:* woman as different but equal is based upon her mind, not upon her body. How do you talk about the body, then? What happens to the assimilative process if her mind is deemed equal to that of the man's but her body is not? How are we to reread "Femininity"?

In the nineteenth century, the concept of "degeneration" functioned as a counterdiscourse to that of evolution and progress. Since the body was now perceived to be mutable and could evolve into an optimum shape, then the converse could also be true: that the body could devolve and degenerate.[80] All sorts of differences were categorized within this terminology: madness, prostitution, racial difference, syphilis, hysteria, all the phobias, sexual deviance, and so on. This particular terminology revealed the anxiety of the bourgeoisie against whose identities the degenerate was constructed. The notion of degeneration historically originated with the fall from grace, from the pre-Adamic state to being the victim of modernity. While on one hand the nineteenth century was invested in progress and reason via the Enlightenment, on the other hand the concept of degeneration became a way of articulating the changing conditions of life. Class conflict and class mixing, the transitory way of life in urban areas, and race mixing all were perceived as forms of perversion and, therefore, degeneration. This powerful counterdiscourse particularly manifested itself within the field of medicine and sexual deviance, and masturbation, incest, homosexuality and any form of perverse sexuality all were categorized as degenerate. Even children were perceived as degenerate, especially in their sexuality. Degeneration was visible on one who had facial tics and other signs, such as the ear of the prostitute or the buttocks of the black woman, the stigmata obvious to the eye. Alternatively, it could also be invisible and reveal itself through behavior. As such, any form of visible or invisible Otherness was categorized as degeneracy.

I suggest that Freud's construction of woman's embodiment and her femininity fell within the concept of degeneration. In his reading of femininity, the female subject, in lacking the penis, lacks perfectability of form. Lacking the penis, she develops a mental defect, penis envy, neurosis, melancholy, hysteria. Lacking the penis, she finds it very difficult to move beyond the Oedipal crisis. Lacking the penis, she cannot develop a superego. Lacking the penis and the superego, she lacks a conscience, a sense of justice, a sense of the public. Lacking the penis, she is closer to the criminal, the pervert, the Other, all of whom also lack a conscience and a sense of the public good. Lacking the penis, and like the racialized Other, she lacks an evolved form. Lacking the penis, she wears her stigmata on her body, in her mind, and in her heart. Lacking the penis, her form converges with all forms of perversion. Lacking the penis, she will never be bourgeois or white in herself, for whiteness, like the perfect form, was masculine.

In this chapter I have examined the whiteness of women and pointed out that she is more black than white. I have suggested that the tension and anxieties of the bourgeois formations of the body converge on the white woman's body. She is neither white nor perfect. She is black, poor, and a degenerate in form. If all women are black and only white middle-class men are white, I wonder: what is the color of heterosexuality?

CHAPTER 3

Victoria's Secret:
The History of White Sexuality

The term "miscegenation," or the sexual union of whites with blacks, was coined in the year 1864 during the American Civil War by two New York journalists who wrote a pamphlet titled *Miscegenation,* which was subsequently reviewed in the *Anthropological Review.* The reviewer of the work was enraged at the promotion of miscegenation and concluded that only a mulatto/"mulatress" could have written this work.[1] Indeed, interracial sexuality becomes visible only within an awareness of racial demarcations. While race-mixing was particularly repulsive to most nineteenth-century Americans who were enmeshed within the trauma of slavery, Great Britain too, with its enormous colonial holdings, formulated its own racialized theories of phrenology, degeneration, eugenics, and evolution in the nineteenth century to demarcate the different races that the British came into daily contact with, in the colonies and within Britain itself.

Can a color be ascribed to Western desire? Can a gender? Are sexuality and sexual practices within modernity raced? Is white sexuality distinctive? I want to focus on these questions, especially within the context of Victoria's white desire that helped shape modern Britishness. In asking such obvious questions I wish to go beyond a mere statement of miscegenation laws that controlled and raced sexuality. Is it possible that our very comprehension of sexuality, its signification and practices, can occur only through its underpinning of racial differences? My exploration of these questions will take me on a circuitous route marked by historical references and citations, legal histories, and issues of embodiment.

The theorizing of Western sexuality was inaugurated in the nineteenth century and the early part of the twentieth century within debates on the nature of the family, the role of femininity, and sexual forms. Included in these inaugural moments are William Acton's *Prostitution* and the regulation and practice of prostitution in the Victorian era. Acton's work was inspired by Parent-Duchatelet's two-volume 1826 work, *De la Prostitution dans la Ville de Paris;* scattered references to sexuality in Charles Darwin's *The Origin of Species* and particularly in *The Descent of Man;* Havelock Ellis's multivolumed *Studies in the Psychology of Sex;* the works of Sigmund Freud, particularly *Three Essays on the Theory of Sexuality;* and even Alfred Kinsey's post–Second World War works, *Sexual Behaviour of the Human Male* and *Sexual Behaviour of the Human Female.*[2] While these scholars and theorists read sexuality, for the most part, as a natural fact, based on the functioning of the body and located outside of history and culture, the second generation of scholarship on sexuality, beginning in 1968, emphasized the constructed nature of sexuality, governed by political urgencies, economic realities, contingencies, cultures of resistance, and the appropriation of the body by the ideological discourse of sexuality. A few of the earliest second-generation scholars of sexuality are Mary MacIntosh, in "The Homosexual Role"; Michel Foucault, *The History of Sexuality;* Arnold Davidson, "Sex and the Emergence of Sexuality"; and Jeffrey Weeks, who wrote innumerable works, notably *Sexuality; Sex, Politics, and Society;* and *Making Sexual History.*[3]

Among all of these texts, it is Foucault's groundbreaking *History of Sexuality* that functions as the urtext of sexuality within modernity. Peopling the nineteenth century with a theater of grotesques—such as the mother who harbors murderous thoughts, the impotent and sadistic husband, the hysterical woman, the precocious and masturbating child, the perverted stranger, the Malthusian couple whose task in life is to reproduce healthy offspring and strengthen the nation-state—Foucault begins this work with the query, Why did an age that seemed to discard sexuality simultaneously proliferate discourses on it? He offers, instead, the notion that sexuality is not only enmeshed within definitions of selfhood, but is also within the grid of power relations and at the site where dense transfers of power occur.[4] In this well-cited work, Foucault urges scholars to turn to an examination of the nation-state embourgeoise-ment for the new technology of sexuality that emerged at the end of the eighteenth century. If previously blood and lineage were important to the aristocrats, the bourgeoisie emphasized the body and its health within reproduction for Foucault. He states, "The emphasis on the body should undoubtedly be linked to the process of growth and establish-ment of bourgeois hegemony: not, however, because of the market value assumed by labour capacity, but because of what the 'cultivation' of its own body could represent politically, economically, and historically for the present and the future of the bourgeoisie."[5] He connects this new obsession with body hygiene, the reproduction of healthy offspring, and longevity with a type of "racism," a term that in this work suggests a nationalistic desire of an elaboration of the same. To this extent, the mentally unfit, the physically degenerate, are Othered because of their flaws and the state need for optimally healthy citizens.

Foucault seems to stop short of analyzing the Other body of state racism, a point that Ann Stoler picks up on. In the incredible *Race and the Education of Desire,* Stoler points out that, notwithstanding the rac-ism of the state and its exclusion of what it deems unhealthy bodies, the boundaries between the healthy and the unhealthy were extremely porous. For her, the formation of the middle class and its values and distinctions was made possible not only in its contrast to the working class in Europe, but also through a "racialized notion of civility that brought about the convergence of—and conflict between—class and racial membership in sharp relief." Stoler's point of origin in *Race and the Education of Desire* is precisely located within Foucault's occlusion of colonialism from his listed sites of knowledges: biology, medicine, psychopathology, sociology, ethnology, education, medicine, and jus-tice. Stoler makes an impassioned case for the centrality of colonialism in the production of nineteenth-century sexuality and the technology of the self. She insists that "Europe's eighteenth-century discourses on sexuality can—indeed must—be traced along a more circuitous impe-rial route that leads to nineteenth-century technologies of sex. They were refracted through the discourses of Empire and its exigencies by men and women whose affirmations of a bourgeois self and the racial-ized contexts in which loose confidences were built, could not be dis-entangled."[6] Stoler focuses on the rise of the bourgeoisie as well, but she emphasizes instead its relationship and construction of/by the colonies and the formulation of its values as central to the construction of sexuality in the West.

Stoler's thesis is an extension of George Mosse's work in *Nationalism and Sexuality,* wherein he explores the relationship between national injunctions and taboos on embodiment and sexuality within the context of Nazi Germany.[7] Indeed, such a line of reasoning has been investigated by cultural theorists such as Marjorie Garber, Eve Sedgwick, R. Radhakrishnan, and Ketu Katrak, among others, who examine discourses of the nation to perceive the shaping and deployment of its sexuality.[8] In her framework and in her analysis of Dutch colonialism, Stoler also extends Sander Gilman's thesis of the relationship between black and white sexuality as elaborated in *Difference and Pathology.*[9] Gilman's suggestive work insists on the metonymic link between the black and white woman, thus locating both of them within the context of degeneracy. Finally, the work of Anne McClintock must be cited within this context. In her analysis of the relationship between Hannah Cullwick and Arthur Munby in *Imperial Leather,* McClintock unravels the tight braiding of the discourses of race and class and the sexualization of these two discourses within the context of nineteenth-century Britain and its enmeshment within high colonialism.[10]

Indeed, my work is much influenced by all of these works that have preceded me, leaving me with little room to say anything new. I therefore want to shift focus slightly to unpack the status of the body produced at the nexus of sexuality and colonialism because the sex/sexuality/gender nexus in the Victorian Age system is predicated on the body. As Roy Porter reminds us, "The body cannot be treated by the historian as a biological given, but must be regarded as mediated through cultural sign systems. The apportionment of function and responsibility between body and mind, body and soul, differs notably according to century, class, circumstances, and culture, and societies often possess a plurality of competing meanings."[11] Is there a history to the nineteenth-century body? Is the notion of difference that underpins the racialized or feminized body different from poststructuralist comprehensions of difference? How does this history of nineteenth-century bodily difference function with that of gender to embody, or disembody, the Victorian subject? How is the comprehension and practice of sexuality enmeshed within the context of difference? Or is the notion of the differentiated body itself central to the production of desire within modernity? I explore these questions to reinscribe the occluded body back into the notion of sexuality in modernity. In so doing, I read the close imbrication of the nineteenth-century white body and white sexuality with their counterparts in the colonies. In particular, I reexamine the silences within Foucault's *The History of Sexuality,* volume 1. Later in this chapter I will read some moments on the legislations on bodies and sexuality in nineteenth-century Britain because these moments in Britain's juridical history do not make sense without considering their relationship to race and their counterparts in the colonies. These moments reveal not only white anxiety, but the centrality of blackness in the production of white desire.

DIFFERENCE AND THE BODY

Jeffrey Weeks draws the determinants of (British) Victorian sexuality within the context of family and domestic life, the split between the public and private, the increasing demarcation between masculinity and femininity, and the "moral and hygienic policing of non-marital, non-heterosexual sexuality."[12] He locates British sexuality within class differences and housing conditions—the Victorian notion of sexual promiscuity and perversion coming into being in the slums, of incest having its origins in the one-room tenement.[13] While he is sensitive to gender and class differences dictating sexual mores in Victorian Britain, his only references to racial difference is his citing of Margaret Mead and her work on Samoa and the miscegenation laws in apartheid South Africa.[14] It is surprising that Weeks doesn't grapple with the embodiment of blackness and the impact of Empire within the scope of his work on British sexuality. Weeks's work has influenced mine incredibly, and I prefer to take as my starting point another nuanced remark by him when he discusses difference in an interview with Ken Plummer in 1993. Here Weeks refers to racial, sexual, and gender differences and suggests that "these differences only become meaningful in certain historical contexts[,] and I'm interested in why certain things become meaningful at that time or this time and not at other times."[15] I want to use Weeks's nuanced suggestion to posit that difference has a history, one predicated on the body.

THE GENDERED BODY

According to cultural and medical historians and theorists, two momentous shifts occurred in the (homogenous) West that relocated the status of the body sometime around the end of the eighteenth century.

Both of these relocations were predicated on new comprehensions of difference—the woman's body as difference, the racialized body as difference—as reinforced by the Cartesian mind/body split. The degradation of the body has a long history as this dualism has been fundamental to Western epistemology and ontology, shaping ethics, linguistic usage, and classificatory schemes. Indeed, the metonymic linking of the racialized and gendered body has shaped modern comprehensions of whiteness.

In *Making Sex* Thomas Laqueur points out:

> Sometime in the eighteenth century, sex as we know it was invented. The reproductive organs went from being paradigmatic sites for displaying hierarchy, resonant throughout the cosmos, to being the foundation of incommensurable difference: "women owe their manner of being to their organs of generation, and especially their uterus," as one eighteenth century physician put it.[16]

In this significant work, Laqueur traces the status of the human body within medical discourse before the eighteenth century and suggests that, far from advances in anatomy, medicine was governed by political discourses of the social and cultural. Before this moment, the model used by anatomists was that of the one-sexed body first posited by Galen in the second century A.D. In this schema based on the Aristotlian-Galenic theory of the four humors—air, water, earth, and heat, which constituted the four elements of the terrestrial sphere—heat was the privileged term. The distinction between the material body and the four elements of the cosmos did not exist as the human temperament was defined by the propensity to be cold or hot, wet or dry. Masculinity and femininity signified differently within medical discourses of the premodern body, wherein male and female bodies were perceived as reversals of each other. The womb was the penis reversed within the body, the bottom of the womb was the scrotum inverted, the cervix and vulva the internal positioning of the glans. Indeed, legends abounded that men could become women and women men if the body changed in the maturation process since notions of hot/cold or formal/informal determined sexed positions. The penis, according to Laqueur, was a "status symbol rather than a sign. . . . Being of one sex or another entitled the bearer to certain social considerations much as noble birth entitled one to wear ermine under sumptuary laws governing clothing."[17]

The discovery of and subscription to the two-sexed model, with woman as difference rather than an inverted elaboration of the same, was a production of the political comprehensions of the body and nature. In its search for justification of hierarchies in the natural world, Enlightenment discourse has presumed a desexed body, but in fact has created the reverse: a highly gendered notion of sex. The two-sexed model of anatomy produced, while being produced by, the political and social ramifications of difference. It directly impacted on the growth of industry and capitalism in the eighteenth and nineteenth centuries: the role of women as reproducers of labor became the cornerstone to a stable political order and the production and generation of wealth in a nation. Thus, the meaning and governance of women's reproductive abilities was a form of the management of capital in the nation.[18] There is a seamless narrative produced here between liberal democratic discourse and medical discourse. For instance, Carole Pateman cites Enlightenment discourse to argue that the perception of woman as difference left her out of the polity because notions of the woman's body excluded them from equal rights in social contract, employment, and citizenship.[19] In *The Disorder of Women,* Pateman critiques liberal democratic theories on citizenship in which women's bodies are perceived as completely opposed to political order. Since women are embodied as disorder, they are brought into democracy differently than men, and are either excluded from or have a different relationship to the public world of freedom, rights, contracts, and citizenship.[20] Pateman suggests that the public/private dichotomy is, in fact, connected by a patriarchal structure that valorizes a civil society over the natural sphere of the family.[21]

While liberal democracy located woman as disorder, gynecological science that developed alongside it also underscored men and women as binary opposites and woman as difference. The history of gynecology was also a history of social relations. As Ornella Moscucci points out, "By presenting historically specific notions about man's and woman's nature as the fruit of unbiased observation, they also conceal the social conditions in which they were produced."[22] It was as recent as 1796 that the first illustration of the female skeleton was drawn.[23] The first illustrations set the course and priority of scientific research of the eighteenth and nineteenth centuries of the study and nature of women. Included in the study and the medicalization of the woman's body in that era, it was not just the genitals that were reevaluated in the eighteenth century, but also all of the female sex organs. Indeed, one can say that the cultural valorization of motherhood was linked to the rising importance of the uterus. The theory of complementarity, which underpinned the notion of difference, suggested that women had specific roles to play, the most important being motherhood.[24]

Within feminist discourse it is a commonplace to conclude that, traditionally, women's roles as difference also simultaneously locates them within the orbit of nature. The opposition between nature and culture has its own history. This opposition becomes particularly meaningful to Enlightenment philosophers who located culture within rationality, education, and city living, and nature within emotions, savagery, and simplicity of thought and rural living. Nature, as Sherry Ortner and Donna Haraway have pointed out, is thus a cultural construct.[25] In the wake of the Enlightenment, in the nineteenth century nature particularly referred to a presocial state, and women, because of their role in reproduction, were closely aligned with nature.[26] This dichotomy maintained peculiar tensions in that the figure of the woman was simultaneously desirable yet threatening. The nineteenth century, because of its subscription to the ideology of progress, perceived that women, with their lack of rationality, their closer adherence to nature, and their conservatism, slowed progress. Humane, rational, and civilized society was only possible via the mediation of culture, progress, and enlightened thought.

The Racialized Body

Before I tease out further political meanings and implications adherent to the notion of difference, I want to juxtapose the feminine body of the eighteenth century to that of the raced body of that era. Tracing the history and system of marks, Collette Guillamin pinpoints the eighteenth century as pivotal in the shift in meaning for the marking of bodies:

> The idea of classifying *according* to somatic/morphological criteria is recent and the date can be fixed: the eighteenth century. From a circumstantial association between economic relations and physical marks was born a new type of mark ("color") . . . [t]he fabrication of taxonomies . . . that were to be progressively qualified as "natural."[27]

Guillamin points out that in the Middle Ages, clothing was used to indicate membership to religious groups (such as the yarmulke for Jewish people and the yellow cross for Cathars), the coat of arms on movable objects to indicate ownership by nobility, and permanent in-delible marks on convicts to indicate the permanence of social relations. However, in the eighteenth century, new classificatory systems and comprehensions of bodies made race/color a new criterion. These new comprehensions of race retroactively conferred the status of natural to its classificatory systems. Guillamin concludes: "For the old mark was recognized as imposed by social relationships, known as one of their consequences, while the natural mark is not presumed to be a mark but the very *origin* of these relationships."[28]

In fact, the genealogy of the modern preoccupation with the ra-cialized body can also be located in the eighteenth century, contem-porary with that over the woman's body. In 1735, Carl von Linné, or Linnaeus, published his decisive work on taxonomy, *Systema Naturae*, which organized plant life as much as it did the four varieties of hu-mans as part of the same natural system that could be classified like the fauna and flora: Europeans, Americanus, Asiaticus, and Africanus. Indeed, Linnaeus's classification of human bodies and definition of the human as *sapientissimum*—most wise—was an extension of John Locke's position that humans were separate from the rest of nature because of their possession of reason. Rewriting Linnaeus's schema, after Captain James Cook's voyage to Australia and Oceania, Blumenbach added one more category: that of the Malay. Blumenbach used circular reasonings to suggest that Caucasians (Europeans) were the most developed and attractive because of the shape of their skull and their beauty. The Na-tive American, the Malay, the Asian, and the African all were inferior.[29] Comte de Buffon, Linnaeus's contemporary and rival, shifted the at-tention from the classification of the variety of humans to that of race by suggesting a history of traits passed down through the generations in multiple forms.[30] He added that the classification of humans should take the whole gamut of physical and mental features such as skin color, stature, hair type, and physiognomy into consideration.[31] The link be-tween the classifications of race and gender becomes clearer when we consider that Buffon's desire to see racial difference in every feature was echoed in that of the German anatomist Jakob Ackermann, who, in 1788, pursued gender differences between male and female anatomy in the bones, hair, eyes, voices, sweat, mouths, and brains.[32]

The scientific revolution of the sixteenth and seventeenth centu-ries had primarily concentrated on physics and astronomy, but in the late eighteenth and nineteenth centuries it developed the biological and human sciences. Such a development was inevitable, given that the latter two centuries coincided with the high colonial period of European powers and the large-scale interaction of people perceived to be of different colors, sizes, and appearances. The dilemma that this ideological and economic development posed for Western Europe was that, if within liberal democracy all humans had the same political rights, how then could it explain or justify slavery and colonialism? This moral dilemma is intimately connected to the development of comparative anatomy and the biological sciences. There was also a revival of the Aristotelian idea of *scala naturae,* which suggested that all living things in nature lived in a ladderlike structure, each being separated from the next by imperceptible differences.[33] Comparative anatomists were thus able to hierarchize humans and give new social meanings to gender. While this Aristotelian idea had its followers, some anatomists like Johann Blumenbach and Georges Cuvier repudiated it, preferring to suggest that definite gulfs separated different humans and the humans from animals.

BODY IN/DIFFERENCE

I want to suggest that Foucault's occlusion of the history of colonialism from the history of sexuality cannot be remedied by merely inscribing that which remains unsaid. In fact, within postcolonial discourse, it is common to see the links between the subject of colonialism and that of the Enlightenment in that the one permitted the formation of the other. Nor is whiteness connected only to the bourgeois formations of Western Europe. I want instead to follow the peculiar trajectory of embodiment that comes into being from the late eighteenth century that located (what is perceived to be as) marked bodies as difference. Within such a formulation, the conflation of the woman's body and the racialized body under the nomenclature "difference" paradoxically suggests the opposite: indifference. Meaning is produced in a loop. Difference must be excluded from the body politic. This exclusion of difference, then, manifested itself as indifference. The indifference to difference resulted in its exclusion from the body politic and representation.

The genealogy of the trope of indifference is located within feminist theory. In *Speculum of the Other Woman* and *This Sex Which Is Not One,* Luce Irigaray analyzes psychoanalytic theory and suggests that, within Freud's work, sexuality that is predicated on sexual difference is problematic because the feminine occurs only within "models and laws devised by male subjects."[34] If femininity is a construction of male logic, then sexual difference was, paradoxically, sexual indifference. Teresa de Lauretis later used this cornerstone reasoning of feminist analysis by applying the notion of indifference within lesbian representation.[35] She speculates on the impossibility of any agency for women in their sexuality, given that femininity was merely a masculine elaboration of the same. For de Lauretis, lesbian representation is possible by separating sex from sexuality because only that locates sexuality outside the orbit of masculinity. In "Woman in Difference," Gayatri Spivak turns around the feminist notion of indifference and suggests a way in which difference can be scripted back into it.[36] Here she reads Mahasweta Devi's novella, *Doulati the Bountiful*, which is the story of a young tribal girl sold into prostitution who eventually dies of venereal disease. Spivak points out that in the homogenizing gesture made by the nation-state, something residual is left behind: that which cannot be homogenized/assimilated by the nation-state. It is this residual that reinstates difference, despite the demand for indifference by the nation-state. For Spivak and Mahasweta Devi, this residual is in the body, whose very materiality resists the assimilative move of the state. The body, thus, post–late eighteenth century, is at the locus of the scripting of difference into indifference.

I want to pursue this cluster of terms—indifference, unassimilability, and residue—and their relationship to the body within the context of my analysis. What, then, can we surmise of difference on the body? Or, approaching this question another way, while the presence of melanin or the vagina governed the atomization of the visibly different body, what underlies the principle of visible bodies? What did the norm refer to? Indeed, there is a body of philosophical writing from Descartes onward equating rationality with disembodiment. In the *Treatise of Man,* Descartes posits that the rational soul was attached to the body in the pineal gland and influenced the actions of the body. While this work led to the theory of bodily reflexes, Descartes amplified on the theme of the devalorized body in other works. In *The Search for Truth* he argues that he is distinct from his body: "I do not even know whether I have a body. . . . [However] this will not prevent me from being certain that I exist."[37] This theme of identity being aligned with the mind and not the body is explored further in *Discourse on the Method,* where Descartes is certain only of his thought and not his body. In the *Meditations,* he indicates that the individual's essence is with one's thoughts rather than one's body. This deprivileging of the body, the split subject within modernity, and contemporary comprehensions of difference as being located on the body are inaugurated in Descartes's works: the mind privileged by its own common sense and ability to perceive itself creates a corporeal structure in which the body becomes completely private. The mind, in contrast, by logic of possessing a *common* sense, becomes public.

This theme of the deprivileging of the body is also fundamental to the formation of aesthetic judgment within modernity as is evident in Immanuel Kant's *The Critique of Judgement.* Kant's work, which deals with aesthetic judgment, makes the link between the mind, common sense, the universal, and the sublime.[38] In this work, disinterest is at the core of the formation of the universal subject who judges; the more disinterested, the more the conformity to universality and the more the elaboration of the same. Thus, there is a value placed on being unmarked, which is also the condition of universality and what David Lloyd calls "the [s]ubject without properties."[39] The body marked as different that also functions as a marker of lack *is dislocated from the space of universality,* common sense, and disinterest. The racialized/marked body, barred from entry into the space of universality, is also simultaneously incarcerated in certain places, held immobile. In contrast the subject without properties, often equated with the ubiquitous white colonist found in every remote part of the globe in the nineteenth century, has the universal right to roam and to mobility.[40] The marked woman's body, prone to hysteria as well, is confined to private spaces, discursively incarcerated among the bourgeoisie as the Angel in the House.

In addition to the spatial dislocation, there is a temporal dislocation in the construction of the modern body. In the process of the naturalizing of marked bodies—their bodily marks indicate their lower social value—women and blacks are dislocated from modernity completely; their bodies are located before the conferring of cultural meanings of them. Further, the atomizing of their body parts locates their anatomy as being lower on the evolutionary ladder, the most evolved body being unmarked. The different body becomes a metaphor for having atrophied or become vestigial—unnecessary to progression, unable to be used, unable to develop. Frozen in a moment before time, the body in difference is dislocated from the normative temporality of human development.

The marked body as granting disembodiment to another group that is posited as the norm is particularly problematic when we consider the terms "identity," "difference," and "citizenship," which are central to the discourses of race and gender. Though the term "identity," predicated on notions of difference, was originally used in logic and algebra, within politico-philosophic discourse it has always been based on the body. For Locke in *The Essay concerning Human Understanding,* the individual can be identified, cohered, and consolidated only through the body. It becomes the essence of the individual. In his discussions of the boundary distinguishing the human from the animal, he insists it is their body and not just their rationality that positively identifies humans. Yet, within liberal humanist thought, the ability to be disembodied has always functioned as the signifier of power. Within this context, the different body, the marked body, be it via race or gender, has functioned not only as the inferior term, but its very hypervisibility has granted powerful bodies the invisibility of the norm.

Contemporary readers, post-Saussure, are aware of the centrality of the concept of difference for meaning itself to come into being. The body in modernity is woven into the comprehension of Saussurian notions of difference in that, as Saussure would have it, "in the linguistic system there are only differences, without positive terms."[41] Saussure's fundamental concept is at the heart of marked and unmarked bodies. Indeed, the unmarked body can come into visibility only in opposition to its marked counterpart. The hierarchical relationship between the two would be unthinkable without the social/cultural meanings and values placed on the body raced as black or the body sexed as female. As Derrida comments on Saussure's notion of the play of differences, "This linkage means that each 'element'—phoneme or grapheme—is constituted with reference to the trace in it of the other elements of the sequence or system. This linkage, this weaving, is the *text,* which is produced only through the transformation of another text. Nothing, either in the elements or in the system, is anywhere simply present or absent. There are only, everywhere, differences and traces of traces."[42] Indeed, if the unmarked body as text is to be read as a positive term, the marked body has to be read as uncivilized. Thus, Kant's Universal and Lloyd's Subject without Properties are inscribed within Saussure's notion of difference; no positive terms, only differences.

Finally, the temporal deferral of meaning, subjectivity, and being unmarked is encapsulated in the Derridean notion of *différance.* While for Saussure the play of differences was the fundamental condition for the functioning of the sign, Derrida goes further to suggest that while a single meaning arises only by the effacement of other possibilities, those other effaced meanings are deferred for their possible activation in other contexts. *Différance*, or making visible this interdiction, is structural. It is material. It must be written on the body. Its movement is constituted historically as a weave of differences. This play of *différance* reveals the body's built-in history, the traces, deferrals, and displacements.

Difference and the History of (White) Sexuality

What I have suggested thus far is that the history of the body must be factored in any study of the history of sexuality, notwithstanding Foucault's insistence on the construction of sexuality as discursive. The history of the body and anatomical science from the Enlightenment, and especially in the nineteenth century, has located bodies within a hierarchical framework. Making this hierarchy visible also reveals the alignment between the embodiment of the Enlightenment and that of poststructuralism.[43] My metonymic linking of the sovereign subject constructed through the Enlightenment framework and valorizing the mind/body split with the poststructuralists flies in the face of logic in that the primary agenda of the poststructuralists has been the *dismantling* of the sovereign subject. Foucault addresses this agenda articulately in the interview "Body/Power": "First of all one must set aside the widely held thesis that power in our bourgeois, capitalist, societies has denied the reality of the body in favour of the soul, consciousness, ideality. In fact nothing is more material, physical, corporal than the exercise of power."[44] In fact, Foucault's works repudiate the denial of the body that links Descartes with the Enlightenment. I want to reexamine the embodiment that is evoked in Foucault's *History of Sexuality*, volume 1, because I think the notion of difference as marked on the body is present everywhere in the text.

Foucault is reputed to have begun work on the last chapter, "Right of Death and Power over Life," of the first volume of *The History of Sexuality* on the same day he finished writing *Discipline and Punish*. In short, the embodiment evoked in the later text is in continuum with the previous work. It also creates a skewed chronology for the reader of *The History of Sexuality* in that the first half makes full sense only in its rereading, after having read the second half of it as well as having read *Discipline and Punish*. His argument in this work is based on two related notions: First, he debates the question, Was sexuality repressed in the Victorian Age? In this he argues against psychoanalysis, especially Freud's theories. Second, he analyzes sexuality and sex as a production of power and not as its Other or its counterforce. Here he examines in detail the bifurcation between the body as disciplined, an anatomo-politics, and the species body, a bio-politics of the body.

Foucault argues against the repressive hypothesis that characterized Victorian society as one of sexual prudery. He posits that, far from re-pression, sexuality spilled over as discourse and produced *scientia sexualis* in the late eighteenth and nineteenth centuries. *Scientia sexualis* ranged from the analysis of populations to the increase in medical knowledges about women's sexuality, to theorizing on eugenics, degeneration, and infantile sexuality. Notwithstanding his impatience with psychoanaly-sis, Foucault reads sexuality from within the psychoanalytic notion of displacement. Further, neither desire nor sexuality exists outside of their discursive status. Such an argument is clear in that, since language is structured specifically and discursively in a historical form and since any discourse reproduces historical relations of power, sexuality and de-sire too are products of discourse. Notwithstanding this close relation-ship between the notion of discursive and the psychoanalytic concept of displacement within his explanation of *scientia sexualis,* Foucault is adamant that sexuality is not a liberatory force or the Other of repres-sive power. For him, since power is "the moving substrate of force rela-tions,"[45] which is unstable and in a constant state of flux, then sexu-ality is about forces, energies, sensations, and pleasures. It is Foucault's revolutionary revision and relocation of sexuality from within the orbit of repression to that of mobile power that has rewritten the history of sexuality in the last thirty years.

I want to explain one other point in Foucault before I evoke the other body that haunts and underpins *The History of Sexuality,* vol-ume I. In his historical excavation of eighteenth- and nineteenth-century sexuality, he insists on the epistemic shift that occurred when the deployment of alliance was replaced by the deployment of sexuality. For Foucault, the deployment of alliance was practiced by the nobility; its purpose was to maintain blood lineage and the threat underlying the purpose was death. In contrast, the bourgeoisie that emphasized the health of the body and the prolongation of life practiced the deployment of sexuality. Sex was at the cusp of both these deployments and became the basis for the regulation of the body and populations. In short, for Foucault, far from a repression of sexuality, there was a *proliferation* of it in power's need to colonize the body. Far from a picture of a sexually repressed bourgeoisie, he evokes one that analyzed and gained knowledge over their own bodies. It is this startling rereading of facts that has made this work fundamental to the rethinking of sexuality.

Yet I suggest that the body that is at the center of Foucault's analysis is marked by a difference. Indeed, I would go so far as to say that it is the marked body that allows for the *very surfacing of sexuality itself* and power's desire to colonize the body in *The History of Sexuality.* The evidence for the different body is everywhere, from his critique of nineteenth-century science to his arguments for *scientia sexualis,* to his assertion of the shift in power's focus from the deployment of alliance to that of sexuality, and it is these specific moments that I wish to analyze.

It is the analysis of *ars erotica* that posts red flags for the postcolonial reader. Here Foucault provides it as a contrast, a counterdiscourse to *scientia sexualis. Ars erotica* is the practice of sexuality that seems dislocated from power, and one in continuum only with bodily pleasure. Furthermore, it is linked to China, Japan, India, (ancient) Rome, and the Arab-Muslim societies. He suggests that

> in the erotic art, truth is drawn from pleasure itself, understood as a practice and accumulated as experience; pleasure is not considered in relation to an absolute law of the permitted and the forbidden, nor by reference to a criterion of utility, but first and foremost in relation to itself; it is experienced as pleasure, evaluated in terms of its intensity, its specific quality, its duration, its reverberations in the body and soul.[46]

The purpose of *ars erotica* is a singular bliss, obliviousness to time and limits, the elixir of life, the exile of death and its threats. If sexuality, as he posits in this work, is discursive and reproduces regulatory practices of power, how can we read *ars erotica,* which seems to be *outside* the orbit of discourse and power? Further, what can we make of the list of societies that he claims practices *ars erotica*? Indeed, all of the societies he lists seem dislocated from modernity and temporality itself. Also, his choice of the societies that practice *ars erotica* seems uninflected by the power relationships between spaces. In his interview "Space, Knowledge, and Power," Foucault is vehement that spaces are not meaningless or outside of the orbit of power relations. He cautions, "Space is fundamental in any exercise of power" (252). But yet such an analysis is missing in his description of *ars erotica*. In short, Foucault's description of *ars erotica* and choice of societies locates them in familiar binaries of the West and the non-West or colonizer/colonized.

Furthermore, the detemporalizing and dehistoricizing of *ars erotica* societies not only dislocates them from modernity, but also seems to make them function as an imaginary space, a retroactive construct of Western desire. It becomes clear that such a theoretical move is necessary for Foucault's disavowal of the forces of colonialism that massively influenced the very construction of sexuality and Western desire. It also occludes the centrality of racial difference from the very production of his reading of Western desire, in that the alterity that these differently raced bodies embody is safely contained within the enclosure of *ars erotica* and untouched by the progress of history. Yet as Foucault himself admits, there was a great awakening to sexual concerns only in the late eighteenth century, which, as I have pointed out, consistently coincided with the location of the gendered and racialized bodies as difference.

Foucault continues to overlook body differences when he tracks the shift from the deployment of alliance to the deployment of sexuality. While he points to the centrality of *blood* for the aristocrats who deployed alliances, he suggests that the bourgeoisie focused on the healthy body: "the bourgeoisie's 'blood' was its sex."[47] In his desire to read the newly formed embourgeoisement in the construction of sexuality, he does not question the displacement of blood for the healthy body. Yet blood-quantum laws prevailed everywhere among the colonizing nations of the West in the nineteenth century. The terminologies for mixed-race people proliferated in that era. For instance, the Spanish had 128 terms to categorize the different combinations of mixed races: mulatto, quadroon, octoroon, Creole, chino-blanco, quintero, zambo, zambo-chino, zambo-negro, and chino-oscura, to name only a very few. Indeed, it is the fear of miscegenation that led to the heightened policing of women's sexuality via law and via the ideological discourse of the Angel in the House. Both the woman's body as well as her sexuality function to mark and to reproduce racial and other boundaries. Women's sexual transgressions could thus prove disastrous to the racial and class hegemonies of the nineteenth century.

Furthermore, the nineteenth-century obsession with heredity and degenerescence causes Foucault to read degeneration as being internal to Europe. Such a reading comes out of a long tradition that perceives the progress of civilization as being countered by increasing diseases. For instance, Daniel Pick suggests that capitalism and social mobility were countered by physiological fluxes.[48] Degeneration thus becomes the binary opposite to notions of evolution and progress and a discourse that reveals the nineteenth-century anxiety caused by the vanquished Chartism, the various economic and political crises in Europe in the 1840s. Gareth Stedman Jones suggests that the poor as degenerate were a discursive construction of wealthy Victorians.[49] For Anne McClintock, the daily interaction of the rich with the poor in crowds, at homes where the poor were domestic servants, in city streets, and when traveling past slums heightened the awareness of contagion from the bodies of the poor masses.[50]

Further, I suggest that the trope of health too is racially laden and points to difference written on the body. Degeneration was not just about the horrified and erotic contact between people of different classes, but also closely linked to the colonies. In fact, degeneration was perceived to be caused by boundary crossing not just of class, but also of space, race, and gender. Race science, in particular, became the site that analyzed sexual transgressions and social/sexual interactions between whites and blacks. Nineteenth-century Britain with its vast Empire also grappled with the idea that races belonged to specific spaces and crossing those limits caused degeneration in both blacks and whites alike. Charles Lyell insisted, "Each race of man has its place."[51] In this perception, white bodies were formed to live in the temperate zones; therefore, moving to the tropics or torrid zones was considered to be detrimental to them. The flora and fauna and the intense heat of the equatorial regions were perceived as causing diseases in whites; furthermore, the change in climate was blamed for the increased alcoholism among the colonists and the heat blamed for their sexual excesses (read: indulging in interracial sex).[52] This notion of degeneration is not obsolete, as traces of it can be perceived even in Ronald Hyam's 1990 description of the British in India:

> Running the Victorian empire would probably have been intolerable without resort to sexual relaxation. The historian has to remember the *misery* of empire: the heat and the dust, the incessant rain and monotonous food, the inertia and the loneliness, the lack of amusement and intellectual stimulus. There were no cars, no radios, sometimes not even white neighbours to make up a proper game of tennis or bridge.[53]

For Hyam, sexual aberrations originate from the ennui of running the nineteenth-century Empire. Indeed, in the nineteenth century, the most problematic form of boundary crossing was that of interracial sexuality. The anatomist William Lawrence insisted that sexual-boundary crossing resulted in the uplifting of the blacks but the deterioration of the European. Commenting on sexual transgressions of racial boundaries, Robert Young suggests, "Such desire, constituted by a dialectic of attraction and repulsion, soon brings with it the threat of the fecund fertility of the colonial desiring machine, whereby a culture in its colonial operation becomes hybridized, alienated and potentially threatening to the European original to the production of polymorphously perverse people who are, in Bhabha's phrase, "white, but not quite.""[54]

Indeed, hybrid degeneracy was perceived to result in disease-prone and short-lived offspring. Such a perception was in continuum with the idea of the hybrid mule as being sterile: racial hybridity/degeneration was not even tolerated by nature. Neither was gender-boundary crossing tolerable. For instance, for Hegel the figure of the Amazon suggested the degenerate sexuality of the female: the Amazon "is said to have pounded her own son in a mortar, to have besmeared herself with the blood, and to have had the blood of pounded children constantly at hand. She is said to have driven away or put to death all the males, and commanded the death of all male children."[55] Thus for Hegel, the Amazon not only crossed boundaries of gender, but in so doing became unmaternal and a man-hater as well.

Foucault ignores this wealth of historical information in his citing of heredity and degeneration; boundary crossing is limited to classed comprehensions of it. The fear of boundary crossing that is also the fear of contamination of the marked body seems to make no appearance in his text. The racially marked body as degenerate not only functioned as sexually taboo, but also as an example of what could happen to the transgressive white body. Blackness thus became a devolutionary condition. By locating questions of health within the context of heredity and degeneration (as if health were not a culturally imbricated term), Foucault seems to foreclose any appearance of the marked body in difference. There is, indeed, an indifference to the body in difference. There is, instead, an insistence on the bourgeoisie's affirmation, and not repression, of the whitened and masculinized body: "What was formed was a political ordering of life, not through an enslavement of others, but through an affirmation of self."[56]

What is even more startling for the postcolonial female reader is Foucault's linking of biopower only to capitalism. Such a linking results in his paean to capitalism—the accumulation of men to capital, the expansion of productive forces, and the investment in the body. There seems no awareness of the system of slavery, indentured labor, or colonialism that made such capitalism possible. His admission of racism is limited to the Holocaust and Nazism. In so saying I do not suggest that the waste of Jewish bodies and lives is immaterial to this reading of Foucault. I think that his citing of only Nazi racism is a narrow view of what constitutes Europe—as if the history of colonialism is irrelevant to Europe or *The History of Sexuality*. Ultimately, his revolutionary work is marked by its own blind spot; *The History of Sexuality* is a limited view of white sexuality, white desire. European sexuality, in this work, can be read only discursively. The pleasures of the body become a marker of black bodies, dislocated from modernity and safely contained in space and time. If, as Saussure points out, meanings can come into visibility only through the system of differences, then it is the occluded, marked body that enables the forces, energies, sensations, and discursive pleasures of the bourgeois/white/European/male body.

Why this occlusion, however? This question haunts Stoler's work as well. She merely states that Foucault's version of the body "eclipses a key discursive site where subjugated bodies were made and subjects formed. . . . The point is to register explicitly that what appeared as distinctively French, Dutch, or generically European in the late nineteenth century were sometimes cultural and political configurations, honed and worked through the politics of empire earlier."[57] I think Spivak explains Foucault's occlusion best. In another context, in "Can the Subaltern Speak?" she points to Foucault's (and Deleuze's) enmeshment within ideology that inevitably locates them on the exploiter's side of the international division of labor. She suggests that it becomes impossible for Foucault to imagine the kind of power and desire that would inhabit the unnamed subject of the Other of Europe. Spivak states, "It is not only that everything Foucault reads, critical or uncritical, is caught within the debate of the production of the Other, supporting or critiquing the constitution of the Subject as Europe. It is also that, in the constitution of that Other of Europe, great care was taken to obliterate the textual ingredients with which such a subject could cathect, could occupy (invest?) its itinerary—not only by ideological and scientific production, but also by the institution of the law."[58] I find Spivak's explanation most useful because the other marked body that historically belongs to that era and that Foucault emphasizes is missing completely from the text. Such an epistemic violence in *The History of Sexuality* is necessary to locate *scientia sexualis,* the history of white sexuality, as normative. The occlusion of the marked body and the history of colonialism becomes a part of the sanctioned ignorance in Foucault's text, but also it is precisely this sanctioned ignorance that allows for the discursive mapping of the body's desire, degeneration, *ars erotica,* boundary crossing.

What I have suggested thus far is the need for the historical excavation and the making visible of the history of difference, the history of marks, in the eighteenth and nineteenth centuries. This excavation needs to be done to see not only the relationship between gender and race, but also the theorizing of the body that valorized the importance of being unmarked in order to be dominant and to be within the nexus of civil rights and citizenship rights. Being unmarked thus meant being right and rational and part of the elaboration of the same. Feminist theorizing has tended to concentrate on the woman's body as difference without seriously theorizing the ghostly, racialized body that haunts it and is in a metonymic link with it. My intention in underscoring the history of embodied difference in the eighteenth and nineteenth centuries was to show the blind spots in Foucault's work. If the theorizing and practice of sexuality is predicated on the sex/gender system, then the status of the body is terribly important to the history of sexuality. In particular, I have concentrated on the history of colonialism that underpins, yet is rendered invisible in, Foucault's history. In volume I of *The History of Sexuality,* the status of the black body and black sexuality has been absolutely central to Foucault's construction of white Victorian desire. The only analogy to the occlusion of the black body that I can make is via Spivak's "Can the Subaltern Speak?" In the construction of the suttee, Spivak uncovers the seamless braiding of the discourse of white patriarchy ("White men are saving brown women from brown men") with that of brown patriarchy ("She wished to die") that results in the erasure of any sense of agency for the widow sitting on her husband's funeral pyre, waiting to go up in flames, to be burned alive. The figure of the woman is necessary for both the enforcement of British rule *and* Indian resistance. Yet the woman who pays with her life itself has no agency or materiality. It is this sort of function that the colonized body and colonialism plays in Foucault's *History of Sexuality.* The black body is absolutely necessary for the propulsion and visibility of white desire. It is necessary for the construction of *scientia sexualis.* It is necessary for the threat of degeneration to work, to send Europeans into a state of panic. Yet it is excised everywhere from Foucault's text. The black body occupies the unfixed place, an erased signifier in the inscription of white desire.

WHITE BRITISH SEXUALITY

Since the meaning of sexuality is predicated on the meaning of the body as much as it is on the sex/gender system, since it needs to be read within the context of race as much as its imbrication within class, since the history of colonialism is implicated in the history of sexuality, I will examine key points in the nineteenth-century history of British sexuality. I want to see how race is encoded within domestic concerns over this issue and if the taboos of the black body, black sexuality, and miscegenation are central to the legislations of and attitudes to domestic sexuality. I will look at three moments, selected and organized not chronologically but incrementally, from the visible to the invisible, from the obvious to the erased, in the racializing of British bodies and sexualities: the Burma Circular and the Crewe Circular, the Contagious Diseases Acts (CD Acts), and the Labouchère Amendment. I have selected the CD Acts yet again because I think notions of British femininity become problematic and racialized in the drama that coheres around them, and juxtaposing them beside the Burma Circular and the Labouchère Act provides new insights into them. In turn, the Labouchère Amendment is interesting because it not only seems to interrogate British notions of masculinity but, in the interrogation of the status of heterosexuality, it also seems to suggest that only the latter could be a properly white practice.

BURMA CIRCULAR AND THE CREWE CIRCULAR

I will start with the practice of British sexuality elsewhere as it sets the scene for the comprehension of the other two moments within Britain. The nineteenth-century fear of miscegenation is immediately perceptible in the taboo enforced against them in the colonies. I want to rehearse this moment, though set in the colonies, because I want to see if the dynamics that racialized sexuality overseas, miscegenation, desire, perversion, and disease were relevant in Britain within the CD Acts and the Labouchère Amendment.

The nineteenth-century British army in India permitted up to 12 percent of the regiment to marry. Since marriage allowances in the army were not paid until the officer was thirty years of age, it was rare for an officer below the rank of major to marry.[59] As a result, white officers posted overseas maintained native mistresses; the enlisted ranks frequented prostitutes. The overvaluing of white femininity as the domestic goddess, the Angel in the House, can also be read as being inflected by the scarcity of white women, especially in the nonsettler colonies, as much as it was by domestic bourgeoisification. The Burma Circular and its clone, the Crewe Circular, should be read within the overvaluation of white British femininity, which is the flip side to the fear of miscegenation. Colonel Fytche, the chief commissioner of Burma, posted the circular in 1867 (just ten years after the Sepoy Mutiny in India), urging British officers posted in Burma to resist having sexual liaisons with Burmese women as they were accustomed to "bribery and chicane and [not] altogether free from evil influences."[60] Further, Colonel Fytche indicates that the personal lives of transgressive officers would be considered in matters of promotion.

The Burma Circular was a model for the Crewe Circular. Circulated as a confidential memo written by Lord Crewe of the British Colonial Office in Kenya in 1909, it threatened disgrace and official ruin to those British officers in the Colonial Office who entered into "arrangements of concubinage with girls or women belonging to the native populations."[61] Thus, the entire range of reasons, from the ideological reasoning of white supremacy to the political need to govern and control territories via the mystique of white supremacy, are covered in the two circulars that are separated by forty-two years. In much of the history of colonial sexuality, London, Rangoon, and Nairobi all are treated as hermetically sealed spaces, unpenetrated by the influence of the other. Indeed, Ronald Hyam's work insists on the sexual opportunity to experiment offered by the Empire. In contrast, numerous historians have marked Britain as a space suffused by the Purity Movement that flourished in the nineteenth century. I, however, want to posit that the whole host of reasons, from the ideological formation of whiteness to political gain, existed in the passing of legislation in the home base as well.

THE CONTAGIOUS DISEASES ACTS

The CD Acts are often central in any assessment of Victorian sexuality or gender relations. As Judith Walkowitz points out, "The CD Acts were consistent with a set of attitudes and 'habits of mind' toward women, sexuality, and class that permeated official Victorian culture."[62] These acts, which forced prostitutes or any woman suspected of prostitution to undergo compulsory medical checks for venereal disease, were passed in 1864, 1866, and 1869. (These acts conflate the status of women with those of cattle in that the CD Animal Acts of 1867, which followed the cattle plague of 1865, were based upon the CD Acts passed to control prostitutes.) Due to the increase in the incidence of venereal diseases among soldiers in towns that had army camps, in July 1864 the first CD Act was passed, which permitted the compulsory examination and hospitalization of infected prostitutes. Among the chosen towns were Aldershot, Salisbury, Rochester, Dublin, Winchester, Devonport, and Canterbury. In 1866 and in 1869 the legislation was amended to provide compulsory three-month examinations as well as to increase the jurisdiction to fifteen miles around the towns. These acts led to agitation primarily from political Victorian women, and in 1886 they were repealed.

Feminist scholars have consistently referred to the CD Acts and their repeal under the leadership of Josephine Butler and the Ladies National Association within the history of white feminism. Women were galvanized into action and politicized by these acts because of their double standards in sexuality: women were legislated against for prostitution but not their male clients. Further, all women could be detained and examined under suspicion of prostitution. While Walkowitz and other feminists locate the repeal within feminist history, Frank Mort reads these acts within the context of the increasing professionalization of doctors. Thus, morality, sanitation, and medicine all are linked in the Victorian Age. Mort points out that "a new and powerful medical ideology, crystallising definitions of normal and deviant female sexuality" developed in the upward social mobility of the doctors.[63] While both these views are relevant to the construction of the white Victorian woman's sexuality, I want to examine another angle to the CD Acts, that which links her to the black woman in India. In her reading of white imperial feminism, Antoinette Burton links the CD Acts with the Indian CD Acts and points out that Josephine Butler was able to turn her attention to the Indian prostitute only after the repeal of the CD Acts in Britain. This chronology becomes central to the narration of Western feminism, for in this reading Indian women's political action can only mimic their white counterparts in Britain. As Gayatri Spivak has suggested, white women's political rights in the West could be won only by juxtaposing them beside black bodies.[64] But the history of the CD Acts is more complex. For instance, the main features of the CD Acts have been the registration of prostitutes, inspection for venereal disease, sanitary detention, the policing of public spaces, and the licensing and inspection of brothels. While historians have cited the use of French models for the regulation of prostitutes (thus making the CD Acts entirely European in genealogy), the trope of containment, the use of lock hospitals, sanitary detention, and the licensing of brothels had their earliest manifestations in India. Lock hospitals were established in Madras as early as 1805. Further, prostitutes were regulated by attaching them to military cantonments where they were strictly used for white clients only. The Indian prostitutes too were subjected to periodical medical examinations and registration. When the regiment traveled, so did the prostitutes.[65] The point is not that the CD Acts in Britain were imitative of the Indian regulations, but rather that notions of race and whiteness underpinned British sexuality in Britain as well. Furthermore, it must be remembered, as Philip Howell has noted, that the French model itself was drawn from the French regulation of prostitutes in Tahiti.[66] The Victorian attitude that prostitutes (and not their male clients) bred diseases was informed by the diseased body of the colonized. The contact and conquest of Africa and India has always been expressed through metaphors of sexuality, contagion, disease, and death.[67]

It is within this context that we must read Philippa Levine's comments on the racializing of venereal diseases and legislation of prostitutes in the Indian context:

> As disease became more and more a convenient metaphor for savagery and primitiveness, the connection between race and "unacceptable" forms of sexual behaviour was powerfully underscored. Venereal disease legislation was justifiable in British eyes, as an agent of progressive civilising Western medicine in its mission to tame the devastating effects of tropical sickness.[68]

The black body as primitive and savage and black spaces as primordial, needing the intervention of Western medicine and law to aid in the evolutionary process, was in continuum with racialized medical science, according to which white bodies suffered and became diseased in degenerate nonwhite spaces. Law and medicine were the only armors against degeneration.

Furthermore, what implications do Levine's analysis of the discourse around Indian prostitutes—that all Indian women were sexually promiscuous—have on British prostitutes? What does the contaminating framework of prostitution as a racially laden term have on British prostitutes? Indeed, the language of disease, which linked the practices of Indian prostitutes with their British counterparts, located both as spreading venereal disease among unsuspecting white British men. There was a further conflation of working-class women and prostitutes in Britain because both were "dirty, clad in unwomanly rags, some appearing half-starved, covered with vermin, causing those near them to shun them with aversion; careless in matters of decency; their conversation having mingled with it such words as made one shudder to listen to."[69]

If the CD Acts led to the Purity campaigns of the nineteenth century that demanded monogamous heterosex among whites, then these attitudes had their origin in their contact and conquest of the colonies. Attitudes toward prostitution, Victorian sexuality, and degeneration of the whites due to urban living and class mixing are imbricated in the colonies and British sexuality is indeed linked to black bodies. In short, white desire, the desire for white reproduction and maintenance of white hegemony, cannot be separated from black bodies. White desire is always already inscripted against black bodies.

THE LABOUCHÈRE AMENDMENT

The CD Acts and their repeal are not only contextualized within women's movements, but also incorporated within the nineteenth-century Purity Movement, which roughly began in the 1880s. The multiple aims of the Purity Movement led to a variety of sexual reforms and legislations that have tended to naturalize sexuality and cover over its intrinsic historical construction. Among the aims and targets of the Purity Movement were the CD Acts, raising the age of consent, a drive against masturbation and schoolboy sex, homosexuality, soliciting, incest, and nude bathing.[70] Earlier I examined the relationship between Victorian femininity and race as encoded within the Contagious Diseases Acts; now I want to examine another legislation, that against homosexuality, because this legislation also encodes within it comprehensions of white masculinity.

The legislation against homosexuality in the long nineteenth century in Britain spanned more than eighty-six years: from the reaffirming of the death penalty for sodomy in 1826 by Sir Robert Peel (which was removed only in 1861); to the Labouchère Amendment in 1885, by which even private, consensual sex between men was punishable by up to two years' hard labor; to the Vagrancy Act in 1898, intended to prevent male homosexual prostitutes from soliciting; to the Criminal Law Amendment in 1912, which punished homosexuals by flogging for their second offense. (In 1921, a new Criminal Law Amendment bill was introduced to penalize lesbians in the same way as male homosexuals, but it was rejected by the House of Lords because it was perceived that the legislations could instigate new longings within women. This omission of lesbians is telling; we can see that the crime of homosexuality has always been a crime against white masculinity.) The Labouchère Amendment, which would prevent juvenile prostitution, had been taken from the French penal code. It was through the enforcement of the Labouchère Amendment that Oscar Wilde was prosecuted for homosexuality.

There has been extensive Foucauldian analysis of the history of nineteenth-century British homosexuality. For instance, in a variety of works, Jeffrey Weeks reads the construction of Victorian homosexual identity. For Weeks, just as the working class formed a distinct identity, so did belonging to the homosexual community produce a collective self.[71] Furthermore, as he states in *Sex, Politics, and Society,* the nineteenth-century legislation against homosexuality must be read against the backdrop of the construction of heterosexuality and its regulation in that period. Ronald Hyam as well reads British homosexuality and the sexual opportunity that the Empire provided quite extensively. In Hyam's work, the Empire becomes interchangeable solely with sexual adventure and deviant sexuality. Indeed, the regulation of British sexuality and the lack of regulation in the colonies seem to imbue Hyam's work with a nostalgia for the unregulated, unbridled sexuality with which the colonized spaces seemed to be analogous. Hyam does not conceive of the forms of regulation of gender and sexuality in other cultures.

I suggest that if sexuality is predicated on notions of difference, then the bodily difference that race provides is fundamental not only to desire, but to the perception of sexuality and sexual practices. In short, if Foucault indicates that sexuality constructs gender, class, and forms of knowledge, then the question of how race constructs sexuality itself must be asked. Earlier I posited that there was a shift in the concept of British masculinity after the Sepoy Mutiny of 1857, so that in the latter half of the nineteenth century it was idealized as being militaristic, homo-social, sporadically heterosexual, and, most important, synonymous with whiteness. I also want to suggest that white heterosexuality itself was constructed against colonial sexuality as can be seen in the Age of Consent Bill, passed in India in 1891, that proposed to raise the age of consent for young girls from ten to twelve years of age under the Indian Penal Code. This bill underscored the Indian male as a rapist whose base desires had to be kept under control through the penal code. The debate around this bill also emphasized the lasting consequences of early sexu-ality among Indian men and women (in contrast to the slower matura-tion processes of European bodies). Repeatedly, scientific and medical discourses were invoked to point to the deterioration and degeneration of the physique of the race. In fact, the effeminate Hindu was perceived to be a direct consequence of early sexual activity among Indians.

The status of homosexuality in the long nineteenth century, which was obsessed with respectability and the insistence of bourgeois at-titudes as the norm, should be read against the backdrop of the 1857 Mutiny and the discourses against the aberrant sexuality of the colo-nized. To some extent, the biopower exerted by the Victorian Age, its construction of racial theories, the value it placed on whiteness, and the limitations it made on women's desire and their expressions of sexuality all are ideologically linked. In short, the European project, the white project, the bourgeois project needed white bodies to govern the colo-nies. Attitudes toward homosexuality and the severe repression that it underwent in that long nineteenth century were an outcome of the per-ception that it was unproductive, unresponsive to the needs of the age, not quite white behavior. Anna Davin's reading of "Imperialism and Motherhood," in which she suggests that the trope of hygiene and its link to the rising status of the mother as being instigated by the needs of colonial/imperial rule, is in keeping with such a reading of homosexu-ality.[72] To that extent, the waste of the body, the waste of body fluids, the excess of sexuality that homosexuality signified required it to be strictly controlled, excised from the body politic.

How would the analysis of homosexuality in that long Victorian Age shift if we read not only within the frameworks of sexuality and respectability, but also those of colonialism and the maintenance of ra-cial demarcations? Homosexuality was not respectable because it was perceived as sexual excess. Sexual excess was not a part of the European makeup; free expression of sexuality indicated degeneration; perverted sexuality characterized black male sexuality. In short, the legislation against homosexuality in Britain was a disavowal of "black" behavior among white men. Thus, there was a consolidation of white, bourgeois comprehensions of heterosexuality, not just in colonial spaces but also in Britain. Underpinning these comprehensions, of course, was that white male desire was for blackness, be it via homosexuality, white women, or black women. I conclude that if blacks (along with women) took on the burden of embodiment in the long nineteenth century, then any notion of sexuality must be mediated also through the category of race. White women as the body were consequently black, even if they were white. Only historical excavation can make the racialization of sexuality visible. White desire, then, is for the lost body—black, marked, and feminized.

PART II

In the South

CHAPTER 4

White Water:
Race and Oceans Down Under

Kevin Reynolds's postapocalyptic 1995 film *Waterworld* concludes with a reference to the postcolonial past: the conquest of Mount Everest by Edmund Hillary and Tenzing Norgay. Though severed from a comprehension of the pastness of history, the movie is set in a future of melted polar ice caps, an Earth that has consequently been flooded, a present without dry land, and the evolution of a nautical society. Land and water are dislocated from their contemporary meanings. References to history, if any, become extremely abstract, and history itself becomes intemporal in this film. There is only the substantiality and expanse of water everywhere. Dry land becomes the lost object of desire, mankind's destiny, and the map to this mythical place is written on the childish but feminine body. Dry land is eventually found to be at the top of Mount Everest with its commemorative plaque, citing and celebrating Norgay and Hillary's feat. Notwithstanding the writing of the postapocalyptic future as completely alien and Other, the yearning for land seems surprisingly familiar to scholars of voyage narratives as well as colonial studies. To select almost at random, Charles de Brosses's *Histoire des Navigations aux Terres Australes* emphasizes a similar search for land and the exploration of the Pacific and the establishment of carefully organized European settlements.[1] Indeed, as Edward Said's now classic work *Orientalism* suggests, the importance of voyaging can be seen not only in Cook and Bouganville, Tournefort, and Adanson, but also in "French traders in the Pacific, by Jesuit missionaries in China and the Americas, by William Dampier's explorations and reports, by innumerable speculations on giants, Patagonians, savages, natives, and monsters supposedly residing to the far east, west, south, and north of Europe."[2]

In Kevin Reynolds's imagined future, water and land show fluidity in meaning, located within difference and desire. I want to look at a snapshot of the almost present—in fact, the recent past—the year 2002. In a special supplement of the *Guardian,* August 2002, during the Earth Summit in Johannesburg, John Vidal refers to water as "Blue Gold" and states that "global consumption of freshwater is doubling every 20 years and new sources are becoming scarcer and more expensive to develop and treat. . . . Water, rather than land shortages, are now stopping agriculture expanding in many regions, and the UN fears that water shortages could jeopardise food supplies and trigger economic stagnation."[3] If in the fictional, postapocalyptic age, dry land becomes the mythical object of desire, it is freshwater that seems to propel contemporary desire. The perspective of the present is shaped by rooted, sedentary, contemporary society unlike the fictional, nautical society of *Waterworld.* This disjunction in the meaning of water between the two ages also dislocates embodiment from the familiar underpinnings of race, class, and gender (and sexuality). In August 2002, at the time of the writing of the special supplement of the *Guardian,* however, these categories prevailed.

Here are some facts on water in 2002: the world is divided into water-rich and water-poor countries. If the human requirement per day for healthy living is 11.5 liters a day (2.5 liters for drinking water and 9 liters for hygiene purposes), then water-rich countries almost use up the daily human requirement each time a toilet is flushed (10 liters). Individuals in water-rich countries use up more than three times the basic per capita water requirements by taking a shower (35 liters) or about seven times when taking a bath (80 liters). Meanwhile 1.2 billion people lack access to clean water, and 2.4 billion have no sanitation. Paradoxically, people in water-rich countries spent less on water per capita than their counterparts in water-poor countries. Interestingly, the water-poor countries were located in Africa, South Asia, the Middle East, and China (and most of Australia). Can even the simple act of flushing the toilet locate you within a geographical, economic, and racial space?

Some of the questions with which I am preoccupied here are: How do we read the substantiality of water? What is at stake in the ownership of or access to water? Can access to water class you? Does its use race you? Are women located differently to water than men? Is water necessary for the evolution of the healthy body? What part does the hygienic use of water play in the racializing of humans? What is the mutual relationship between land and water? What is the relationship between colonialism and water? Does water have a history? Does the water closet? What does an awareness of sanitary engineering in Britain have to do with the production of whiteness in the colonies? I will attempt first to address the history of water, concentrating on the eighteenth and nineteenth centuries because I think the tropes of hygiene and mercantilism converged with that of colonialism and differently produced the racialized body in its relationship to water. Then I will examine nineteenth-century Australia's relationship with water, in particular the futile, yet desirable mirage—the inland sea—that propelled explorers and shaped the contours and experience of the continent. I make the link between Britain and Australia because I want to see if water can travel; in particular, how can we link the embodiment of class in Britain with that of race in Australia? How does the race for water down under race Australians?

Women's Waters

Is water essentially the same always or does it have a nuanced history? There are at least two different ways in which one could read the meaning of water. Traditionally, it is the primordial stuff of mythology and genealogy. In the Book of Genesis in the Old Testament, water precedes the formation of land: God first makes heaven and the formless Earth, then light, then the sky gathers the waters under heaven to one place and thus allows dry land to appear. They are named seas and Earth. In Hindu scriptures, in the *RG Veda,* the God Indra begins as a germ in the water. Rising like a fiery column from the limitless flood, the water droplets on his body glow and sing. In Maori mythology, waters fuse in the womb leading to creation. Tane, the firstborn, wedged himself between his father, Rangi, and his mother, Papa, and separated them. The world was formed out of the blood that oozed out of the separation.

This link with creation mythology and especially the maternal is particularly visible within popular comprehensions of this term. For instance, for Jules Michelet, a contemporary of Herman Melville, the sea was like mucus that caused the slipperiness of the fish. Conflating the milky sea with mother's milk, Michelet characterizes the sea as nourishing:

> These nourishing waters are thick with all sorts of particles of fat, suited to the soft nature of fishes who lazily open their mouths and breathe, nourished like an embryo in the womb of a common mother. Do they know they are swallowing? Scarcely. The microscopic food is like milk that comes to them. The great fatality of the world, hunger, is reserved for the earth. Here it is prevented, unknown. No effort is needed to move, there is no search for food. Life must float like a dream.[4]

The sea, for him, teems with life and its maternal form offers nutrition, warmth, and refuge like a woman's breast. This conflation of the milkiness of the ocean in the moonlight and woman as mother leads Gaston Bachelard to speculate that the ocean's whiteness is a retroactive construct in that the waters of the sea evoke in the viewer a certain fullness of being from early life and "of the most pleasant of foods . . . whiteness never comes until afterward."[5] Further, Bachelard suggests that both water and milk are equally nutritive for the unconscious; water is the milk of Mother Nature: "the liquid element then appears as an ultra-milk, milk from the mother of mothers."[6]

Gaston Bachelard's monumental *Water and Dreams* examines the close relationship between images and the imagination and attempts to read the two through water because this substance has clarity and permits seeing ideas in depth and through reflection. Bachelard states: "I cannot sit beside a stream without falling into profound reverie, without picturing my youthful happiness. . . . The nameless waters know all my secrets. The same memory flows from all fountains."[7] Bachelard's work attempts to suture the split between the self and the world and dissolve the boundaries between mind, body, and the material world. He does this by pursuing the trope of water, the substance of materiality and reflections. He genders some water as feminine, part of motherhood, with its flows contoured to the environment. The sea, however, is masculine with the adventures it offers. For Bachelard, the sea provokes narratives before it does dreams; therefore, terrestrial, everyday water, the stuff of dreams, is superior to marine life.

This link between the waters and the maternal is a trope often evoked by feminist scholars as well, the waters of the ocean being linked to the intrauterine fluids within the pregnant mother; in this metonymic link, the ocean is feminized. This metonymic and then metaphorical link between the oceanic water and the maternal causes both water and mother to be located as before meaning, a constant and a universal. Indeed, the reproductive mother and her maternal instinct becomes the source for the ocean's miming of her. The ocean performs maternity. As the material from which life originates, both the mother and the ocean remain constant before the cultural construction of meaning superimposed upon their materiality and substantiality. It is this structure of meaning that leads to a naturalization of water, particularly in its connection to the maternal and its representation as part of nature. Yet, as Sherry Ortner and Donna Haraway have pointed out, nature is a cultural construct. Enlightenment discourse influenced the nineteenth century; definitions of nature referred to a presocial state, and women, because of their role in reproduction, were perceived to be closely aligned with nature.[8] As Maurice Bloch and Jean Bloch have pointed out, there are four main areas of the meaning of nature: as a presocial contract state; man as a natural being, with bodily processes such as the senses and instinct being perceived as natural; nature as a guide for future society, with man's nature in harmony with environmental physical nature; and primitive people as being closer to nature.[9] Within this context of the valorization of culture, a woman's bodily form that is perceived as less evolved than that of man is inevitably more closely linked with the maternal substance of the ocean and with nature.

The woman's relationship to water can be evoked on yet another plane. The woman and the water closet (WC) function in an analogous relationship. In addition to the link between femininity, intrauterine fluid, and water, the bourgeois woman's enshrinement as the Angel in the House that confined her to the private in the Victorian domestic ideology mimes the increasing privacy that the WC (historically) offers to its users. Beyond the nineteenth century, in the early twentieth century, within the context of modernism, there is a schism between the way buildings in general became more public with their use of light, glass, and transparency while the toilet became secreted further and further into the recesses of the building.[10] This link between the woman and the toilet is also made via the nomenclature "porcelain," the gleaming material used in the manufacture of the toilet bowl and the description of a woman's delicate skin and body. Painters are reputed to have used the same colors for Venus riding the waves (on her porcelain shell) as for the shell itself.[11] Venus, the woman, and her toilet bowl all converge under the signifier "porcelain." The distance between the woman and the toilet and the woman as toilette (as in combing, grooming, applying makeup, and dressing) decreased in the nineteenth century with innumerable artists who painted the nude woman in the bath. In nineteenth-century Paris, the well-known sanitation engineer and sociologist of prostitutes, Alexandre Parent-Duchatelet, conflated the two forms of sewage—"putrid matter" and prostitutes—and posited that "the vaginal filth of fallen women is naturally linked to the mire and to excremental effluvia."[12] The domestication of waste thus coincides with the domestication of woman and, like the woman, bodily waste becomes located within the private. It reinforces the public/private split within liberal democracy and modernity. It is not just that bodily waste must be kept private, but also its odor must be secreted within it. It is this structure of public and private that suggests every home with a WC, that marvelous product of sanitation engineering, as being included within modernity.

VICTORIAN WATER

If the meanings of the oceans and water are constructions, if their mythical meanings and gendered meanings reflect social constructions, how else can they be read? How else are they perceived? I begin by suggesting that there are two different strands to the meaning of water in the nineteenth century: water as part of hygiene and the water of oceans, its currents, its dominance, and its yielding of wealth. Both are interlinked as they function to produce the background of Empire and black embodiment. Each facilitated the other; the former justified, to some extent, the latter because the lack of "hygiene" was incorporated as the bourgeois white man's burden. The wealth of the oceans also becomes the rightful inheritance of the bourgeois white man.

First, the tropes of cleanliness and sanitation within the context of access to clean water allow for the convergence of racialized and classed bodies. Elsewhere I have argued that race and class compose a double-bodied discourse, which allows for the experience of geographical spaces as discrete.[13] The discourse of race gets grafted onto that of class (or it can be posited as the other way around as well) and allows for the perception of them as mutually exclusive zones: one about the heterogeneity of whiteness and the other about the homogeneity of blackness. It is not surprising that the historical, material, and cultural conditions that allowed for the emergence of Marx's theories coincided with the age of colonialism. The concerns about the living conditions of the Victorian working class, its poverty enmeshed within anthropological discourses on morality (or lack of it), are strikingly familiar to the scholar in colonial studies. Sewage is not only conflated with the fallen woman, but its contents link race and class as well.

In the summer of 1846 in Britain, a serious outbreak of typhoid occurred, a disease that is waterborne, like cholera, and flourishes when the source of drinking water is contaminated. The summer of 1846 merged with 1847 when the Irish, who were perceived as having brought typhus to England and Wales, immigrated in mass numbers. Within this period of a year and a half, thirty thousand deaths occurred through waterborne diseases.[14] The waterborne epidemics were largely linked to poverty. In the rapidly expanding cities in Britain, caused by the mass migration of populations internal to Britain, poor people had little access to the few water resources. For instance, the poor would rely on one pump in a street that served twenty to thirty families. In St. Anne's parish in Soho, for instance, the feces of a child with cholera was washed down to the water reserve and infected almost every user of a local pump.[15] Again, the Thames, which was the chief source of water supply for Londoners, was so polluted with sewage in 1858 and 1859 that Parliament could conduct business only by hanging cloths that had been soaked in disinfectant over windows that opened to the river.

The link between the circulation of water and embodiment also becomes visible in the ideas of Vincenz Priessnitz of Silesia, who established a water university in the 1820s. A farmer by profession, Priessnitz suggested that humans, like animals, should drink more water and bathe more frequently. This continental idea took off in Britain, and soon a number of hydropathic spas were established. A wide range of clients, such as George Henry Lewes, George Eliot, Thomas Carlyle, Charles Dickens, Thomas Maucaulay, Charles Darwin, John Ruskin, and Alfred Tennyson, all tried the spa treatment.[16] At spas in Cheltenham, Leamington, and Malvern, patients used water in a wide variety of ways: they sat in water, bathed in it, had it sprayed on them, and drank it. Unlike the waters of Bath and Tunbridge Wells, these spa waters were plain and considered better for health.

Dirty, stagnant water and the diseased and degenerated body are further linked through the notion of circulation. While Ibn Al-Nafis, a physician from Baghdad and Cairo, first posited the circulation of blood as early as 1288, it was left to William Harvey, the court physician of King James I and King Charles I, to popularize this concept within medical circles. The link between the purification of blood by the heart and the cleansing of the city through the circulation of water was finally made in the nineteenth century by Sir Edwin Chadwick, who began his career as a literary assistant to Jeremy Bentham (of the Panopticon fame). Chadwick wrote a report on the sanitary conditions of the laboring population of Britain, "The Health of Nations." For Chadwick, only the constant circulation of water through the mean and dirty streets of metropolitan areas would make it habitable, washing away the accumulated sweat, sewage, and shit. In the seventeenth and eighteenth centuries, latrines were suspended directly over urban waterways. Households and businesses such as butchers, slaughterhouses, and brick and dye works discharged their rubbish to cesspits, to be later removed to sewage ditches or made to flow directly to drains and local bodies of water. Residents of houses often crossed sewers as they crossed the street since the ditches ran at the center of the street rather than at the two sides.[17] In the mid-nineteenth century, most households still used privy pails, which were emptied onto the streets. Street cleaners, in turn, cleaned up the waste. However, the infrequency of street cleaning contributed to the hovering miasma—night gases—which also emanated from the bowels of the homes. The history of the water closet, the privacy required for the expelling of bodily wastes, is a phenomenon of modernity and can be noted in Marie Antoinette's installation of a door to her closet. In the late eighteenth century the British upper classes designed the water closet, which consisted of a closed cupboard connected by an unventilated pipe to the cellar, which also housed a cesspit. In the fabulous *H2O and the Waters of Forgetfulness,* Ivan Illich contextualizes this moment within the history of smells:

> The unintended feedback from this progress in hygiene was the saturation of English townhouses with a new type of gas resulting from more advanced stages of decomposition. While the English got used to it as the appropriate aura of elites, foreign visitors during the entire century commented on this peculiar phenomenon without, however, recognising its technical source.[18]

The middle class had their mania for cleanliness and the means to maintain it, and the upper classes, who had previously become used to the smell of shit in their cellars, were frequenting health spas, but what about the poor working classes? Any notion of the privacy and domestication of the smell of bodily waste bypassed them as they shared a common privy with numerous other households. Even by the end of the long nineteenth century, the washing of bodies was problematic, as bathrooms were rare for the poor. Weekly washes at the local public baths were indulgences for the working poor because they cost twopence each.[19] While there was a bourgeois flight to the suburbs for a better lifestyle, the working classes were concentrated in the city, near their workplaces. The cleaning of streets in residential areas varied according to class differences. For instance, the bourgeois areas had street waste removed every night; the working-class areas were cleaned far less frequently. The link between race and class becomes particularly evident in the 1883 pamphlet *The Bitter Cry of Outcast London,* in which Andrew Mearns analogizes working-class homes to the middle passage of slave ships:

> To get to [working class] homes you have to penetrate homes reeking with poisonous and malodorous gases arising from accumulation of sewage and refuse scattered in all directions and often flowing beneath your feet; courts, many of which the sun never penetrates, which are never visited by a breath of fresh air, and which rarely know the virtues of a drop of cleansing water. You have to ascend rotten staircases, which threaten to give way beneath every step, and which, in some places, have already broken down, leaving gaps that imperil the limbs and lives of the unwary. You have to grope your way along dark and filthy passages swarming with vermin.[20]

The descriptions of Victorian tenements are particularly gruesome, and contemporary social historians and commentators obsessively comment on the degeneration of whiteness in these tenements. Charles Booth's breakdown and analysis of the impact of poverty on the physique of third-generation Londoners (Holborn, 70.8 percent born in London and 48.9 percent in poverty; St. George's in the East, 71.38 percent born in London and again 48.9 percent in poverty, etc.)[21] is fascinating because underlying the analysis is the notion of urban degeneration, debilitated white bodies, and the decay of whiteness. Fears were rife that urban decay could cause the progressive deterioration of the race. The chronic poverty also seemed linked to a poverty of morality. The Victorian philanthropist Octavia Hill subscribed to an evolutionary model of humans and posited that improving sanitation led to improved self-worth. Hill, the granddaughter of the sanitary reform worker Dr. Southwood Smith, became a manager of houses, buying leases of slum property and improving them. She set up a narrative of self-improvement for the poor whose homes she managed. Her philosophy of the maintenance of clean surroundings as being linked to the inculcation of thrift, and eventually happiness, among her tenants made her suggest: "You cannot deal with the people and their houses separately. The principle on which the whole work rests is, that the inhabitants and their surroundings must be improved together. It has never yet failed to succeed."[22]

The various epidemics in Britain caused by dirty water eventually led to the reformation of the sewage system and the disposal of waste in the mid-nineteenth century. In 1855, the Metropolitan Board of Works was established in London, and Sir Joseph Bazalgette was appointed engineer to the board. Bazalgette designed a new sewage system for London (a blueprint for other metropolitan areas as well), which is still at the basis of the city's sewage system in the twenty-first century. Until 1855, the sewage in London was carried out through old watercourses that flowed into the Thames and polluted it. Bazalgette suggested a plan to build large new sewers that ran parallel to the Thames, the main water supply for Londoners. Thus, the waste in the sewage system and the Thames, the source of water and life, flowed side by side to merge downriver, in the country. The city's shit flowed into the country, which functioned as the site of recycling waste into water again. Further, a new embankment was built for the Thames and thus reclaimed thirty-seven acres of land that was once a quagmire of mud and sewage.[23] The breakdown of sewage is as follows: Every household's sewage consists of 99.9 percent water. The remaining one-tenth of 1 percent consists of sand and grit, feces, fat, and vegetable matter. The need to recycle waste is obvious because untreated organic material decomposes, traps oxygen in it, and releases foul-smelling gases. This consumption of oxygen, in turn, leads to the denuding of fish and plant life in rivers. In Victorian Britain post-Bazalgette, the waste was treated and the water was recycled into the river to be reconsumed by the population. The sludge of organic material was pumped into containers and dumped out at sea.[24] Thus, water transformed into sewage was retransformed into water to be consumed again. The cycle is endless. Water required water to be decontaminated and functioned like a camouflage, masking the fact it was shit once. Human bodies were just the transitional state of the transformation of water to water. Inscribed within these details is the emergent meaning of water as that which is fundamental to the evolution of lives and subjectivity within secular life; as that which facilitates the visibility of cleanliness, health, and whiteness; and as that which brings about cleanliness, a central aspect of Norbert Elias's thesis on the civilizing process. Yet the material conditions of working-class lives made it difficult to access that water. In this framework of the comprehension of the body's relationship to water—the centrality of its deodorizing effects on the body—some bodies continued to smell like shit.

BODY ODOR

The history of the senses—the history of smells—and water as deodorant are all interconnected in that contemporary notions of human development and progression are predicated on the subordination of the sense of smell to that of visuality. For instance, Freud's and Lacan's theoretical frameworks—be they via the notion of penis envy or the mirror stage and *méconnaisance*—valorize the sense of sight for the construction of gender and subjectivity. In *Civilisation and Its Discontents,* Freud posits that the human adoption of an erect posture in the history of mankind led to an aversion to smells:

> The diminution of the olfactory stimuli seems itself to be a consequence of man's raising himself from the ground, of his assumption of an upright gait; this made his genitals which were previously concealed, visible and in need of protection, and so provoked feelings of shame in him. . . . The genitals, too, give rise to strong sensations of smell which many people cannot tolerate and which spoil sexual intercourse for them. Thus, we should find the deepest root of the sexual repressions which advances along with civilisation is the organic defence of the new form of life achieved with man's erect gait against his earlier animal existence.[25]

For Freud, then, contemporary human civilization demands the repression of smells and insists on the deodorizing of the body. A hierarchy of humans based on their approach to smells can thus be discerned; the smellier the race or class, the less evolved it is. Indeed, this line of thinking is prevalent in Enlightenment thought, as well as the idea that the formation of aesthetics demands a circumventing of the sense of smell. For instance, in Condillac's work on the hypothetical statue, he bestows it with the sense of smell first because, "of all senses, it seems to con-tribute least to human understanding."[26] Again, in Immanuel Kant's key work, *The Critique of Judgement,* the sense of smell is located in the subjective (unlike aesthetic judgment, which is disinterested or objec-tive, and therefore universal). For Kant, in the history of mankind there is a narrative progression from the charms of the senses to universal communicability, the latter of which is central to the emergence of the individual in the public sphere. Kant states that the judgment "'the rose is agreeable' [to the smell] is also, no doubt, an aesthetic and singular judgement, but then it is not one of taste but of sense. For it has this point of difference from a judgement of taste, that the latter imports an aesthetic quantity of universality, i.e. of validity for everyone which is not to be met with in a judgement upon the agreeable."[27] Thus, in the history of the senses, and of aesthetics, the sense of smell belongs to a more primitive way of being, and in the hierarchy of mankind, the emergence of universality demands almost deodorized bodies. It is this narrative progression that is referred to in Dominique Laporte's fas-cinating *History of Shit.* Laporte refers to the cesspool disinfectors of France who sniffed at "bergamot, orange and lemon essence, distilled lavender, orange blossom essence, cloves, and countless other essences and oils" as they worked because sucking on orange-blossom-scented drops while working metamorphosed "shit . . . into sparrows."[28] The collection of sewage and the suppression of smells become important to the emergence of subjectivity within modernity.

In summary, I have suggested that water is not an inert substance, but within the construction of its meanings, it is connected to myth and maternity. I have pointed out that the Enlightenment preoccupation with sight rather than the other senses devalorized the sense of smell in particular, so that all smells, by implication, were bad. I have also sug-gested that aesthetic sensibility is predicated on sight rather than the other senses. I have explored the significance of water within the grow-ing awareness of hygiene in the eighteenth and nineteenth centuries and their relationship to sewage and water's increasingly deodorizing effects. Most important, I have suggested that, notwithstanding the discourse of development, which is marked by indices of proper plumbing and efficient sewage systems and their implications to health, the material conditions of the majority of people in Victorian Britain, their occupa-tions, and their paltry incomes effectively excluded them from being within the orbit of these indices. In short, the trope of water as hygienic was a bourgeois construction and preoccupation, more appropriate to people who could afford better housing, live in gentrified neighborhoods, and had the disposable income that could be indulged in developing good health. I want to see if these determinants of water as part of development could be transported across the oceans to the colonies. How does the trope of water as important to hygiene and health manifest itself in the colonies? How does the colonized black body compare with the poor white body in Britain? How smelly were they? Did they smell the same?

THE EMPIRE OF GERMS

Previously, I examined the cleansing role of water and the history of sewage in the production of white embodiment within modernity and suggested that the notions and determinants of whiteness could function only within a bourgeois framework; any deviation from that framework destabilized the unmarked (by class and gender) status of the universality of whiteness. In fact, this fantasy of whiteness, not riven by class, gender, sexual, and regional demarcations, could be played out only in the colonies because it is only there that the white can function as universally representative. One could say that racial theories and the excruciatingly detailed racial demarcations that nineteenth-century race science developed can be seen as props that maintained the fantasy.

In the classic work *Purity and Danger,* Mary Douglas points out that the two main differences between the contemporary European notion of defilement and that of "primitive," non-European cultures are connected to hygiene.[29] First, Douglas suggests that in European cultures, hygiene and not religion governed aesthetics. Second, European ideas of dirt are dominated by the knowledge of pathogenic organisms. She states: "The bacterial transmission of disease was a great nineteenth century discovery. It produced the most radical revolution in the history of medicine. So much has it transformed our lives that it is difficult to think of dirt except in the context of pathogenicity."[30] Indeed, there is a link between the knowledge of hygiene, the formation of Empire, and the construction of Western subjectivity. In this version of history—that Empire would not have been possible for the English or the Spanish without the aid of the empires of germs and pathogens—people of the Old World (Africa, Asia, and Europe) had built an immunity over the centuries to certain germs and diseases unlike the isolated and indigenous peoples of the New World. This resistance to germs facilitated the conquest of the New World and the formation of Empire. For instance, just as Spain conquered Native Americans, as much through disease as through military means, so did the English conquer Native Americans. As Alfred Crosby says, "When Francis Drake raided St. Augustine in the 1580s, he brought an epidemic with him. The local Florida Indians 'died verie fast and said amongest themselves, it was the Inglisshe God that made them die so fast.'"[31] In this pathogen theory of conquest and Empire, the indigenous people are not native to the New World; immigrants themselves, albeit tens of thousands of years ago, they arrived into the New World before the existence of crowd diseases like smallpox and measles, which need higher densities of populations to spread. Furthermore, killer infections are perceived as by-products of agricultural/pastoral peoples who live in dense populations in close proximity to animals.[32]

One can suggest that the comprehension of hygiene developed not only through breakthroughs in medical science, but also through the witnessing of diseases in the New World, whose natives died in similar proportion to that caused by the Black Death, which decimated European, African, and Asian populations in the fourteenth century. In the beginning of the sixteenth century (post-1492), it is estimated that Native Americans numbered five million. In about 1800, there were a mere 600,000 Native Americans left in the United States—a paltry 12 percent of the original number at first contact. Europe's population was 18 million in 1492, but by 1800 it had increased to 180 million, ten times greater. The English, Welsh, Scottish, and Irish had increased from 5 to 16 million, more than 300 percent over their numbers in 1492, and all this shift in demographics was due to diseases, pathogens, and a sharper medical awareness of bacteria and the need to keep environments clean and washed.

The connection between health and hygiene became particularly evident under colonialism and in the slave colonies. In the eighteenth century, colonialism in the Caribbean and other torrid climates presented European physicians with new, bewildering pathogens and a growing awareness that European bodies responded differently to them than the native, indigenous population or the slave populations. The emphasis on the use of water and its hygienic properties arose from the comprehension that it was easier to preserve health rather than attempt to cure a diseased body. As a result, a Galenic/Arabic approach to hygiene was developed through the control of the "six things non-natural" that are important to life: air, meat and drink, sleep, exercise and rest, evacuations and obstructions, and the unstable passions of the mind.[33] As Sean Quinlan points out:

> Through active knowledge of the Galenic/Arabic 'six things non-natural', and the corollaries of hygiene and regimen, the individual mediated the physiological processes within the organism—particularly the more visible bodily functions of excretion, physical activity and nutritional intake. What made this doctrine so novel was that physicians encouraged the middle classes to actively control their own bodies. By separating the exogenous and endogenous causes of disease, physicians enclosed the body from its environment, and disassociated one bodily experience from the other. Health became the self-disciplinary mark of the middle classes. However, this self-regulating control demarcated not only social class in the colonies, it also distinguished race.[34]

Furthermore, the increase in health care for Europeans in the colonies not only led to an awareness of pathogens and cleanliness, but also connected that awareness to the discourse of degeneration. One of the many ways proposed to countereffect degeneration promoted sober living at all times: by avoiding overexposure to the sun, by perspiring and not sweating, by drinking fruit juices and not alcohol, and most important, by avoiding dancing. Personal hygiene became paramount to prevent degeneration, and the enslaved black bodies, poor with few resources, could not maintain the same standards of hygiene, further evidence of their degenerate condition. Furthermore, autopsies of slaves in the Caribbean led physicians to perceive large amounts of black bile underneath layers of skin, revealing the "humoral imbalance" of black slaves.[35] The enslaved black body itself was perceived as pollution and physicians urged that contact, particularly sexual, was to be avoided.

The link between race and disease becomes visible within the framework of degeneration; races prone to certain diseases are also prone to the same sort of physiques. Such a comprehension of disease is evident in the fight against malaria within the period of high colonialism. The pathologizing of India as diseased led to certain characterizations of Indians—docile, with delicate physiques, timid.

I want to make one final point before I analyze the material on water, hygiene, and disease that I have presented so far. Connected to all of these peripherally linked points is the history of soap and soapmaking in the production of the modern deodorized body; indeed, soap makes visible the intersections between capitalism, race, and class. Just as the poor were those who smelled without being particularly aware of or bothered by their odor, racial Others were also perceived to smell differently than Europeans: the Indian, the African, the Hottentots all had different signatures of smell that located them in some sort of a Linnaean map of civilized bodies. The more deodorized the body, the higher it is on the evolutionary ladder. As Dominique Laporte puts it, "Civilisation despises odor and will oust it with increased ferocity as power strives to close the gap between itself and derive purity. The ferocity reaches its peak when imperialism punishes color. Smells have no place in the constitutive triad of civilization: hygiene, order and beauty. In the empire of hygiene and order, odor will always be suspect."[36]

Saponification, or the process of making soap, has its own history that is enmeshed with the history of colonialism. Like water, soap is not naturally associated with cleanliness, but is a culturally manufactured and orchestrated event within the aegis of capitalism. Obviously, it could not be manufactured in places where fat was meant to be consumed solely as food. In the fourteenth century, principally in Italy, Spain, and France, soap was produced from olive oil. In 1622 in Britain, King James I granted a monopoly to soapmakers for a price every year. Until the nineteeth century, soap was heavily taxed and was therefore a luxury item. While in the eighteenth century whale hunting and whale oil produced soap and perfume, industrial soapmaking was not possible until almost the middle of the nineteenth century.[37] Soap was made in America as early as the late seventeenth century, when several soapmakers arrived in Jamestown, Virginia. In fact, one could say that commercial soapmaking required the colonies in that Malaya, Ceylon, and West Africa produced the cheap palm, coconut, and cottonseed oils required to produce soap within the new technology of saponification invented in France and Belgium. It was 1884 before the first commercially packaged and branded soap was sold. The commercial packaging of soap also inaugurated the insertion of the colonial and classed Others within the discourse of deodorants.

The binary structure between water and sewage that occludes the tight relationship between the two is not unlike the relationship between capitalism and colonialism; though capitalism denies any relationship between the two, the latter provided the capital to enable the former. This economic relationship becomes obvious in the Indian con-

text when, on July 10, 1833, T. B. Macaulay delivered a speech defending
the East India Company to the House of Commons:

> It is scarcely possible to calculate the benefits which we must derive
> from the diffusion of European civilisation among the vast population
> of the East. It would be, on the most selfish view of the case, far better
> for us that the people of India were well governed and independent of
> us, than ill governed and subject to us; that they were ruled by their
> kings, but wearing our broad cloth, and working with our cutlery, than
> that they were performing their salams to English collectors and English
> magistrates, but were too ignorant to value, or too poor to buy, English
> manufactures. To trade with civilised men is infinitely more profitable
> than to govern savages.[38]

Macaulay's words foretell the story of globalization and the imposition
of crippling demands on the economies of colonized nations, forced
to purchase goods from overseas that were either unwanted or easily
manufactured domestically at a fraction of the price charged for its importation. His plan for the British in India also dovetails with the development of advertising strategies of soap companies within capitalism
that made clean and whitened bodies desirable for both the working
class in Britain and the black bodies in the colonies. Soap companies
repeatedly evoked the racialized body in its images, be it as the primitive black body in the colonies or the work-darkened body of the poor
in Britain. The history of capitalism, with its insistence of whiteness as
a desirable universal condition, is enmeshed within that of colonialism.
Anne McClintock points out that soap

> emerged commercially during an era of impending crisis and social ca-
> lamity, serving to preserve, through fetish ritual, the uncertain bound-
> aries of class, gender and race identity in a social order felt to be threat-
> ened by the fetid effluvia of the slums, the belching smoke of industry,
> social agitation, economic upheaval, imperial competition and anti-
> colonial resistance. Soap offered the promise of spiritual salvation and
> regeneration through commodity consumption, a regime of domestic
> hygiene that could restore the threatened potency of the imperial body
> politic and the race.[39]

While McClintock's emphasis is on the commercial aspects of peddling
soap in the Empire and how the advertising industry combined with

the colonial machinery in selling goods, particularly soap, I want to analyze something quite different. What does sewage have to do with soap? How does the trope of cleanliness function here? I suggest that, first, the manufactured desire for cleanliness and whiteness was the desire for bourgeoisification. The bourgeoisie, in their insistence on hygiene, created a niche market for their products, but in so doing also idealized their social class and their sense of whiteness. Second, coupled with a fading sense of smell, the idealized body became the disembodied body. To be middle class and white was to be dislocated from carnality and smelliness, to be released from the grossness of the body. In *The History of Sexuality,* Foucault suggests that the Victorian Age did not bring about an asceticism of the body but rather an "intensification of the body."[40] Here, Foucault discusses the sensations and pleasures of the bourgeoisie that affirmed itself through its body:

> The emphasis on the body should undoubtedly be linked to the process of growth and establishment of bourgeois hegemony: not, however, because of the market value assumed by labor capacity, but because of what the "cultivation" of its own body could represent politically, economically, and historically for the present and the future of the bourgeoisie.[41]

I refine Foucault's position by taking into account the importance of water, washing, soap, cleanliness, hygiene, and the water closet, and posit that the bourgeoisie's intensification of the body was precisely to disembody itself, to deodorize itself, to whiten itself, because the desirable quality of whiteness was to be not only hegemonic and dominant, but also permitted an invisibility, a scentlessness, leaving no spoor of itself. Health was important, as Foucault would have it, but also particularly because it would permit no lingering odor of the person. Washing and hygiene allowed for the deodorized and hegemonic individual to become (in)visible. It permitted the inscription of the unmarked individual that didn't smell of the unwashed body or sewage or shit. This tasteful, aesthetically developed, disinterested subject, disembodied from the body, engendered among its racial and classed Others a bourgeois desirability for the condition of universality. Foucault's thesis of the bourgeois promotion of health, read against this backdrop of water, narrates a different meaning than he imputes to it. The mind/body split, with its long history of the denigration of the body, takes on a different meaning within the context of hygiene, propped by water, whiteness, and a bourgeois sensibility. The degradation of the body within early Christianity, in which it was perceived as radically sinful, in the eighteenth and nine-teenth centuries takes on racial and class significations, and it is the trope of water that makes clear this new signification lodged within the mind/body split. The carnality of the body needs to be washed away, deodorized, derealized to become only a metonymy of its former self. In its new condition, the body, though it cannot yet be wholly absent, at least need not be fully present either and thus can be exscribed from day-to-day living. The inability to completely excise the body displaces its unruliness, its secondary nature, its rebelliousness onto the working class and nonwhite bodies (and, for that matter, feminine ones as well). They take on all the aspects of the ignoble body and signify as the body. But the close proximity within which the bourgeoisie and the working class live and the interpenetrative relationship in the lives of the white and black in the colonies become problematic because the working class and the black function as daily reminders that the body cannot be so easily got rid of. I want to suggest that the increased significance of the function of water is precisely to wash away the dirt of the body, to cleanse the blackness, to provide a forgetfulness to the bourgeois self, that in Othering Others, it also does the same for a part of itself: its body. The injunction faced for the emergence of the bourgeoisie is that it must forget its forgetfulness, and water, lethe-like, provides its double forgetting.

It is within this context of the status of the body that the notion of abjection comes in useful. As it will be remembered, Julia Kristeva's notion of abjection has its origin in both Sigmund Freud's *Totem and Taboo* and in Mary Douglas's work on the boundaries between the clean and the unclean. From within different frameworks, Freud and Douglas analyze the expulsion of the improper and disorderly from the proper for achieving an acceptable subjectivity and sociality. Freud in-sisted on the structure of the binary opposition between the subject and the object as central to the construction of subjectivity. Within anthro-pological discourse Douglas examines religious prohibitions of filth, which alone can ensure the cleanliness of the subject. The concept of defilement is an assertion of boundaries. In *Powers of Horror,* Kristeva commingles Freud's framework with that of Douglas to produce the notion of abjection.[42] According to Kristeva, in the construction of subjectivity, that which is expelled can never be completely excised. It haunts the contours of its culturally orchestrated subjectivity and the mediated physicality like a ghostly image, threatening its very clarity.

The desire within modernity to transcend corporeality inevitably results in the condition of abjection.

I suggest that the Victorian insistence on the trope of hygiene, and the colonization of water that enables this trope, is precisely to ward off the threat of abjection that besets bourgeois subjectivity and its desire to transcend corporeality. The flow of water and its cleansing properties that can deodorize and disembody can thus control abjection and disperse its threats. Water is the natural ally of strong subjectivity within modernity and postmodernity. It keeps strong-smelling black corporeality in abeyance. It functions like the repressive mechanism wherein there is an overinvestment in the energy expended on avoiding pain. Therefore, the subject washes, mops, deodorizes, sweeps body parings (skin, nail, hair), cleans toilets till they sparkle and smell sweet, and shits and urinates in the private bowels of the home so no one can suspect the subject's corporeality. And water is crucial for all of this repression to happen.

But as with the nature of repression, that which is repressed eventually escapes the censoring mechanism by assuming disguises, taking new forms through the process of condensation or displacement. The body just cannot be repressed. In the end, the truth, like shit, will out. The disgust of the body gets displaced on the black; they wear their color on their body. The slave and indentured laborer sweats; their dwellings stink; they are dirty. Similarly, notwithstanding the similarity of whiteness written on the working-class subject's body, the abolition of difference, and the assertion of unity between bourgeois and working-class embodiment, the latter have dirt on their bodies; they are surrounded by dirt in their daily work. Thus, far from seeing unity, there is only the infinite play of differences between the two groups, reiterating the hierarchy of bodies.

To sum up, what I have examined so far is the status of dirt, washing, cleanliness, and hygiene in the construction of hierarchized embodiment. I have suggested that the racial construction of whiteness is always already enmeshed within its relationship with race and class, which, in turn, are in a metaphorical relationship with each other. The availability and use of water is a race and class issue, but its political enmeshment is occluded by its location within the scientifically neutral discourse of hygiene and medicine. This occlusion becomes visible only by tracing the materiality of the history of Victorian water, hygiene, and health. When the history of water is retraced, you see the whiteness that plentiful water can bestow.

Pacific Crossings

In the previous sections, notwithstanding its subject being the fluidity of water, my chapter was sedentary, rooted in the fixed, geographical points of Britain and its colonies. Do dislocation and movements, a mimicking of the flow of water, provide a different comprehension of water in the nineteenth century? I want to cross the oceans in the next section to examine the story of the Pacific man, the quest for water, and the construction of whiteness down under. I want to take a slow boat across the Pacific to examine how ocean crossings contribute to the whitening of the Pacific man in the final section of this chapter.

Though this chapter is about the relationship between race, class, and water, my references to the Pacific of necessity remind the reader of the rise of Pacific Rim discourse within postcolonial scholarship on globalization. The Pacific Rim is a newly imagined zone constructed through the flow of commodity and capital that, because of its anti-protectionist ideology in trade, is also posited as the postnational and postmodern. The connection between economics and bodies of water, the fluidity of oceans, has been central to the rise of civilizations, the wealth of nations, and antisedentary ontologies. The fluidity of oceans has also caused the mass movements of people from one social, economic, and geographical space to the New World. Fully fifty-five million Europeans moved to the colonies, traversing the oceans between 1815 and 1914. Janet Abu-Lughod suggests that the works of Immanuel Wallerstein, Eric Wolf, and Fernand Braudel locate the year 1400 as a defining moment for the beginning of modern world systems and for the advances of capitalism, both of which were dependent on trading and sailing the oceans, especially the Atlantic. She adds that this premise now needs to be recontextualized as the commercial importance of the Pacific Rim, and the contemporary global economic system was *predated* by the commercial importance of the Indian Ocean around the beginning of the Christian era, and the eastern Mediterranean and China seas from the ninth century onward.[43] Indeed, the rise of the Atlantic was merely a phase in the construction of identities. In short, one can argue for the importance of the fluidity of oceans and crossings in the development of commerce *as well as* the construction of racial identities. Crossing the oceans racializes the subject. Like intrauterine fluid, the ocean is the origin of emergent (economic) identities.

But if we were to use the year 1400—the onset of Western modernity—as the starting point, the term used for the perfect commonwealth, half-idealized and half-real, is "Oceana." Sir James Harrington in the seventeenth century insisted that this commonwealth was the destiny of the Scottish, English, and Anglo-Irish.[44] Like the imagined zone of the Pacific Rim, James Froude defines Oceana to comprise North America, Australia, New Zealand, and Ireland: the Anglo-Saxons spread across the globe in the name of personal and economic freedom and enterprise. Oceana is the place that dislocates Englishmen (and Scottish, Welsh, and Anglo-Irish) from the reductions of class and rebirths them as youth in the settler colonies: "Those poor children of hers now choking in the fetid alleys" would go to the colonies "where there was still soil and sunshine boundless and life-giving; where the race might for ages renew its mighty youth."[45] Oceana thus becomes the clichéd and mythical land that contains the fountain of youth that recirculated the polluted English into the Pacific man. But beyond its life-renewing properties, Oceana is the place where England can dump both, its excess of manufactures and its excess of population, for profit. Froude's work prophesies the desire of Australia, New Zealand, South Africa, and Canada to seek independence, become republics, but he posits that they could be kept together as a commonwealth, for then,

> in the multiplying number of our own fellow-citizens animated by a common spirit, we should have purchasers for our goods from whom we should fear no rivalry; we should turn in upon them the tide of our emigrants which now flows away, while the emigrants themselves would thrive under their own fig tree, and rear children with stout limbs and colour in their cheeks, and a chance before them of a human existence. Oceana would then rest on sure foundations; and her navy—the hand of her strength and the symbol of her unity—would ride securely in self-supporting stations in the four quarters of the globe.[46]

In this economic and racial narrative of Oceana, Froude concludes that the future of the British lies in the sea, "the natural home of Englishmen."[47]

The natural and easy relationship between the Anglo-Saxons and the sea is particularly manifest within the history of swimming. England's dominance in the sport surfaced in the nineteenth century, to be superseded by the American and the Australian only from the twentieth century on. Elizabethan swimmers used the dog as their model for swimming, but overarm strokes were inspired by Caribbean and Pacific Island swimmers.[48] Early nineteenth-century swimmers, pre-Victorian, swam mostly in the nude to achieve a oneness with nature. The Etonian swimming society used as its motto the line from the Greek poet Pindar, "Water is best." As Christopher Connery points out, "Classics and empire-building were water sports."[49]

This paean to the ocean is sung under the auspices of the whaling industry by Herman Melville and Charles Olson. For them, the whaling industry converted the Pacific into the world's first sweatshop. With its division of labor and a proletarian crew, it provided the first blueprint of nineteenth-century factories. For Melville, the Pacific was an extension of the West Coast of the United States. The western border of the United States touches the Asian countries of the Asia-Pacific Rim. The Pacific is perceived as belonging to the Americans. It resembles the Great Plains, the motions of its wheat; the immensity of the Great Plains was a mimicking of the Atlantic. Yet the Pacific was the mother of the Atlantic: "It rolls the midmost waters of the world, the Indian Ocean and the Atlantic but its arms."[50] The Pacific with its abundance of whales located the United States as the leader of world trade. The fluid oceans functioned as the highway for Anglo-Saxons, leading them to populate and whiten the New World. The nonwhite Pacific body thus gets superseded by the (white) Pacific man.

This valorization of water, of oceans, within modernity is saturated with and underpinned by certain historical details pertinent especially to Britain. From the seventeenth century and especially in the eighteenth and nineteenth centuries, oceangoing commerce and enterprise expanded. Between 1660 (Restoration) and 1689 (just after the Glorious Revolution) English shipping tonnage doubled. (This was also caused by the capture and addition of Dutch ships to the English fleet after the Dutch wars, especially the merchant marine, which drastically improved long-distance overseas trade.) The ports of London, Liverpool, Bristol, and Whitehaven were filled with ships sailing to the Mediterranean, America, the West, and East Indies.[51] Commerce expanded with colonial products such as tea, tobacco, sugar, and cotton, and timber from Scandinavia; colonial products reexported throughout Europe traversed the world.

The burgeoning of English trade, and even European trade, in the eighteenth and nineteenth centuries is linked to the rise of colonialism and the traffic in slaves, especially from West Africa. The ports of Bristol and, later, Liverpool grew in importance with the slave trade. By the middle of the eighteenth century, the port of Bristol rivaled that of London in trade and commerce. In total, it is estimated that twelve million slaves from Africa were transported to the New World, in which Britain played the major role. Products such as gold, ivory, beeswax, and cloth also used the same extensive network that was established for the slave trade and were transported in the same ships as well.[52] James Walvin locates the British weakness for sugar not with just slavery and colonialism, but also with the development of domestic industries, as for instance, the popularity of tableware such as china from manufacturers such as Wedgwood. As Walvin points out, Jamaican plantation ledgers record the importation of tools for slaves, clothes and fabric, firearms for their owners, metal goods for their factories, and foodstuffs for both slaves and owners. In short, the boom in British commerce and capitalism in the eighteenth and nineteenth centuries and its superior mercantile power, which made it a major player among European powers, is closely linked to the system of slavery and colonialism.[53]

British commerce and capitalism and the traversal of oceans are also linked to the system of indenture. The four main colonial crops—sugar, tea, coffee, and rubber—led to the diaspora of the Chinese and the Indians as indentured laborers in the eighteenth century to the West Indies, Malaysia, Ceylon (Sri Lanka), Fiji, Mauritius, Réunion, and South and East Africa. The nineteenth-century form of indenture was instituted after the abolition of slavery and the transportation of slaves. The indenture of laborers in the plantations, notwithstanding the free will of people signing up, carried vestiges of slave laws within it, especially for vagrancy.[54] Among Indian indentured laborers alone, it is estimated that 525,482 went to French and British sugar colonies, 30,000 went to Mauritius, and 1,446,407 went to Ceylon between the years 1843 and 1867, of whom about 90,000 returned. Overall, it is estimated between one and two million went to tropical plantations between 1830 and 1870.[55]

If previously the sea was an enclosure that protected a hermetically sealed Britain, by the eighteenth century the sea shifted in cultural meaning to become a ubiquitous and fluid roadway that led to its prosperity. Britannia, indeed, ruled the waves.

THE WATERY ROAD FROM BOTANY BAY

Crossing the Pacific, I have reached the final geographical section of this chapter: Australia. Postcolonial studies have been overwhelmingly preoccupied with the materiality of land masses, their unlawful usurpation, and their continued occupation, especially in settler countries such as Australia. The fluidity of water, its ambivalences and shifts, has not factored much in postcolonial studies. Indeed, though much discussion has been devoted to terms such as landscapes, place, site, space, territory, margin, ground, and maps, the trope of water has been left out of the loop, notwithstanding the histories and meanings of oceans and water in the eighteenth and nineteenth centuries. Yet Australian explorers were obsessed with the discovery not just of suitable land but also of water. In fact, the latter preceded the former. It is the base, the ground upon which the whitening of Australia has occurred. I want to follow seas and rivers and streams in the Westernized landscape of Australia. The discourse on the pursuit of water takes place on two levels in Australia, at that of trope and at that of the "real." Water as trope is particularly evident in the pursuit of the inland sea, salty as the Mediterranean, in the early exploration journals of the nineteenth century. On the level of the real, the search is always for fresh potable water, a search replete with the anxiety of settlement and the whitening of landscape. Often the same explorer journal conflates water as trope with water as real. Thus, there is a convergence of meaning of the occupation of land and the signification of water. Like the dry land in Kevin Reynolds's *Waterworld,* in the nineteenth century the mirage of water beckons and leads a westward and inward movement of settlement into the interior spaces of the continent.

Nor is the pursuit of the inland sea just a marker of the Victorian Age. In the twenty-first century, Australia's quest manifests itself on Web sites on its geological formations. Among others, there is a Web site that allows you to download images of plate tectonics on a QuickTime Player and suggests that the nineteenth-century search for the inland sea was late by seven hundred thousand years. We find that millions of years ago in geological time, another plate beneath the Australian plate caused the land mass to be sucked downward by 350 meters, which led to the flooding of low-lying areas. However, when the land mass drifted northward and eventually rose again, the sea receded; in turn, the new sediment prevented flooding when the sea levels rose again.

Indeed, the Murray-Darling Basin is a remnant of that original flooding and, perhaps, the ur–inland sea. (We are also informed that while the Northern Hemisphere's rivers and waterways changed courses since the last ice age and are therefore only less than fifteen thousand years old, the Murray-Darling Basin has remained the same for millions of years or, at least, for seven hundred thousand years.)

However, it was not geological ponderings that led Joseph Banks, the botanist who voyaged with Captain Cook to Eastern Australia, to speculate in one of his reports to the Colonial Office in 1792: "It is impossible to conceive that such a large body of land, as large as all of Europe, does not produce vast rivers, capable of being navigated into the heart of the interior." This speculation was reiterated by Matthew Flinders, who navigated the HMS *Investigator* in 1801 and 1802 to chart the southern coastline of Australia. Taking his cue from Joseph Banks, Flinders attempted to find a shortcut into some other part of terra Australis.[56] Flinders's *The Journal on the Investigator* is interesting for its un/awareness of water. While it does figure too prominently as the subject of the text, all the crew are aware of water only peripherally. Yet they are surrounded by it, float in it; the *Investigator* leaks because of it, and the crew also need to find channels deep enough for their ship in their mapping of the contours of South Australia. Most of all they need fresh water for drinking and staying alive. In the *Journal on the Investigator,* two sorts of water, potable and floatable, conflate, and their presence becomes equated with white existence:

> The port itself may be of much utility, since its depth of water is equal to any want, and the shelter it affords complete. . . . I did not find any water worth the attention of a ship during my excursion, but upon both sides of the Northern entrance it was found by our gentlemen in various ponds and swamps; and there is little doubt but that a days *[sic]* examination for water would find it in sufficient abundance.[57]

This passage, recorded on Sunday, August 8, 1802, goes on and on with its obsession of water: its presence, its absence, its depth, its potability, and the abundance of food it contains. In fact, it was Banks's influence that permitted Flinders to imagine a Mediterranean in the interior of Australia.[58]

Not finding any significant river mouth along the coastline, Flinders posited that the rivers could flow into an inland sea. Both Flinders and Banks, notwithstanding their discoveries, seemed unable to comprehend that in the positing of the inland sea as similar to the Mediterranean, Australian difference in its landscape, fauna and flora, and evolutionary history itself becomes a copy modeled on a European template. Australian landscape, then, functions as mimicry in these texts, deprived of its own history, specific geological formation, and historicity. The hunt for the Mediterranean in Australia, or at least a great river, is not then just a scrambling of geographies and specificities, but also a form of citationality in that Europe's specificities are naturalized as the norm, and the repeated citing of the inland sea or the Mediterranean reinscribes Europe as superior in the ambit of power and authority. Every foray into the interior of Australia, as, for example by Oxley, Sturt, Hume, and Cunningham, functioned to reiterate and cite European knowledges as dictating Aussie reality. For instance, while Charles Sturt in 1833 finds a salty river and refers to it as the Mediterranean,[59] the eerie resemblance to Europe also disconcerts him. He queries:

> Where, however, are the inhabitants of this distant and singular region? The signs of a numerous population were around us, but we had not even seen a solitary wanderer. The water of the ocean was not, by any means, so salty as that of the ocean, but its taste was precisely similar. Could it be that its unnatural state had driven its inhabitants from its banks?[60]

This is an important moment in the geological (white) history of Australia because we later find that Sturt names his discovery the Darling River. (Ironically, Sturt had, indeed, found the scattered remnants of the seven hundred thousand-year-old inland sea on the Murray-Darling Basin, though he was not to know it.)

In another context in the relationship between the dominant Western subject in the space of the non-Western Other, Gayatri Chakravorty Spivak remarks on the imperialist notion of the "worlding of the world on uninscribed earth,"[61] thus suggesting the violent erasure of a prior set of meanings inscribed to the landscape by its indigenous populations. Indeed, such a reinscription or a reworlding of the world as a copy reforms, regulates, and disciplines the new landscape. In re-presenting the Australian landscape as functioning within a logic set by Europe, it is reduced to a metonymy, in which the whole is reduced to parts with the difference between the whole and its parts simultaneously maintained and visible.

This hunt for the inland sea, predicated on Northern Hemisphere and European assumptions of land mass, also subscribes to the theory of the upside-downness of the antipodes. Etymologically, the term "antipodes" encapsulates within it an upside-downness—the soles of the feet of inhabitants of the Northern Hemisphere rubbing against those of their counterparts down under—the function of the Australian continent being to serve as a balance for Europe and Asian land masses. Australia is the ballast. The concept of the upside-downness of the antipodes pervaded the classical as well as the medieval and contributed to it, becoming the site of fantasy and Otherness. Stories abounded of the aberrant nature of the fantasized occupants of the antipodes, a space where hermaphrodites proliferated, women ruled, and servants dictated masters.[62]

The hunt for water in the explorer journals also has a practical element to it, in that white immigration is predicated on its availability and the access to it. Most of the explorers are sharply aware of the issue of immigration. John Oxley's account concludes with a short and mournful abstract of the general population of New South Wales: 12,911 in 1815, 15,175 in 1816, and 17,265 in 1817, along with a statement of the land in cultivation and quantities of stock, thus expressing the need to increase white population. Again, Charles Sturt remarks on the beauty of New South Wales: "most delightful under heaven," but simultaneously underscores that "the climate may be said to be too dry."[63] John Oxley, at the onset of his expeditions into New South Wales, states on June 3: "The country [New South Wales] is so extremely impracticable and so utterly destitute of the means of affording subsistence to either man or beast; water is so precarious, and when found is only the contents of small muddy holes, which under different circumstances would be rejected equally by horses and by men, that I much fear we shall not be able to proceed much further."[64]

The mapping of the landscape can be done only from one water hole to the next because without it, the explorers know they won't be able to survive in the outback. Indeed, some of the expeditions, such as that of Edward John Eyre, can map only landscapes along the coast or within easy proximity of it because ships carrying drinking water were needed to accompany expeditions. Eyre is obsessed not only with charting landmarks and finding water, but making sure his horses get water too. Like water, horses become a precious commodity, providing transportation and, in a pinch, food.

The difference between the heroic and the illogical often completely collapses in the journals, showing close metonymic ties between the two. For instance, Oxley was sent on two different expeditions, first on the Lachlan River to see whether it fell into the mythical sea and if it could be used for shipping and trade purposes. On the second expedition, after not having discovered the inland sea, but having discovered the Macquarie River instead in the previous expedition, Oxley floated on the Macquarie to examine if it led him to a tropical region with valuable possibilities. At one point, Oxley literally burned his boat, taking a calculated risk, and headed on land toward the coast. Instead, his gamble proved wrong and his crew/team suffered severe privations on the muddy trails as a result. Again, Edward John Eyre was so aware of the importance of water that he buried containers of it in a form of hoarding.[65] Yet he was all too aware of the shifting landscape, making previously visited places not quite recognizable in subsequent visits. Commenting on the explorer journals as narratives in *Living in a New Country,* Paul Carter suggests that the explorers

> singularly failed: for instead of capitalising on such external phenomena as they did find, whether human or geological, the explorers steadfastly drew attention to their absence. Far from seeking to "bunch" their day-to-day entries into significant (if fictional) episodes serving to advance the narrative, they dwelt on their failure to advance, the repeated experience of disappointment. Far from suppressing intervals of inactivity as uninteresting, they expatiated on their cloudy lack of definition. Signs of change, far from indicating a change, usually foretoken the opposite: the absence of change, a deferral of dramatic action.[66]

In the now classic work *Imperial Eyes,* Mary Louise Pratt suggests that the European systematizing of nature consisted of three different aspects, all mimetic of each other: the circumnavigation of the globe, the mapping of the world's coastlines, and the classification of nature, as, for example, by Linnaeus.[67] Indeed, miscalculations notwithstanding, the explorers were obsessive in their recording of precise locations, landmarks, passageways, the availability of water, and the noting of latitudes and longitudes. As such, in their mapmaking they participated in what Pratt describes as European consciousness of knowledge production. The governor of South Australia, who commissioned Eyre's expedition, indicates his European consciousness:

We are assembled to promote one of the most important undertakings that remain to be accomplished on the face of the globe—the discovery of the interior of Australia. As Captain Sturt in substance remarked in a recent lecture of the five great divisions of the earth—Europe is well known, Asia and America has been generally searched out; the portion that remains to be known of Africa is generally unfavourable for Europeans, and probably unfit for colonization; but Australia, our great island continent, with a most favourable climate, still remains unpenetrated, mysterious and unknown. . . . Mr Eyre goes forth to brave a battle [which] may present the dangers of Waterloo. May triumph crown his efforts.[68]

This passage is remarkable not only for its promotion of European consciousness—the undertaking as a discovery of the Australian interior—but also for a European perspective, that Asia and America have been searched out (even though they had been constantly occupied for tens of thousands of years by Asians and Native Americans) and that portions of Africa are irrelevant because they are unfavorable to whites. Further, Eyre's expedition is perceived as a defining European moment, like the Battle of Waterloo. Heroism, perceived as evident in Eyre's mapmaking, is also conducted under the aegis of science and exploration and objective reality. However, by now it is common to point out the intimate bond between maps, mapping, and power relations. Maps are never objective reality, but are cultural meanings that always already present the hegemonic viewpoint. As Chandra Mukherjee suggests, "The meanings of land as property [in the New World] to be consumed and used by Europeans was written into the language of maps."[69]

But do indigenous Australians not map? Where does their system of marking, knowing, and territorializing the landscape fit in with the white quest for water? The white explorers were often aware of the indigenous Australians' knowledge of the landscape, water holes, and rivers; Oxley reveals an awareness that indigenous hatchet marks on trees could signify the presence of water. But while precise latitudinal and longitudinal information is constantly recorded, native methods of marking landmarks are often ignored. Yet Eyre is constantly dependent upon and directed by indigenous Australians to water sources. In fact, he is all too aware of European and indigenous difference in their use and consumption of water:

The natives generally resort to such places [as one ten miles up a stony hill] when the rain water is dried up in the plains or among the hills immediately skirting them. Far among the fastness of the interior ranges, these children of the wilds find resources which always sustain them when their ordinary supplies are cut off; but they are not of corresponding advantage to the explorer, because they are difficult of access, not easily found, and seldom contain any food for his horses, so that he can barely call at them and pass on.[70]

Eyre is aware that water is to be found everywhere in this "wretched and impracticable"[71] land and, in fact, finds native tracks leading to them most times. At an interesting moment in Eyre's journals, Eyre's team attempts to dig a well in the sand to access water and are unable to do so. Indigenous Australians observing them help out and dig one for them in "an incredibly short time."[72] Their economy of movement is coupled with the economic sensibility with which they dig a deep, narrow hole instead of the massive well that Eyre's team attempts. In short, their economic use of water, their engineering skills organic to their landscape, the abundance of food they seem to find even in places the explorers consider wretched, suggests the alternate indigenous consciousness that slowly occurs to Eyre.

Eyre's text has a self-aware moment when he perceives or, rather, hypothetically posits the Europeans as the invading Other. He ponders over the fact that the indigenous are right to conclude that Europeans would dispossess them; that Europeans are going through the act of usurpation of the best spaces for themselves; that European customs and prejudices and habits are cultural constructions as are those of indigenous. He wonders:

Suppose the case of a settler, who, actuated by no selfish motives, and blinded by no fears, does not discourage or repel the natives upon their first approach; suppose that he treats them with kindness and consideration . . . , what recompense can he make them for the injury he has done, by dispossessing them of their lands, by occupying their waters, and depriving them of their supply of food? He neither does nor can replace the loss.[73]

Ultimately, as history proves, European consciousness prevails. In a poignant moment in Sturt's text, which functions as a metaphor for

Australian history, his team sees water and, upon their approach, the natives flee. Soon Sturt and his team enjoy the watery site that the natives had enjoyed just moments before.[74] The indigenous Australians are displaced by the explorer's team at the water hole: the history of Australia. In the last instance, the pursuit of the inland sea, the obsession with finding water in Australia, is also a metaphor for the occlusion of native knowledges, of resources, and of ownership of land. The hunt for and the finding of water becomes a code for the ownership (or usurpation) of land. On the level of the "real"—as much as one can access it—water and its availability, its access, signifies the ownership of land, the usurpation of rights in Australia.

The pursuit of and quest for water by the explorers can also be read from within the Lacanian notion of desire. Lacanian desire is principally informed by Hegel's explanation of desire as an absence and a lack. For Lacan, desire in a subject is inaugurated at the moment she or he comes into meaning and language and is accompanied with the formation of the unconscious. At this inaugural moment the subject is split from personal drives and is always in a state of nonfulfillment and nonrepresentation. Thus, the Lacanian notion of desire also bespeaks a lack. Desire is intransitive, in that it has no specific object; it is not for another but rather indicates a place, language, and the Symbolic that generates it. The acquisition of language functions as a compensation for this lack.

I interpret the quest for water by the explorers from within this framework because I cannot comprehend why their search for water did not make use of indigenous mapping more, especially as Edward John Eyre had discovered that their tracks led to most of the water-hole sites that he found. No, water must also function as a metaphor for the explorers. The explorers want land to settle; water is needed; an inland sea needs to be discovered; yet like desire, it is destined to a nonfulfillment. There is water everywhere in Australia, yet this is not the water that Eyre or Flinders, Oxley, or Sturt seem to want to find. The search for the inland sea becomes a quest with no fulfillment, an intransitive moment, bespeaking a settler loss and lack. Yet, as the Web sites on the inland sea indicate, the search for water constantly propels Australian settler identity forward.

I end where I begin—with another newspaper supplement. A year after I read the first supplement with which I began this chapter, I came across the monthly *Food Magazine* for the *Observer* (August

2003, no. 29), which pointed out that bottled water was a two-million-pound-a-day habit in the United Kingdom. In the United Kingdom, in 2002, £847 million was spent on two billion liters of bottled water. Kaballah Mountain Spring water costs about £3.90 a liter. The water labeled Fiji costs about £1.95 a liter and tastes of nothing. In postmodernity, water needs to taste of nothing—no additives, no chlorination, no fluoridation—and we pay through our nose to taste nothing. Nothingness takes us to a preindustrial, premodern space before the rise of the West. It represents a sense of purity, a fullness of being. Our digestion improves, our skins get supple, and most important, it is noncaloric. In postmodernity the quest is not for the inland sea, but the perfect liter of water. Meanwhile, in the same year, in 2002, 1.2 billion people in other places had no access to clean water to drink, for sanitation, or to survive.

CHAPTER 5

Mourning and Melancholia:
The Wages of Whiteness

The landscape in New Zealand is still saturated with the remnants of melancholy: it is said that the pohutakawa trees that spill their crimson blossoms on the white beaches of New Zealand at Christmastime symbolize the blood—Maori and Pakeha blood—spilled on them during the New Zealand land wars of the 1860s.[1] I have before me a collage of nineteenth-century texts, all of which marvel at the indescribable, blinding beauty of the New Zealand landscape—its beaches, bushes, the silvery foliage, the clarity of the air—but hovering over all of these texts is the whiff of tragedies past. Sailing into Auckland Harbor on Friday, June 24, 1842, Sarah Selwyn, the wife of the first bishop of New Zealand, exclaims that they were in "the middle of a New Zealand winter, equivalent to Christmas in England, but very bright and warm, the sun shining hotly upon us."[2] Notwithstanding she had just arrived in this barely settled colony that had become part of the Empire only two years before in 1840 with the signing of the Treaty of Waitangi, her husband, George Selwyn, left her to her own fate on July 4, less than two weeks after her arrival. He was away for six months, sailing to the south, tending to his flock and trying to increase it. In his wife's *Reminiscences,* George Selwyn is frequently away, and she has to cope with the strangeness of the country and losing her young baby to it on her own. Next to Sarah Selwyn's text is the bibliographic index of the work *Mission and Moko,* which includes a list of the Church Missionary Society (CMS) missionaries and workers among the Maori in New Zealand.[3] This index is a mournful roll call of loss and uncertainty: James Boyle is dismissed from the CMS by Samuel Marsden for swearing; Robert Burrows of Gloucester, whose children die in 1841 and 1842 in New Zealand, is diagnosed with consumption in 1853; Samuel Butler, who served as teacher and catechist, is dismissed from his job in New Zealand and drowns in the Hokianga River in 1836; Elizabeth Colenso separates from her unfaithful husband and is left with an uncertain future; William Charles Dudley, who studied at Oxford and Cambridge, suffers a mental breakdown at Turanga; William Fairburn, who was a catechist, develops severe depression and becomes an alcoholic. This list of CMS workers who meet disastrous ends is quite extensive. One final text to finish the collage: Lady Mary Martin's patronizingly titled text, *Our Maoris.*[4] Mary Martin's husband had been the first chief justice of New Zealand. Arriving in New Zealand just three weeks before Sarah Selwyn, Mary Martin exclaims, "How pretty everything looked! The blue water lay like a lake below. There was a strip of white shelly beach. The little bay was shut in by sandstone cliffs, and these were over-hung by huge forest trees. . . . The clear air seemed to quiver and sparkle with light."[5] She lived in New Zealand through the land wars of the 1860s and left only in 1876, but not before burying a large number of Maori friends and acquaintances. In the final chapters of her work, she celebrates the democratization that the church, along with English law, brought to New Zealand. She says, "The young chiefs go to English schools, and mix on equal terms with all the nobodies in their village."[6] Notwithstanding the disappearance of hierarchy among Maori, the democratic spirit does not mediate Maori-Pakeha (Pakeha is the Maori nomenclature for immigrants of white British origin in New Zealand) relations in Martin's text. If the missionary services are lauded for bringing an egalitarian spirit, it becomes the mechanism through which the denigrated Maori are preserved. Haunted by the ghostly image of the dying Maori, this text accounts for the guilt, yet through a denial of it. It is a text that simultaneously blends shame *and* dominance, emotions that are also always racially marked. Melancholia and whiteness are mutually imbricated in pioneer New Zealand. Melancholia that hovers over the New Zealand landscape functions in two ways: first, there is the obvious meaning in the vernacular sense of the word as affect, a sadness; and second, it functions in an identificatory sense, in the formation and loss of the self, an illegitimacy at the heart of racial identity.

What did it mean to be white in nineteenth-century New Zealand? How was whiteness forged in the other land down under, whose history of colonization and settlement follows a completely different trajectory from that of Australia? Within whiteness studies, there is often an uncritical, unquestioned acceptance of this term, wherein it is perceived as a homogenous site of power without any indication of the tense negotiation between various groups to appropriate the status of being white. This approach is evident in a lot of scholarship, where it is examined only within contemporary notions of subjectivity, citizenship, and nationhood.[7] Its dislocation from historical and geographical specificities permits whiteness, like capitalism, to be an assimilative machine that allows for the incorporation and homogenization of all various groups, and the erasure of their historical and physical specificities. Whiteness in this framework of multiculturalism becomes a marker of upward mobility, a bourgeoisification of the bodies. In this chapter I want to slow down the assimilative machine so we can see how whiteness has different effects and components in the geographically different New Zealand. I want to track the wages of whiteness in New Zealand. I want to suggest that the white settlers who exchanged Britain for New Zealand also acquired along with the stunning landscape an overwhelming sense of melancholia: nineteenth-century New Zealand history is also the history of loss, grief, and desire, aesthetics compensating for bitter emotions. Melancholia functions not just as a mourning for England lost, but also, perhaps, as a major condition for white identity in New Zealand.

I also want to contextualize the mourning and melancholia not only within the comprehension and assignment of race, but also within that of the humanitarian movement that underpinned the various missionary services in New Zealand. Following the collapse of missions in the South Pacific, in Tonga, Tahiti, and the Marquesas, Samuel Marsden, the Anglican chaplain of New South Wales, established the first Church Missionary Society in the Bay of Islands in 1814. Between the Church Missionary Society, the Wesleyan Missionary Society, and the Catholic Church, as many as forty-eight mission stations had been established by 1845 in New Zealand.[8] Indeed, the primary texts that I examine in this chapter are linked to the church, including Mary Martin's work, which was published in 1884 by the Society for Promoting Christian Knowledge. I want to ask if melancholia is connected to the recognition and maintenance of racial difference. How can we read the relationship between melancholia and the missionaries? How does the structure of melancholia pervade the agenda and effects of the Church Missionary Society in New Zealand? How do the missionary services and the humanitarian bent participate in the framework of loss, grief, desire, and incorporation of Otherness that constitutes melancholia? I will explore the genealogy of mourning and melancholia as formulated by Freud and practiced by subsequent critics. Here, I want to attempt to map the relationship between racial formations and the structure of melancholia that they partake in. Later, I will locate New Zealand within the history of the Treaty of Waitangi and the wars of 1860 to see how racial identities and historical specificities can bring about the effect of melancholia. Finally, I want to locate early New Zealand texts against the backdrop of mourning theory and New Zealand history to trace the contours of whiteness that intersect with a settler melancholia. In so doing I would like to see what conclusion we can arrive at about the status of racial identifications themselves.

THE FREUDIAN FRAMEWORK

Freud formulated his theory of mourning in two stages. Written alongside other influential and well-known essays between 1914 and 1915, such as his "On Narcissism," "Instincts and Their Vicissitudes," "Repression," and "The Unconscious," Freud's essay "Mourning and Melancholia" marks the first stage in his link between mourning theory and that of the structuration of identity. "Mourning and Melancholia" (written in 1915, but published in 1917) distinguishes between these two emotions and posits mourning as healthy and normal and the latter as pathological. Both arise as a reaction "to loss of a loved person, or to the loss of some abstraction which has taken the place of one, such as one's country, liberty, an ideal, and so on."[9] In 1923, in "The Ego and the Id," Freud reworked his theory on mourning to suggest the very construction of the subject's ego as partaking in a bereavement. In these two essays ("Mourning and Melancholia" and "The Ego and the Id") he distinguishes between mourning, an emotional reaction to loss for a finite period of time, and melancholia, a pathological condition wherein the subject cannot and will not accept a substitution for the loss of an object. Mourning is the emotional condition of the subject when an object that one had loved for its intrinsic qualities as separate and distinct from oneself is lost. In contrast, in melancholia, the pattern by which loss is worked through is different because the loved object fulfilled a different function in the psychological life of the bereaved. Psychically stuck, the melancholic subject incorporates the lost object into the self and develops a profound ambivalence to the object (and by extension, to oneself). The incorporation of the lost object permits the melancholic subject to experience loss as ongoing. Not only do the subject in mourning and the melancholic differ in their abilities to recover, but they also differ in their regard for themselves. For Freud, while the former eventually reverts to his/her normal attitude to life, the latter has

> a lowering of the self-regarding feelings to a degree that finds utterance in self-reproaches and self-revilings and culminates in a delusional expectation of punishment. . . . [The melancholic displays] an extraordinary diminution in his self-regard, an impoverishment of his ego on a grand scale. In mourning it is the world which has become poor and empty; in melancholia it is the ego itself. (244, 246)

In this first topography of the psyche drawn by Freud, we see the connection to his work "On Narcissism," in which the narcissist treats his body as a sexual object. Like the narcissist, the melancholic too seems unable to form attachments outside of the self.

By the time Freud formulated "The Ego and the Id" in 1923 in his development of the second topography of the psyche, this over-development of the narcissistic libido, a hallmark of the melancholic, becomes central to the very formation of the normative subject. In this later essay, Freud suggests that one's very ego is formed as a response to a loss and the incorporation of the characteristics of the lost object within oneself. If ambivalence was a strong component of "Mourning and Melancholia," in this stage the subject starts loving itself because it is now so similar to the lost object. Freud claims, "When the ego assumes the features of the object, it is forcing itself, so to speak, upon the id as a love object and is trying to make good the id's loss by saying: 'Look, you can love me too—I am so like the object.'"[10] Thus we can see that, in the second essay, sadness becomes part of the founding process by which the self is constituted. The ego, then, is a composite of losses, and the history of the self is the sum of one's losses. The ego itself is narcissistic in this later formulation, and the cannibalistic incorporation of the features of the lost object transforms the subject; only such a transformation can permit the id to give up its libidinal hold on the object and permit a strong foundation for the ego.

While Freud's mapping of mourning and melancholia was primarily for therapeutic purposes, his location of the structure of melancholia as partaking in the very structuration of normative subjectivity links his framework to the elegiac character of language. The loss of the loved object, which transforms and causes the plenitudinous subject to compensate the loss by incorporating those lost qualities inside the ego, is not unlike the loss of the originary plenitude of the subject within psychoanalytic discourse being offered the compensation of language. Thus, the mournful incorporation of the loved object by the ego nevertheless bespeaks a loss not unlike the metaphorical structure of language bespeaking a loss. Indeed, in poststructuralist thought, particularly in the work of Paul de Man, the speaking subject signifies a bereft condition: "Writing always includes the moment of dispossession in favour of the arbitrary power play by the signifier and from the point of view of the subject, this can only be experienced as a dismemberment, a bleeding or a castration."[11] For Eric Santner, de Man's focus on the elegiac nature of language is problematic:

> The error of Paul de Man [was] . . . that he sought to *displace* and *disperse* the particular, historical tasks of mourning which for him, as is now known, were substantial and complex, with what might be called structural mourning, that is mourning for those "catastrophes" that are inseparable from being-in-language.[12]

For Santner, de Man's mourning for his collaborationist writings during the war is manifest in the funerary speech present in his later theorizing. Further, the link from de Man to other poststructuralists has resulted in a privileging of "an abstract mode of bereavement."[13] Indeed, this linking of the structure of mourning to poststructuralist approaches to language and subjectivity, with the resultant dilution of the meaning of *actual mourning,* has elicited sharp criticism elsewhere. For instance, Greg Forter is insistent that the loss that language initiates us (within poststructuralist thought) is not the same as actually losing loved ones or being victimized or losing one's life to certain ideologies. Forter criticizes the depathologizing of melancholia, especially when millions of people experience "the bleak and joyless deadness of depression."[14]

Forter's criticism is valid because contemporary mourning theory has a tendency to celebrate melancholia. For Julia Kristeva, melancholia becomes a source of creativity: "For those who are racked by melancholia, writing about it would have meaning only if writing sprang out of that very melancholia."[15] Thus, aesthetics develops through the process of melancholia. In Kristeva's text, the melancholic subject suffers from a problem of differentiation and cannot separate from his/her mother. As a result, there is an inadequate enmeshment within the symbolic for the melancholic subject, exemplified in his/her problematic relationship to language. The lost object of libidinal desire in Freud becomes the lost mother in Kristeva, and in suffering over the loss the subject recalls the mother into his/her psychic life.[16] The only solution left to the melancholic to escape the web of sadness and grief is an oedipal one: that of committing matricide. For Kristeva, the works of Heraclitus, Socrates, Kierkegaard, Heidegger, Aristotle, and Dostoyevsky, as well as the paintings of Dürer, Marsilio Ficino, and Holbein all are marked by melancholy. Her work *Black Sun* is divided into chapters on Holbein, Gerard de Nerval, and Dostoyevsky. With the exception of a chapter on Marguerite Duras, the women beset by melancholia all are case studies: Helen, Marie-Ange, and Isabel. Feminist scholars have pointed out that such a connection between melancholia and language has resulted in gendering melancholy as male. Here, the male artist speaks the authoritative truth about the withdrawal of God and the division in the self. Women's melancholia in her text is reduced to something banal, a mere depression.

While mourning theory has been used extensively in explorations of gendered identity, it has also become significant within theories of minority identity. Since in the Freudian framework, mourning and melancholia are designations for psychic responses to loss, these terms become useful in analyses of a minority's relationship to majoritarian culture and their incorporation within the hegemonic state. Minority identities ranging from homosexual to racial groups have made use of this theoretical framework.[17] This framework resonates particularly in racial discourse, in that just as the melancholic subject cannibalistically consumes the lost Other to make him/herself palatable to the id, the dominant subject within the multiracial society also absorbs the less politically powerful racial Other. This embodied image from the digestive process, wherein food is broken into its basic elements to be digested, expresses the relationship between the racialized minority and the dominant culture. In Freud's framework, the lost Other also functions as a ghost, disembodied and with a partial presence, to be assimilated within the ego. In the fascinating *The Melancholy of Race,* which deals with racial minorities in the United States, particularly Asian Americans and African Americans, Anne Anlin Cheng states:

Racialisation in America may be said to operate through the institutional process of producing a dominant, standard, white national ideal, which is sustained by the exclusion-yet-retention of racialised others. The national topography of centrality and marginality legitimises itself by retroactively positing the racial other as always Other and lost to the heart of the nation. Legal exclusion naturalises the more complicated "loss" of the inassimilable racial other.[18]

Notwithstanding the legitimation for the cannibalistic assimilation of the Other by law, it must be pointed out that this act of swallowing is never smooth or unambivalent. David Lloyd suggests that rhetorically and politically the assimilative process functions to prioritize similarities above that of differentiation "such that its rhetorical structure is that of metaphorisation."[19] While Lloyd focuses attention on the (ghostly) Other consumed by the dominant subject, the Freudian framework concentrates on the melancholic cannibal, who transforms the object of desire by eradicating any separateness and then transmuting this swallowed Other into excrement. This eradication of boundaries transforms the melancholic subject into the image of chaos. In swallowing the Other, the melancholic subject risks pollution and contamination in an attempt to contain the Other within the confines of one's own body. The melancholic subject functions as a crypt that contains the politically weak and inadequately digested racial minority. Indeed, the rage, guilt, resentment, and denigration aimed at the initial object of loss suggests the indigestion that the swallowed Other can cause.

The trope of cannibalism has been very important in Freud's various formulations as in *Totem and Taboo* and *Three Essays on Sexuality* and is used to signal a threat to the progression of the individual's development. While the infant can live in the world of symbiotic oneness with no separation between the self and the Other, the melancholic's desire to consume the Other becomes pathological in that individuated identity is deemed psychically most healthy for the adult. One can infer that in *Beyond the Pleasure Principle* the death drive is itself cannibalistic; it is a desire to return to its original state of unity and a countermovement to the progression to individuated identity. In her reading of cannibalism as a trope, Maggie Kilgour suggests that

the cost of modern autonomy is solitary confinement, isolation in the prison-house of the self, in contrast to which cannibalism becomes an ideal of a Golden Age of a larger corporate social identity. Cannibalism is thus associated with the desire to return to an original state of unity.[20]

Most significant, Freud's melancholic as cannibalistic becomes a new manifestation in the stockpile of images accumulated on the cannibal in the late eighteenth and nineteenth centuries. Notwithstanding William Arens's contention that there is insufficient evidence for customary cannibalism anywhere,[21] it has functioned as a trope that demarcates the opposition between civilization and culture, modernity and primitivism, innocent and depraved, white and black, and victim and predator. For Arens as well as for Peter Hulme, cannibalism is a construction with "no application outside the discourse of European colonialism."[22] Hulme also suggests that the epistemological boundary between Europe and America in 1492 is predicated, among other things, on the representation of the cannibal.

Yet as H. L. Malchow suggests, the association of the cannibal only with the black colonized Other (as Hulme and Arens would have it) is belied by the presence within popular imagination of the stories of the Scottish cannibal, Sawney Deane, and of Sweeney Todd.[23] Within folk traditions, the depravity with which cannibalism is associated is also metonymically linked with women who function both as victims as well as cannibals. This relationship between women and cannibalism appeared in multiple ways in Britain with stories of perverse appetite, of desires to eat body parts of sexual partners, of women serving pieces of children to fathers, of the linking of working-class women to black cannibals. For instance, John Hawkesworth in his observation of cannibals in the Southern Hemisphere states, "Those who have been so accustomed to prepare a human body for a meal . . . with as little feeling cut up a dead man, as our cook-maids divide a dead rabbit for a fricassee."[24] Cannibalism, particularly mortuary cannibalism, was also associated with the hungry working class and the poor, with folktales of cadavers being eaten by the poor. Malchow comments, "The underclass as imaged by the sensational press were alternatively represented either as criminal fiends or pauper victims—the former driven by the blood lust that produced both metaphoric and actual deeds of cannibalism, the latter fearing . . . a workhouse diet with the dissected bodies of diseased fellow-paupers."[25] Thus, the stories of the colonized, depraved blacks in Asia, Africa, and the Pacific were merely extensions, or vice versa, of the discursive constructions of the underclass in Britain: the poor, the women, the prostitutes, and the Jewish. The domestic underclass and the overseas colonized black, both feared and repulsive, thus mirrored and referred to each other in their discursive construction by the bourgeoisie. Furthermore, neither preceded the other but were instead displacements in that they were inversely related to what bourgeois Europeans sought to incorporate in themselves. Cannibalism functions as a catachrestic term that covers over the usurpation of land or labor by focusing on constructions of perverse appetites of the disenfranchised. The brutality and greed of bourgeois white policies are thus spoken as are the unnatural appetite or the consuming mouths of cannibals.

Thus, mourning theory lies within a dense web of metaphors, of ghosts and cannibals, of digestion and assimilation, of bodies and crypts, of displacements and catechrisms, domestic and international anxieties, and the underclass and the colonized. It is inevitable, then, given the implication of primitivism in the cannibalistic swallowing of the Other, that mourning theory, when used within racial discourse, has made critics tend to focus attention on the racialized Other, the ghost of the Other that must be swallowed, assimilated, and digested.[26] But what about the dominant subject who is also the melancholic subject? How does race function for this subject?

Notwithstanding her focus on racial minorities such as Asian Americans and African Americans, Anne Cheng makes a passing comment on white identity in America as "operat[ing] melancholically—as an elaborate identificatory system based on psychical and social consumption-and-denial."[27] It is this notion of whiteness itself as being a melancholic formation that interests me here.

The formation of the racially melancholic subject does not necessarily oscillate around cannibalism and the social and racial demarcation that it provides, but rather at the enforced rupture of individual egos from the ego-ideal that the nation holds out as a promise for its citizens—as, for instance, in the repeated and ongoing violations of founding documents or constitutions. Alexander and Margerete Mitscherlich first posited such a location of the betrayed subject-citizen-as-melancholic in 1975 in *The Inability to Mourn*. The Mitscherlichs offer an interpretation for Germany's collective behavior when Germans switched allegiance from having followed Hitler to an immediate identification with the Allied forces in the aftermath of the Second World War. For the Mitscherlichs, Hitler had functioned as an ego-ideal for the Germans during the war, and instead of plunging into a collective mourning for their lost vision of Germany, they worked on its economic revival.

Germany's inability to mourn, according to the authors, resulted in a derealization of the past and a perception of themselves as the true victims of the war:

> Only certain acceptable fragments of the past were admitted to memory. All events in which we Germans were guiltily implicated are thus denied or reinterpreted, with responsibility for them pushed onto others. . . . The general public reacts ever more strongly against those "spiteful people" who are unwilling to forget and who feel the so carefully warded off past still at work in the present.[28]

These melancholic reactions, according to the authors, inhibited Germans from achieving any responsible, reconstructive, individuated practices. In this work we can see that, notwithstanding German ideals and fantasies for racial purity during the Second World War, which drove Hitler's agenda as predominantly narcissistic, the melancholic reactions that resulted in the aftermath of the fantasy of impotence are still racially underpinned. Since the ego-ideal is the representative of the internal world, and if its dictum for white supremacy had been properly internalized by Germans in the Third Reich, this hierarchization of races would be indelibly etched in their internal world. As Freud insists, "Social feelings rest on identifications with other people, on the basis of having the same ego-ideal."[29] Despite the removal of Hitler from the position of ego-ideal, he and his philosophies would have been melancholically kept alive, incorporated, and assimilated within postwar Germans, hence their inability to mourn (and consequently recover).[30]

Finally, it must be pointed out that the framework of melancholia is particularly compatible with matters of race and racism in that each needs the Other to function. The melancholic identity is at its clearest in the anxiety caused by the continued presence of the Other. The ambivalence that it feels, like that of the racist, is out of a nexus of fear, desire, repudiation, need, and hate. The white settler subject is peculiarly located, in that he or she doesn't fit neatly within the binary opposition of colonizer/colonized. The white settler's relationship to the metropolitan society, that is, at the settler's point of origin, is marked by the discourse of degeneration that is attributed to colonized society. Yet, notwithstanding their metonymic link to the designated degenerate (indigenous) population, white settlers simultaneously embody the authority of an imperialist Europe. Their bodies thus function at the intersection of degeneration and white supremacy. The settler white embodies the working-class, disenfranchised metropolitan white, in that the latter is the defiling and impure materiality of white bourgeois identity. It muddies any notion of whiteness that functions within binarities in order to attest the impossibility of demarcating between the proper and the improper. White settlers attest to the constructed condition of whiteness; their presence attests to the denaturalization of race and the subjective political nature of nineteenth-century racial biology.

THE TREATY OF WAITANGI

The white New Zealand subject is constructed within a context of racialization that dates back to 1840. Two specific moments—1840 and the early 1860s—in the history of New Zealand were central to the melancholic formation of white subjects; the legacy of these key moments underlies even contemporary relations between Pakeha (white settler) and Maori (indigenous) New Zealanders. Both these dates grapple with the issue of ownership of land. Though Captain Cook (or Pakeha Kupe, in Maori myth) visited New Zealand five times on three different voyages in 1769–1770, 1773–1774, and 1777 while mapping the contours of Australia and New Zealand, the latter country did not become a British colony until 1840.

The Treaty of Waitangi, which made New Zealand a part of the British Empire, was signed between the Crown and more than five hundred Maori chiefs in 1840. The signing of the treaty needs to be contextualized not only within the growing influence of the missionary service in the South Pacific, but also within the larger arena of a bourgeois reformist discourse in Britain that had resulted in the abolition of slavery as well as the Poor Law Reform Act in 1834. Indeed, both the Poor Law Reform Act as well as the abolition of slavery were specific measures taken in response to outbreaks of resistance at different locations in the Empire.[31] As Alan Lester points out, "As far as British reformers were concerned, then, the enslaved abroad and the poor at home 'occupied similar moral space,' and had to be treated in similar, if never identical ways."[32] It is within this context of reformist discourse that the British humanitarian Thomas Fowell Buxton established the Select Committee on Aborigines (British Settlements) in 1835 to investigate colonial policy in Southern Africa, Canada, New South Wales, and Tasmania, as well as to advise on New Zealand and the South Sea Islands. Buxton succeeded William Wilberforce as leader of the anti-slavery lobby in the House of Commons; he was also the vice president of the Church Missionary Society and had close connections with the London Missionary Society as well.[33] The purpose of the committee was not only to make sure that a particular vision of justice underpinned profitable economics; their desire was to encourage "peace and mutual good understanding" so that it would "promote the civil and commercial interests of Great Britain."[34]

There is a close link between the rise of capitalism and the origin of the humanitarian sensibility in the cognitive shift in perception of causality that led to a bourgeois acceptance of moral responsibility for others.[35] Thomas Haskell suggests that this approach does not treat capitalism and humanitarianism as "two expressions of a single form of life but does argue that the emergence of a market-oriented form of life gave rise to new habits of causal attribution that set the stage for humanitarianism."[36] While Haskell argues for the imbrication of benevolence with capitalism as part of the new approach to life, Thomas Laqueur locates the epistemological shift elsewhere.[37] He suggests that the late eighteenth and nineteenth centuries formed a new awareness of the suffering body that found its way into humanitarian narratives. For Laqueur, there was a minuteness, an intensification of observation of people who were deemed previously as socially unworthy of scrutiny. This minuteness led to a reality effect in that there was an emphasis on representations of the material body in humanitarian narratives that included medical and forensic discourses. What is relevant to both Haskell's and Laqueur's work is the simultaneity of the rise of capitalism and the awareness of one's dominant position in the globe along with that of the suffering of distant others.

For practical reasons as much as for humanitarian ones, the Select Committee on Aborigines wrote up their report by interviewing witnesses for the various colonial territories. Buxton insisted that the only way out of the impasse of the extraordinary expense of maintaining a huge military presence was "to enter into amicable relations with the people and treat them with justice."[38] The Select Committee also felt that both indigenous corruption as well as unruly (read: working-class) British could be brought to proper governance only through a properly constituted government. Furthermore, the fifteen members who composed the Select Committee leaned toward Christian solutions. There was a general consensus that particularly Christianity and (to a lesser extent) "civilization" were adequate and just compensations for the indigenous loss of land. Reverend William Elles, upon being questioned by the committee, insisted: "An inferior kind of civilisation may precede Christianity and prevail without it to a limited extent; such for instance, as the adoption, by comparatively rude tribes of the dress and modes of living of more cultivated society. . . . All this may occur without any change of character. This kind of civilisation is only superficial."[39] Thus, foreign policy in Britain in the nineteenth century was driven by an amalgam of capitalism, colonialism, and Christianity. Pakeha hunger for land in New Zealand is always also tinged with the humanitarian spirit, evidenced in the signing of the Treaty of Waitangi.

It is against this backdrop that 1840 rolled into New Zealand. In 1839, at the eve of the signing of the treaty, it was estimated that 2,000 Pakeha and anywhere between 70,000 and 200,000 Maori lived in New Zealand.[40] Between 1769 and 1840, European settlers in New Zealand were composed of escaped convicts from Australia, missionaries, and whalers and sealers.[41] Initially, New Zealand was a desirable location as a whaling station in the Pacific due to the demand for whaling oil. (London alone required £300,000 worth of whale oil for its street lamps in the 1780s.)[42] Furthermore, by 1837, Edward Gibbon Wakefield established the New Zealand Association (later the New Zealand Company) to populate it with a "good" stock of immigrants who were to buy land at inflated prices after it had been purchased cheaply from the Maori. The New Zealand Company wanted to set up instant townships with the British government's backing. In this scenario of the gradual whitening of New Zealand, in 1831 the Maori had became concerned that the French were intent on colonizing it as well. (In fact, the French did establish a settlement in Akaroa on the South Island.) Preferring the English to the French, due to the influence of the English missionaries, thirteen North Island chiefs signed a petition in 1831 appealing to the Crown to help them against the French. In this appeal, the chiefs acknowledged the primacy of their relationship with the British and requested that George IV become a "friend and guardian of these islands" and protect them from the misconduct of British subjects as well.[43] This appeal resulted in the appointment of James Busby, the Crown representative resident in New Zealand in 1833. Busby's six-year term as the "kaiwhakarite," or intermediary, between the two races resulted in the incremental presence of not only the British but also its law in mediating problems between Maori and Pakeha. The need for a legal structure to protect the indigenous and settlers alike led to the signing of the Treaty of Waitangi in 1840.

The treaty, written in English and translated into Maori, has five different copies and versions that were circulated throughout New Zealand. Containing three different articles that spelled out the contract between the Crown and Maori chiefs, its purpose was to "establish a settled form of civil government to avert the evil consequences that must result from the absence of the necessary laws and Institutions alike." In Article 1, the chiefs and tribes of New Zealand ceded all the rights and powers of sovereignty to Queen Victoria. In Article 2, the queen in return confirmed and guaranteed to the chiefs and tribes of New Zealand their full possession of lands, estates, forests, and fisheries as long as they wished it. In return, the chiefs and tribes were to sell their lands only to the Crown. In Article 3, the queen transformed all Maori into British subjects.

The problems of translation were many. The use of the term "kawanatanga" in Article 1 of the Maori version of the treaty was perceived by them to mean governorship, whereas in the English version it read as sovereignty, with completely different implications. Further, in the Maori version, assurances of "rangatiratanga," or chieftainship, were made, though in the English version there was only a confirmation of Maori possession. In short, the English version gave Queen Victoria sovereignty and did not mention the role of chieftainship. The Maori version merely conceded governorship to the queen and maintained the right of chieftainship. This slippage in meaning lies at the heart of the continued clashes between Maori and Pakeha and the tribes and the Crown to the present day. Nopera Panakareao, the paramount chief of the Te Rarawa tribe, exclaimed in 1840, "Ko te atakau ote whenua i rori I a te kuini, ko te tinara o te whenua I waiho ki nga Maori" (Only the shadow of the land is to the queen, but the substance remains to us). But the Pakeha, William Colenso noted wryly in his journal in 1840, on the event of the signing of the treaty, said, "Sic Transit Gloria Nova Zealandia" (This is the way the glory of New Zealand passes).[44]

It is easy to comprehend the Maori interpretation of the treaty, particularly the various articles—of the role of the governorship of the Crown and that of the Maori retaining of the chieftainship—if it is contextualized within the demographics of New Zealand. In 1840, as mentioned before, the number of Pakeha was a scant 2,000, and Maori outnumbered them at 70,000. In the first fifty years of the occupation of New Zealand, between 1831 and 1881, the Pakeha population exploded to 500,000, 400,000 of whom emigrated from Britain, whereas the

Maori population had shrunk to 48,000 in 1874 and to 42,000 in 1896. The Pakeha population doubled in the 1860s and doubled again in the 1870s. In the 1870s, the New Zealand government advertised for immigrants in no fewer than 288 Scottish newspapers and had no fewer than seventy-three immigrant agents in Scotland alone. In 1881, Maori were 8.6 percent of the population; by 1901, they were 5.5 percent, and in 1921, they had been reduced to 4.5 percent of the population.[45] The meaning and interpretation of the treaty changed with the proportional shift in population. Maori were first surrounded, then cannibalistically consumed, and finally ingested by Pakeha. Yet as late as 1855, immigrants were informed that their flesh was not considered to be tasty to the cannibalistic Maori.[46]

Between 1860 and 1872, land wars (or the 1860s war) broke out in New Zealand. Triggered by a civil war among Maori over anti–land selling, or whether to sell land or not to the Crown, the land wars soon spread to the Waikato and drew in Pakeha who wished to suppress the king movement, which, among other things, was a pan-tribal movement. The 1860s war was decisive and firmly established Pakeha dominance in New Zealand. By 1864, there were 12,000 imperial troops in New Zealand, and in total by the end of the 1860s there had been 20,000 Pakeha troops involved with the war, of whom 18,000 were members of the British army. The significance of the 1860s war becomes visible when we realize that there were more members of the British army fighting in New Zealand during this decade than were sent to India during the Sepoy Mutiny of 1857. As a result of the war, the Tainui of the Waikato, the most powerful tribe, lost most of their lands. In total, 3.25 million acres were confiscated (by the Crown) from tribes in the Waikato, Bay of Plenty, and Taranaki in Central North Island alone.

If the discovery of the New World was fundamental to the formation of the modern European subject, as Stephen Greenblatt and other new historicists have insisted, and the cannibal became the symbol of the New World and the symbol of the force hostile to the civilizing process, I suggest that the reinscription of the treaty and the 1860s war in the representation of nineteenth-century New Zealand reveals the inversion of the trope of cannibalism. If the cannibal represents consumption and the annihilation of discrete identity, it is the Pakeha that consumes land and, in becoming settler white, annihilates clear demarcations between the colonizer and colonized. If cannibalism is an image of hunger, and a hunger for corporate identity (and a rejection of individuated identity), then the Pakeha settler's hunger for land asserts a corporate identity with the Maori as a New Zealander and with the British as white. If the cannibal represents consumption with no limits, then it is Pakeha's limitless hunger that reveals a consumption with no limits, not even one the treaty can enforce. If the cannibal, in his consumption of the Other, is the embodiment of the melancholic, then the Pakeha in his consumption and incorporation of the (land of the) Other, through treaty and land wars, scrambles demarcations of the civilized and savage, subject and Other, and victim and predator. Who is the melancholic cannibal now?

New Zealand Melancholia

In the previous section I suggested that the reinscription of the dense materiality of New Zealand history allows for a reinterpretation of the trope of cannibalism. Furthermore, while the valorization of the Treaty of Waitangi legitimizes Pakeha presence in New Zealand—"We acquired New Zealand legally"—there is a simultaneous denigration of it in its proximity to the 1860s war, which thus displaces its effects as the illegal outcome of the treaty, the indigenous deprived of their own land. The melancholic, ingesting and developing an ambivalence to the Other, directs an action against the past, remembering while trying to forget, and it is these contradictory operations that the settler embodies. I want next to examine a few settler texts that are engaged with the initial moment of identification as New Zealander in the newly formed nation—indeed, "intelligibility is established through a relation with the other."[47]

One can posit that New Zealand identity is defined around a sense of loss that permeates the psychic apparatus of the nation: the loss of the land (for Maori) or the loss of home (for Pakeha), the sense of unbelonging for both groups, whether politically disenfranchised or geographically marooned, both groups caught in the web of denial of loss and the incorporation of the Other. Pakeha and Maori are melancholic differently and in the same way: the one from dislocation and disenfranchisement, and the other from disenfranchisement and dislocation. For Pakeha, the wages of whiteness might have been good, but the costs of whiteness, of being far away from the resources of home, were quite dear as well. The treaty covers over the traces of grief over loss of home and the cultural and bodily safety that the familiar conveys. Becoming Pakeha was a melancholic formation. As a raced subject, Maori, though warlike, were melancholic (as in sad) as well, with an overwhelming sense of the lack of economic and social privileges, their race and their melancholy, a sign of their rejection by the state that was formed around 1840 and based on the treaty. It had been their land, after all, to begin with.

In the pivotal work *Nation and Narration*, Homi Bhabha suggests that "nations, like narratives, lose their origins in the myths of time and fully realise their horizons in the mind's eye."[48] But what if the myths of time are a mere 167 years ago? How completely do you lose a sense of its origin or forget it? What if its foundational document is a treaty, filed away and preserved for posterity? In his work, Bhabha focuses on the distance between pedagogical definitions of the nation and the practice of it by its citizens: the ambivalence and differences of class, taste, politics, sexuality, and justice. It is this notion of ambivalence that provides us a map for reading New Zealand Pakeha identity. The ambivalence that Bhabha notes is a strong feature in Bill Ashcroft et al.'s definition of settlers:

> Settlers may seek to appropriate icons of the "native" to their own self-representation, and this can, itself, be a form of oppression where such icons have sacred or social significance alienated by their new usages. On the positive side, as settlers themselves become indigenes in the literal sense, that is, born within the new space, they begin to forge a distinctive and unique culture that is neither that of the metropolitan culture from which they stem nor that of the "native" cultures they have displaced in their early colonising phase.[49]

I examine the ambivalences, silences, and loss to see how the very landscape of New Zealand is seeped with white melancholia. The theme of loss plays a major role in the recording of history, especially in Sarah Selwyn's *Reminiscences*. Compiled from her journals maintained during her years in New Zealand, she writes this work as one long letter addressed to her sons: "I do not very willingly comply with your request that I should leave some record of my life." Though Sarah Selwyn lived to be ninety-eight years old, in this work she concentrates in particular on her years in New Zealand. It is a memoir that evokes, and then silences, traumatic moments. Selwyn was born in a colonial family; her grandfather was a West Indian merchant and landowner in Dominica. Her father became a judge after having been educated at Harrow and Oxford, followed by a legal career. She was married to Bishop George

Selwyn at thirty, and there is a fundamental difference in the way she handles her memories of her childhood in Britain and those of her adulthood in New Zealand. In Britain, Sarah Selwyn lived within the enactment of history and a historiography that perceived Europe as the land that initiated meaningful temporality. For instance, her father and uncle's subjectivity are shaped by the French Revolution and are marked by events such as the murder of Louis XVI and Marie Antoinette and the Reign of Terror in France; the history of Europe in Selwyn's text is intertwined with familial history such as the Battle of Trafalgar and Lord Nelson's funeral. Her memories of her early years, the houses they lived in, her relationship with her parents are all triggered by English political history. Her family memories include the crowning of George IV and eventually Victoria. Metonymically and geographically linked to this history, her life embodies history.

If historiography is predicated on the separation of the past from the present and a clean break between the two, and if it takes the position of the subject of action whose objective is to make history as Michel de Certeau suggests,[50] then in Sarah Selwyn's colonial text Britain makes history. It is the subject of history. It is the subject of action and marks the founding moment of colonial historiography. This positioning of Britain is maintained throughout the text; in her subsequent trips home from New Zealand, major political events in British imperial history keep occurring: the Crimean War, the Sepoy Mutiny, and the Morant Bay Rebellion. Emphasized as well are relationships to historical figures: dining with Queen Victoria, meeting the royal children, and having Prime Minister Gladstone as her son's godfather.[51] In contrast, temporality functions differently in New Zealand. There is a geological slowness to the passage of time that is marked by the availability of food, the primitive times when "a large kete of anything, potatoes, kumara, peaches, cape gooseberries, quinces all alike were 1 shilling each."[52] This is followed by the pork period; in a week they eat hot pork for three days and cold pork for four days. (John King, a missionary, had sent fifty-six pigs in three ships between 1804 and 1805 to the Te Pahi tribe in the North Island. Recognizing the pig's value for trade purposes, the Te Pahi and soon the North Island Maori had bred a surplus of them by 1808; by 1815 pigs were widely available in the South Island as well.) In Selwyn's text, the pork period is followed by the beef period.[53] She mournfully remarks, "We could turn the beef to more account than the pork."[54]

If Europe represents significant temporality in her text, then New Zealand is represented as the land that time and history have forgotten, caught in a temporal, seasonal cycle and marked only by the availability of certain forms of food. Indeed, history in New Zealand is so new that it is not yet meaningful. Attempts to initiate history consist of Hone Heke's rebellious acts, when he cut down the flagstaff twice in Paihia in a Maori protest of the violations of the Treaty of Waitangi. Selwyn barely notes this moment in her text as if it is insignificant or meaningless. Yet it is necessary to repress the agency of Maori in the text to valorize the treaty, and hence an untroubled white identity in New Zealand. It is necessary to place precontact Maori history and Maori subjectivity under erasure to naturalize Pakeha. New Zealand history in Selwyn's text reveals that it is not particularly meaningful for a woman who had dined with Queen Victoria. The only historical event that intertwines white temporality with Pacific time is when she visits Norfolk Island, where the crew and family of Captain Bligh of the HMS *Bounty* were evacuated from Pitcairn Island in 1856 on the order of the governor of New South Wales. She pronounces it "a beautiful island with its most dreary and hopeless population."[55] Not only is New Zealand cut off from meaningful history, but also Norfolk Island is even more provincial than New Zealand. She passes her stay there by teaching children hymns and teaching in the school. Conversations to be had are minimal. At one juncture, out of desperation, Selwyn asks of a Pitcairn Islander: "Are not cows better than cocoanuts?" To this the Pitcairnite replies, "Cocoanuts are the best of cows."[56] In a subsequent visit to Norfolk Island in 1857, a loaf of her bread was stolen and becomes the topic of a Thursday morning sermon.[57]

De Certeau suggests that psychoanalysis and history partake of the same structure: time, memory, and return of the repressed. The past haunts the present even though the latter attempts to expel the past:

> The dead haunt the living. The past: it "re-bites" (it is a secret and repeated biting). History is "cannibalistic" and memory becomes the closed arena of conflict between two contradictory operations: forgetting, which is not something passive, a loss, but an action directed against the past; and the mnemic trace, the return of what was forgotten, in other words, an action by a past that is now forced to disguise itself. . . . What is eliminated . . . reinfiltrates the place of its origin. . . . It resurfaces, it troubles, it turns the present's feeling of being "at home" into an illusion. (*Heterologies,* trans. Brian Massumi [Minneapolis: University of Minnesota Press, 1986], 3–4)

I want to work with this notion of the return of the repressed and its relationship to history and historiography to see how the loss of England and its history is processed in this text. If England is the site of history-making in its connection of knowledge with power, how would the memories of it and its absence in New Zealand and Norfolk Island have affected Selwyn? Gayatri Spivak's classic essay on "The Rani of Sirmur" describes the moment of colonizing or power's incursion into the colonized world as "the worlding of the world on uninscribed earth that obliges the native to cathect the space of the Other on his home ground."[58] While the presence of Sarah Selwyn and her husband is a large part of this worlding, what are its effects on memories and embodiment? How does the body react to powerful memories of a powerful home and what it deems as a meaningful past when it is dislocated from it and inserted into a new world with sparse population and hardly any history? In Enid Evan's introduction to Selwyn's work, she notes that Sarah "had poor health—severe headaches which prostrated her, and which appear to have been as she admits in a letter, nervous in origin."[59] Further, in her trips back to England, her friends remark on her aged appearance.[60] How does one deal with living on an island that entered modernity only two years before her landing there? If the past haunts the present, how would the present appear in the material absence of and geographical and physical displacement from the past?

While within the discourse of imperialism, the very presence of the British in foreign spaces suggests not so much a loss of Britain for them but a somatic incorporation of it, such that in the physical constitution of the British they represent Queen Victoria more than they are individuated subject. In Freud's "Ego and the Id," the subject, whose bits of ego mime the lost object, performs a kind of sublimation. This switch from the object libido to the narcissistic libido is also key to the development of the superego. Thus, Britain within imperialistic discourse functions as the superego, an ideal propagated through the influence of authority, religious teaching, schooling, and reading. The superego is, indeed, imperialist in nature. Reading Sarah Selwyn's nervous headaches from within Freud's framework, I suggest that loss becomes an exclusion. The hustle and bustle of British life is a contrast to hers in the antipodes. With her husband away, establishing the Anglican Church, one of her few outlets is figuring out different ways of serving pork and beef. Her infant daughter dies while George is away, and her sons are sent to England for their schooling. Lady Martin at one juncture refers to Sarah as a "brave wife"[61] when George leaves her yet again to tour New Caledonia and the Loyalty Islands. However, even in Lady Martin's text, there is an elision of Sarah's life because George and his voyages are deemed more interesting to its readers.

While white settler men, for the most part, embodied imperialism and Britain as superego, the women, particularly missionary wives, signified differently. The perception of Pakeha women's disaffiliation from the colonial and political process is particularly underscored, as in the letter that William Richmond (minister in charge of native affairs in 1859 in Auckland) wrote to his wife: "It was indeed a most exceedingly foolish thing to cry about the Native Policy. What, my pussy, have you got to do with the Native Policy? Never mind it. Don't cry about it till I do."[62] I suggest instead that Pakeha women's lives literalize white settler melancholia. While white male settler bodies embody colonialism, be it through settlement or through missionary services, Pakeha women's bodies, like some sort of Wildean portrait of Dorian Gray, embody the melancholia, filled with a sense of loss and a sense of their own obscurity. If in Freud's framework the ego mimed the lost object in order to say, "Look, you can love me too—I am so like the object," for these women, the incorporation of the lost object made them completely Other, obscure in New Zealand. Frances Porter notes of Marianne Williams, one of the missionary wives, who, when overcome with fatigue, would throw herself on her bed whenever possible "to refresh [herself] with a good cry." Sarah Selwyn was not the only one filled with grief. So was Elizabeth Harris, mother of twelve, who on one occasion expected her husband, James Hamlin of Wairoa Mission Station, to help when her Maori domestic help deserted her. James Hamlin's cross reply, "A strange way of preparing sermons. Washing plates etc I have never before done."[63] Missionary wives—Jane Williams, Anne Wilson, Ellen Spencer, Marianne Williams—were melancholic, all having to deal with routine flood and fire. While women were mostly filled with melancholy as an affect due to their isolated condition, the structure of melancholia did not necessarily exclude men from it. The remoteness of New Zealand must have been underscored to them as well; even in the 1830s most British had never even heard of it. Vaguely associated with Australia (yet Australia has always been the better-known colony) and convicts, New Zealand was perceived to be populated with cannibals. Even as late as 1855, cannibal jokes were routinely made to immigrants to New Zealand. Pakeha must have been filled with their sense of antipodean obscurity. Francis Hall, one of Samuel Marsden's missionaries, wrote of the loneliness of New Zealand as well:

> None but married men should go to New Zealand. Single men will continually be exposed to trial; and if through the grace of God, they are able to withstand the temptations of the native women, they will be constantly assailed with cruel mockings and abominable speeches.[64]

John Butler wrote of the Maori "noise, singing, talking, laughing, ochre, lice, and other filth."[65] The missionaries were Europeans first, then Christians.

The missionaries were perceived as being fundamental to the Pakehaization of New Zealand in that they were culturally and economically useful. The missionaries often ran schools, brought books, and supplemented the literacy of Maori. In the church rush that took place in the 1840s, eleven Catholic chapels in the Tauranga/Whakatane region and fourteen in the Rotorua region were established in the middle of the North Island. There were so few converts, though, that each chapel had an average of thirteen people attending it regularly. Though the population of Maori could be estimated at about 70,000 in 1840, all the various missionaries—the Anglicans, Methodists, and Catholics—claimed to have saved 103,700 Maori between them. Te Heuheu Iwikau of Ngati Tuwaharetoa explains this miraculous phenomenon: "When you in Taupo, I am churchman, when the Wesleyan missionary is here, I belong to his church, when the RC priest calls, I am papist, and when no European is here, I am a heathen."[66] The missionary services in New Zealand focused on alterity, silencing and consuming the Other to come into intelligibility. In its cannibalistic urge of ingesting the Other, while simultaneously requiring their very presence to constitute itself, the Pakeha in the missionary services produce a discourse of conquest. Pakeha missionary subjectivity can be seen as also being inscribed in its aggressive relation to an Other.

But are the senses of sadness and loss the only ways in which melancholia manifests itself? Within dominant Pakeha identity, there is an elaborate identificatory system that is based on psychical and social consumption. This system, operated by a melancholic retention of the Other, was used by all Pakeha in New Zealand in that they all needed Maori to memorialize them; like melancholia, racism needs its Other. The foundation of a settler nation embodies a complex relation to other raced bodies. In this complex framework of race relations first mapped by the Treaty of Waitangi in 1840, and then later in the 1860s land war, Maori are buried and then resuscitated to function as serviceable ghosts, to give meaning and coherence to Pakeha identity. I will examine how Maori are treated, being the group directly affected by the formation of a melancholic Pakeha identity. I particularly look at Lady Martin's book because it spans the secular as well as the missionary responses to the role of the Maori in the Pakeha-ization of early New Zealand.

Lady Martin's text is fascinating for its ambivalence, not only toward Maori but also the Pakeha presence in New Zealand. Initially describing the sense of peace and justice and the civilizing presence of British law, Mary Martin becomes increasingly confused, especially in her description of the 1860s land war. In a letter to Mrs. Anne Palmer dated May 21, 1860, she writes:

> You will be sorry to hear of our war at Taranaki. It has come like a black cloud over all the cheering hopes of the last few months. . . . If there were a cause for the war, if it were, as the papers now try to say, a rebellion against the Queen's authority, we would not complain. But that is merely an afterthought. . . . The Taranaki settlers wanted [Wiremu] King's land and had coveted it for years.[67]

The disenchantment about Pakeha presence begins as early as 1847 when Lady Martin, though not medically trained, begins treating Maori patients at the newly built hospital. She uses safe drugs to treat common complains—rosemary tea with treacle for coughs, the tops of elder shoots and Spanish broom for dropsy, and poultices of seaweed and mustard plasters.[68] The text becomes replete with touching stories of Maori postponing, defying death, waiting to die, until they are baptized. But soon Maori patients start dying in large numbers and she narrates episode after episode of Maori death. Soon, the text takes a turn; instead of the British saving Maori lives and souls, they start appearing as some sort of Typhoid Mary, their very presence annihilating Maori. In the chapter on the New Zealand land wars, she records the death of one of her favorite Maori, "a native teacher" called David Te Mania. Lady Martin describes at great length the close relationship that they share with David and his wife, Rebekah. During the land wars David dies, having contracted tuberculosis. Rebekah too flees to the King country for refuge. Lady Martin describes the end of her relationship with Rebekah with a note of ambivalence:

Once only she wrote to me, and they were the words about our English people, though full of expressions of personal regard. A house had been set on fire after a skirmish, and one or two Maori women and children were, as it was believed, burnt. Of course the men who did this supposed the house to be a lurking-place for the enemy. She asked me whether it was part of our Christian religion to burn women and children alive. Poor soul, she died before the war was over.[69]

David Te Mania's text is followed by descriptions of further Maori deaths. There is Roto Waitoa, the first native clergyman, some Melanesian schoolboys' deaths, and even references to Pacific narratives about death. For instance, Lady Martin narrates the story of a Loyalty Island legend in which a young man named Larona has magical powers and replenishes fish and sugarcane while distributing them to his tribe. Finally, Larona is transmuted into a big yam before he is killed by foreigners for profit. Lady Martin does not comment on the intersection of Christian and capitalistic imagery, or the significance of Larona's death within the context of Pakeha–Pacific Islander relationship. The final chapter records some more deaths. Here Mary Martin muses over the query if the Church Missionary Society has not been a failure in New Zealand. She concludes by reiterating the beneficial lessons that Christianity has taught Maori: to cease in the practice of cannibalism and infanticide. Yet there is a grudging admission that Christianity has not spread as widely and rapidly as it was hoped for.

I conclude by briefly discussing the dynamics of Mary Martin's text, which seems to obsess over Maori death to a large extent, and its relationship to the larger framework that is the topic of my chapter. How does the death of the Other affect the melancholic subject? Could the image of dying Maori be connected only to the diseases that Pakeha have brought with them? Indeed, such a thesis has been put forward by writers such as Alfred Crosby, in whose analysis the catastrophic deaths of the indigenous populations of Native Americans are perceived as having been caused by the pathogens inadvertently brought by the settler population. I want, however, not to focus on the actual deaths of the Maori, but to see how death functions as a trope that signals Pakeha melancholia in Mary Martin's text. In her text there is a romanticism as well as a naturalization of the vanishing Maori, which, while serving to legitimize the future white presence in New Zealand, also seems to question it. If the church and the missionaries in her text function to save Maori, then they have not been particularly successful. The principle of egalitarianism that underpins the practice of Christian religion is doomed to fail within the imperialist ambitions of Britain. To this extent, the philosophy of egalitarianism is violated. The ambivalence in Martin's text oscillates around the question: how does the church go on while remembering the violations and transgressions of being an instrument of Pakeha in New Zealand? How does it reconcile its continual location of Maori as Other with its own ideological and religious principles? How does it come to terms with its own cannibalistic urges of swallowing the Other? Thus, her text accounts for the guilt while denying any guilt. It is ashamed and dogged in its sense of superiority, all at the same time. Christianized Maori thus allegorize white melancholy, the melancholy by which a whiteness is formed by a refusal to grieve for the inequality among Christians. Indeed, the deaths of Maori in Mary Martin's text can be perceived as a displacement of white guilt so it can deny any guilt.

I will leave the analysis at that. I have attempted to make some preliminary statements about the white settler and map two different aspects of their melancholic formation: their whiteness formed through the sense of their loss of Britain and whiteness in their melancholic introjection of Maori that it can neither fully relinquish nor accommodate but whose ghostly presence they needed to guarantee their own racial formation. I have suggested that mournful Pakeha embodiment that depends on the consumption of the Other—not unlike the process of colonialism and the structure of the missionary services—in fact functions as a memorial for the Other. Pakeha whiteness is at the intersection of the indigenous Maori and imperial white bodies. It is the porous nineteenth-century Pakeha women's bodies that bear the markers of melancholia—the sense of isolation, the unremitting labor, the profound loneliness (this theme, I would suggest, from the 1940s manifests itself as that of Man Alone in New Zealand fiction), the constant fear for their lives (at the hands of the "vengeful" natives), the transmutations of these emotions into the wonderment at the breathtaking landscape. The beautiful landscape puts a lid on the seething subterranean emotions. If modernity (and postmodernity) insists on individuated identity, Pakeha identity lays bare the fiction of such a requirement. The Other is essential; individuated identity is in an aggressive relation to the Other. In short, individuated subjectivity can only ever be an intersubjectivity. Whiteness can only ever be an aggressive construction. Racial identification can only ever be a melancholic formation.

I have not attempted to analyze the melancholic object's relation—Maori's relation—to Pakeha, for that would have been a completely different chapter.

CHAPTER 6

Dermographia:
How the Irish Became White in India

In the magnificent *Discipline and Punish,* Michel Foucault enters into a seamless discourse with E. P. Thompson on the shifting embodiment of Europeans under the aegis of capitalism.[1] In this text, Foucault describes the docility encoded within white European bodies in the late eighteenth century: the soldier is taught to stand and hold his head in particular ways; his movements, gestures, attitudes controlled; he is made to function with economy and efficiency; taught to pick up and handle his rifle so that it mirrors his body and functions as its analogy. The description is that of a hall of mirrors in that this discipline of the soldier is further reiterated and reflected within civilian life. In the factory, the workers are distributed on the floor for maximum efficiency; the worker's positioning in the factory floor is a reflection of the carefully considered schema that allows for optimum positioning of machines, the surveying gaze of the supervisor, and the skills of the coworkers.[2] By this moment in history—the late eighteenth century—the civilian body, bludgeoned into docility by capitalism, was on its way to becoming an economically efficient entity. Meanwhile, E. P. Thompson, in his pivotal "Time, Work-Discipline, and Industrial Capitalism," discusses the temporal shift under capitalism and the consequent shift in the production of the subject. Thompson begins the essay by citing the non-West, where the indigenous people of Nuer, Madagascar, Chile, and Algeria neither have control over time nor any desire to save it. In contrast, industrial capitalism in the West, with its time sheets, timekeepers, informers, and fines, produced workers who knew that time was money. As a result, these workers and their committees learned to fight for overtime as well as time-and-a-half salary. Thus, in the late eighteenth century, new labor habits and new labor disciplines were learned. Thompson points out that by the mid-nineteenth century, the English industrial worker not only had a capacity for hard work but had also simultaneously lost his capacity "to relax in the old uninhibited ways."[3] Thompson ends the essay by urging the non-West (and the nonindustrialized) to shift their awareness of time, to gain time-discipline, to bow to its inevitability. Here the othering of the sensibility that lacks time-discipline becomes a simultaneous endorsing of the disciplined capitalistic body with its perception of control and precision over temporality.

Foucault's and Thompson's texts beg to be juxtaposed with the now classic text, "A Manifesto for Cyborgs," in which Donna Haraway suggests that the cyborg or the cybernetic organism is "an offspring of militarism and patriarchal capitalism, a hybrid of machine and organism, a creature of social reality as well as . . . fiction."[4] For Haraway, the cyborg is beyond gender, beyond sexuality, and follows a different teleology; it does not subscribe to an origin myth and signifies boundary transgression between human and animal, between organism and machine, between the physical and nonphysical. The model of worker evoked by Foucault and Thompson is cyborgian, then, homogenized and functioning within the nexus of difference. If the embodiment of the worker in the industrialized West is homogenized through the use of machinery, becoming a cyborg because of a precision with temporality, then what happens to the raced body in Nuer, Madagascar, Chile, and Algeria? Does the raced body in nonindustrialized spaces eventually homogenize and assimilate with Western counterparts? Does it become a cyborg eventually as well? Is this the difference between the Western and non-Western individual? Additionally, how does it fit in within the framework of temporality and time-discipline that is produced by industrialized capitalism? Alternatively, if notions of skin and skin color bring with them cultural assumptions of raced or life histories, how does industrial capitalism in modernity (and now within the decline of the nation-state)—with its growing emphasis on the internationalization of the economy, global mass culture, and increasingly rapid labor migrations among both elite and subaltern classes—erase or reinvent raced specificities? Is there a connection between skin, history, and capitalism, and if so, what is it? One can begin by suggesting that the relationship between capitalism and racialized bodies is established in the convergence of their genealogical origins. The discourses on both follow a similar teleology, predicated on an evolutionary model, a historicism that conceives of history as narrating the evolution and development of modern subjects and cultures. Within the nexus of the Enlightenment and democratic discourse, the temporality evoked by historicism follows a trajectory of the emergence of civil society and the evolution of the cyborg subject.

In this final chapter I work on the surface, on the skin, the site that manifests in modernity one's enmeshment within power relations, one's entire history. Skin functions as a boundary; it is a bodily envelope that marks the material limits of the human body; it coheres bodies and identities and is present at the interface, mediating between the internal and external worlds. It charts a history, the meaning of the individual, his/her social, national positioning made clear in the transition made by the skin from pre-Enlightenment discourse, wherein bodily marks were arbitrary, allegorical, but with no biological meanings imputed to them, to those within Enlightenment discourses when they became symbolic, natural signs. I focus on skin, which within modernity is synecdochic of race, for several reasons. First, while within the context of diaspora studies the black diasporic subject (who has been displaced from her nation or land through slavery or indenture, immigration, or by seeking asylum) has been emphasized, the white diasporic subject has largely been ignored. Such an occlusion of white European subjects in diaspora has resulted in their right to movement and a naturalization of their body, with a simultaneous marking and a discursive incarceration of and setting limits to the black subject's right to exist only in specific places. Indeed, much of contemporary Western discourse of the post/modern nation treats black refugees, and immigrants in particular, as a contamination, as a pathology, even as a pathogen that should have remained in its place of origin. Yet in the long nineteenth century (1820–1914), one-fifth of the population of Europe moved to the colonies in non-European spaces. Whiteness, then, comes into meaning within the context of this movement and becomes a shape-shifter, especially in the colonies. A close examination of the meanings of skin will allow for an unpacking of whiteness, its disparate significations, and make visible some final statements on the relationship between race and class.

Second, it is within the context of the visual index (of race, class, or gender) that markers of difference and identity become most pronounced. Difference written on the skin becomes *visible* at a glance. Indeed, notions of subject formation, be they within the context of psychoanalytic theory, such as those by Freud (castration anxiety) or Lacan (mirror stage), Enlightenment discourses such as those by Linnaeus (types and hierarchy of humans) or John Beddoe ("degrees of negrescence"), all rely on and valorize the appeal to visual immediacy. The insistence of physical difference in these frameworks functions as a metaphor for the difference that is *internal* to the constitution of the subject's identity itself. Within the context of race, skin becomes the shorthand for the meaning of racial and national characteristics.

Yet, finally, perceptions of skin and their meanings are very problematic; skin's visual immediacy and the truth that it purports cannot be relied upon, as theories of racial passing and racial hybridity have made clear. Seeing is not necessarily always believing. Furthermore, there is also the fluidity of nomenclatures: groups categorized as belonging to a race or color at certain historical or political moments need not retain these categorizations at other moments. Two instances that exemplify the shifting goalposts of nomenclatures are Eastern European Jews being perceived as black at critical moments in Nazi history or southern Italian migrants to Australia being deemed black in the postwar period before they eventually became white in the 1960s.

I concentrate on racial meaning assigned to skin. I particularly want to read the significations of Irish embodiment and skin. The Irish are so problematic: their practice of Catholicism, the history of their colonization, their political sympathies all scandalize and problematize British whiteness, revealing the limits of its assimilative processes. Are they black or are they white? The visual index of difference is so minimally written on their skin that their presence causes a severe disturbance to the notion that race and the authority of whiteness become perceptible at a glance. The insertion of the Irish into whiteness in colonial discourse makes them function like Freud's fetish, a substitution, a trompe l'oeil for the constructed authority of whiteness, its fictional nature constantly soothing while simultaneously evoking the anxieties of white identity. The changing hues of the Irish—from the Cromwellian era of the seventeenth century, when thousands of the Irish were sent to the Caribbean as indentured servants to work alongside slaves of African descent,[5] to those who went to the United States after the famine and gradually whitened through their integration into the legal and political landscape of the dominant American culture[6]—suggest that their skin and embodiment made them ambiguous figures. Sometimes white, at others black, their racial categorization is tightly and completely imbricated within colonialism, be it in their colonized status or in their roles as settler whites in other colonies. I will examine a literary text set in India around the Mutiny of 1857, Rudyard Kipling's *Kim,* whose protagonist is of Irish parentage and thus marked by all the ambivalences of being Irish white. I examine Irish presence in colonial India to see how ambivalent whiteness is layered onto the skin in a black country. I read this text to see how difference is constituted, since whiteness here can be seen as an aggregate of perceived attributes that is metonymically superimposed onto white skin. This text records the failure of Irish whiteness, the gaps in white logic.

I need to ask: How does the skin come to be written and narrated? Since skin is a boundary object, it is not only assumed to be the sign of the subject's interiority, it is also to reflect the truth of the Other. Skin has a testimonial function, in that it bears witness to injustice, violence, and trauma.

Skin/Matters

What is the connection between skin and history? One can say that the history of the individual is marked most visibly on the skin. Sleepless nights, cigarettes, harsh weather, and other excesses that the body is subjected to get written on skin. Veins become prominent, dark red and purple on the nose of the subject who has drunk too much alcohol for too long. With the passing of years, the skin loses elasticity, wrinkles, lines, peels, coarsens, and fades. The pores enlarge, thus becoming a signifier for the loss of innocence. It is the most likely surface to betray the age of the individual it surrounds, as well as being the first surface where sensory perception develops: the fetus develops a skinlike membrane that precedes all other sensory systems.[7] This ur-skin of the fetus is transparent and diffuse and does not participate in the perception-consciousness system until after the baby's birth. Once the baby is born, its developing consciousness teaches it to zone the surface of its own body as separate from the others. Indeed, the envelope of the skin aids and abets in the making true of the Lacanian notion of *méconnaisance.* Notwithstanding its flailing arms and legs and its gawky, awkward motor responses, the child looks in the mirror and its enveloping skin produces the fiction of its sense of coherence and completion. If the role of the skin is to function as an envelope, a body bag of sorts, then the maternal body functioning as the fetus's skin, its body bag, soon gets relegated to the realm of the abject, as Julia Kristeva would have it. In *Powers of Horror,* abjection occurs when the boundary between subject and object is violated, breached.[8] Skin is always in the process of becoming abject since we shed it constantly. If the formation of the abject is predicated on the boundary breach between subject and object, then molting, powdery skin suggests that the subject is always the object: abject.

But skin has another history as well, fundamental to the history of the senses. The sense of touch recorded on the surface of the skin provides a direct, though considered sometimes as an unreflected, comprehension of the world, and as such is associated with a dense materiality in the sense that it is most closely associated with empiricism.[9] While the rest of the senses are related to specific sensory organs, such as the nose for smell and eyes for sight, the skin's surface is spread over the entire body and registers sensation over the entire body—heat, cold, pressure, vibration. It also has a socially constructed meaning, in that a person's character is written on it: the coarseness of the skin is a sign of the individual's coarse personality, its smoothness and clearness those of its innocence. Within Western epistemology, the sense of touch is deemed the lowest within the hierarchy of the senses, while that of sight the highest; yet both function together to produce the sense of the erotic.[10] In *The Three Essays on the Theory of Sexuality,* sexuality associated with the sense of touch (touching the other, touching oneself) is repressed and results in its displacement onto the act of seeing. In Freud's explanation of the sexual, libidinal maturation of the child, there is a narrative movement, a maturational development, from the masturbatory touch and polymorphous perversity to eventual sublimation caused through "shame, disgust, morality."[11] The narrative of development moves from skin to sight, from masturbation to "a lively interest in the genitals of their playmates."[12] Castration complex does not merely put an end to polymorphous perversity, but also sublimates these energies. Thus, the rule of the father shapes the development of the sense of aesthetics in the individual in that it demands the subordination of the sense of the touch to that of sight principally and is then transmuted to the role of the superego. For Immanuel Kant, sight exemplified the triumph of the rational as opposed to the sense of touch, which, because of its association with empiricism and an unreflected knowledge of the world, becomes the site of the irrational.[13] In the Middle Ages, the sense of touch is associated with the libido; in the Renaissance too the touch is associated with sexuality. By the eighteenth century, in John Locke's work, it became the most basic of senses, an ur-sense, upon which the rest are built.[14] For Johann Gottfried von Herder, the touch, the feel of the object, produces a desire to name it.[15] Thus, the touch is linked to the origin of languages.

There is yet another history that is imbricated within that of the skin, one that is fully pertinent to this work: that of its racialization. One can state that modern, scientific racism is a product of the Enlightenment.[16] Several factors contribute to the locating of modern racism to this time period. First, while the sixteenth and seventeenth centuries brought about new ways of thinking, it was the development of the biological and human sciences that led to racial classifications. As Nancy Leys Stepan suggests, "A science of human beings could develop only when the entire globe had been explored, some knowledge of the entire range of human types gathered, and this knowledge evaluated for its accuracy."[17] While morphological markings such as skin color became the primary signifier of racial difference, a logic of a system of marks worn on the body to denote identity prevailed before the Enlightenment as well. For instance, the use of the yarmulke by Jewish men, the tonsure of Catholic priests, a coat of arms on movable objects to indicate ownership by the nobility—all are examples of this system of movable marks. The immovable mark such as a tattoo or a branding indicated the permanence of the hierarchical relationship and the utter subjection that the wearer of the mark underwent.[18] In *The Problem of Slavery in Western Culture,* David Brion Davis suggests that slavery was not new to the eighteenth century, but in the ancient and medieval world the slaves were distinguished by impermanent marks like a shaven head, which allowed them to merge into the local population upon receiving their freedom.[19]

The notion of the movable sign also suggests that the marking of bodies before the Enlightenment veered more toward religious, moral, and political customs and not necessarily within physical racial criteria. Within the history of the biological sciences, racial markings on the skin were often imbricated within the debate between polygenism and monogenism in the eighteenth and nineteenth centuries. While monogenism insisted on a common humanity and was a marker of universalism, egalitarianism, and humanism, polygenism propagated the multiple origins of humans in their multiple geographical spaces. A subscription to polygenism indicated that "human races were separated from each other by such profound mental, moral and physical differences as to constitute separate biological species of mankind."[20] The eighteenth and nineteenth centuries also saw the shift from a sacred history of monogenism (that justified the prejudice toward dark-skinned Africans by citing the biblical story of the curse of Ham and that toward anti-Semitism by attributing the death of Christ to the Jews) to a secular history that emphasized a polygenism.

Un/Natural

This movement from monogenism to polygenism is anticipated in the development of the natural sciences in the Enlightenment, in its classifications, distinctions, and categorizations of species. The development of the natural/biological sciences did not mean that there was a discarding of the Christian faith, but rather showed the influence of central issues as emerging from philosophy, aesthetics, politics, *and* the Christian faith. Classifying humans, like fauna and flora, reiterated that the underlying hierarchies were established by God. In *The System of Nature,* Carl von Linné, or Linnaeus, attributed as being among the first to categorize nature (and thus to bring order to the chaos of nature), suggests that the urge to classify by humans who are "the last and best of created works, formed after the image of his Maker, endowed with a portion of intellectual divinity, the governor and subjugator of all other beings, is, by his wisdom alone, able to form just conclusions from such things as present themselves to his senses, which can only consist of bodies merely natural."[21] Thus, Linnaeus's categorization of Homo sapiens not only sets up strict racial distinctions, but also posits these distinctions as belonging to the realm of the natural. Linnaeus distinguishes between five types of Homo sapiens "varying by education and situation":

Four-footed, mute, hairy. *Wild man*

Copper-coloured, choleric, erect. *American*

Hair black, straight, thick; *nostrils* wide, *face* harsh; *beard* scanty; obstinate, content, free. Paints himself with fine red lines. *Regulated* by customs.

Fair, sanguine, brawny. *European*

Hair yellow, brown, flowing; *eyes* blue; gentle, acute, inventive. *Covered* with close vestments. *Governed* by laws.

Sooty, melancholy, rigid. *Asiatic*

Hair black; *eyes* dark; *fevere,* haughty, covetous. *Covered* with loose garments. *Governed* by opinions.

Black, phlegmatic, relaxed. *African*

Hair black, frizzled; *skin* silky; *nose* flat; *lips* tumid; crafty, indolent, negligent. *Anoints* himself with grease. *Governed* by caprice.[22]

Thus, in such a positing of the metaphysics of order, the classification of nature was not perceived as an invention that displays a European bias, but rather an *essence* that Linnaeus *discovers.* This distinction between discovery and invention is important, for it is precisely through this difference that racial marks that come into visibility within the context of a hierarchy of development can be posited as natural. Linnaeus's taxonomy remakes attributes into attributions, thus granting privileges, capacities, and powers to the fair, brawny, and sanguine European or a denial of political agency to the silken-skinned but crafty, indolent, and negligent black. This categorization permits the switch of racial attributes from the social to the natural, and in so doing contributes also to the traveling of whiteness and white power under the logic of the Enlightenment. The argument for racial hierarchy builds up thus: the categories and hierarchies are determined by God; therefore, they wait to be *discovered* and articulated by biologists. Being dislocated from the notion of a construction embedded within biases, these hierarchies are put forward as natural and unchanging. Thus, the notion of the natural and nature themselves are ripped away from the sedimentation of history. Within this system of classification, the notion of natural is a misnaming, a perversion of a trope or metaphor, a catachresis.

The trope of nature and the natural are reinforced through the image of a tree in the biological sciences. As John Dupré explains:

> The part of biology that is concerned with the classifications of organisms is taxonomy. . . . [A] complete taxonomic theory could be displayed as a tree, the smallest branches of which would represent species. Rules would be required for assigning individual organisms to species, and an individual assigned to a particular species would also belong to all higher taxa in a direct line from the species to the trunk of the tree.[23]

The image of the tree in a tree diagram evoked by taxonomists, with an emphasis on the arborescent, functions to naturalize constructs such as nation and national identity, origins, ancestries, racial lines, and evolutions. The implied roots of the tree establish the genealogy, the autochthony, the rootedness of this construction deep within the trope of nature. Yet it is a theoretical commonplace to state that the notion of nature is itself problematic in that it is a trope that functions by emphasizing the similar and covering over the dissimilar. Thus, the view of nature is always only partial, a fetish made to appear as a substitute for the whole. In "The Promises of Monsters," Donna Haraway suggests: "Nature for us is made, as both fiction and fact. If organisms are natural objects, it is crucial to remember that organisms are not born; they are made in world-changing technoscientific practices by particular collective actors in particular times and places."[24]

How are the notions of nature and the natural constructed within Enlightenment thought? Is it a discursive linguistic construct as postmodern cultural theory would have it or a domain of truth, value, and authenticity?[25] Indeed, nature and culture are terms that function within a dichotomy; they function as shorthand terms for the difference between the human and the nonhuman. It is this distinction that situates nature to function as an object, without a mind. Thus nature, while it becomes the subject of thought, is itself incapable of thought. Within a Cartesian framework, the mind–body split means that the body is devoid of thoughts, that quality belonging to the realm of the mind. As a result, within this framework, nature is metonymically linked to the mindless body. The mind–body split, metonymically linked to the split between nature and culture, also includes other dichotomies, such as those between animal/human, woman/man, and non-Western/Western. Thus, culture or humanity can come into inscription only though the exclusions of the body, the primitive, the animal, and the feminine.[26]

Included within the context of the "natural" is the essentially political comprehension of the term. The notion of nature varied in its interpretation among the various contract theorists of liberal democracy in the Enlightenment. For instance, in *Two Treatises of Government,* John Locke describes the "law of nature" within the context of the basic and minimal social rules of mutuality that are required of any organized society. In the administration of communal life, all individuals have equal rights: "preserving all mankind and doing all reasonable things . . . in order to that end."[27] But as feminist philosophers have indicated, not all humans have equal natural rights, as women cannot even accede to the status of the individual in Locke's framework. In *The Sexual Contract,* Carole Pateman indicates why women are excluded:

> Locke assumes that marriage and the family exist in the natural state and he also argues that the attributes of individuals are sexually differentiated; only men naturally have the characteristics of free and equal beings. Women are naturally subordinate to men and the order of nature is reflected in the structure of conjugal relations.[28]

Pateman suggests that it is not only women but also slaves who are incarcerated within the space of the natural. If individuals with free will and political judgments construct culture, and if contractual agreements between people with equal rights form the backbone of a liberal democracy, then women and slaves, spatially dislocated into nature, are precluded from the polity, as well as prevented from making contractual agreements. Thus, Locke's concept of nature permits the establishment of hierarchy among those who are deemed individuals and those who are not. Among other Contract theorists it was only Hobbes who insisted that both men and women are equally free, but in general the Contract doctrine insists on men's rights over women.[29]

Thus, within the context of the eighteenth and nineteenth centuries, the opposition between nature and culture gained greater significance. Nature gained multiple meanings: a presocial state, a synonym for the internal processes of the human body, the world of plants, animals, and the countryside, and the life of "primitive" people. While in the binary opposition between nature and society, the latter was considered the more advanced; it was also perceived as leading to depravity and enslavement. Thus, there was an ambivalence toward society among writers such as Rousseau. The term "natural" also referred to all things related to the body: physical, instinctual, sensory. In the temporal movement from the natural to the social, there is embedded an evolutionary discourse that follows Linnaeus's distribution of Homo hierarchichus that latches on to the Cartesian notion of the mind–body split. The premise of the inferiority of the natural or the bodily and the need to transcend the body can be seen at all levels in the production of the theoretical frameworks of the nineteenth century. For instance, it underpins Freud's theory of the maturation of the human: from instincts and drives, the human has to progress to repression and the construction of the superego. Within his theoretical framework, culture is fundamental to overcoming the weaknesses of the body.

This prolonged unpacking of the notions of the natural and nature is important, in that these concepts are central to the genealogical shifts that the meaning of races underwent in this time period. The genealogical shift records the movement in the classification of people according to somatic and morphological criteria, from symbols of physical difference to signs of racial characteristics, from allegorical marks (with its implication of arbitrariness to social constitution) to natural marks with a one-to-one correspondence between outer marks and inner constitution of the subject. This genealogical shift is also a chronological one because only then can there be a basis, the very ground, for racial discourse. Only then can the conceptualization of racial characteristics become meaningful and homogenize entire groups of people, even though the differences *within* racial groups are as or more varied than those *between* groups. Only then can the switching from arbitrary marks to natural marks legitimate the violence meted out to the millions of Africans transported into slavery and to the millions of indentured laborers, especially the Chinese and Indians transported into the New World. This switch also permits a synecdoche—a part for a whole—in that the marks of race on the skin become a direct way to categorize domination or subordination. The skin functions as a catachrestic fetish, the color on it suggesting the visibility of the *entire* subject, her interiority, her inferiority, at a glance. It permits for a Linnaean model for the categorization of Homo hierarchichus. The genealogical shift in the premises made of the skin permits it to function as a metaphor, but one that makes visible both the like and the unalike elements in the comparisons.

In the now classic work *Essentially Speaking,* Diana Fuss points out that the doctrine of essence denies or annuls "the very radicality of difference."[30] In its premise of the fixedness of an identity, its irreducibilty, its unchangingness, the doctrine of essence celebrates the natural and its purity. While notions of essence and the natural dislocate themselves from temporality to posit themselves as unchanging, I suggest instead that the racially marked body is also located within a temporality, but one different than the one in which the unmarked individual lives. This temporality is located within a geological time. This temporality lags behind the post/modernity occupied by Western (white) subjects. It is a temporality that calls forth an evolutionary model. Indeed, for a marked body to become unmarked, it takes a very, very long time.

Why does the metamorphosis of the marked body into the unmarked literally take eons? Could it be that marks on the skin carry memories that prevent a quicker osmotic process? In fact, the framing of the skin as the borderland between internal psychic structures and external reality is suggested by Freud in "The Ego and the Id" and "A Note on the Mystic Writing Pad."[31] Freud renders the ego itself as a skin—"The ego is first and foremost a bodily ego; it is not merely a surface identity, but is itself the projection of a surface," and when he states, "A person's own body, and above all its surface, is a place from which both external and internal perceptions may spring. It is seen like any other object but to the touch it yields two kinds of sensations, one of which may be equivalent to the internal perception."[32] This theme of the skin negotiating between the inside and the outside is continued in "The Mystic Writing Pad." Inspired by the recent invention of what we now call the "Magna Doodle," the learning tool for children, Freud makes an analogy between the way writing is inscribed on the pad and how memories are retained in the unconscious. Thus, in Freud's work, the ego is not only based on the perception of the skin, but the skin also becomes the site on which the faint traces of the unconscious are perceptible. Skin can, therefore, be seen as the site of bodily memories, covering over the demands of the unconscious, protecting the latter from the forces of external reality, forming a mantle, like the Earth's crust. It is this interface between the skin and ego that allowed Didier Anzieu, a psychologist who worked at a dermatology unit in a hospital, to posit the notion of the skin ego. For Anzieu, the actual material skin was a highly sensitive surface that bore the sense of trauma that the patient might psychically feel. Anzieu suggests that "skin ailments are closely related to stress, to emotional upheavals . . . [;] the irritation of the epidermis becomes confused with mental irritation."[33]

It is this notion of the skin functioning as the surface that makes visible the internal trauma of the subject. It is the process through which skin becomes the master signifier and leads to the collapse of the boundary between the internal and the surface or the psychic and the physical that haunts Frantz Fanon in the famous scene in *Black Skin, White Masks*. Here the child exclaims, "Look, a Negro . . . Mama, see the Negro! I'm frightened." To this reduction of him to his skin, Fanon claims he felt "an amputation, an excision, a hemorrhage that splattered [his] whole body with black blood."[34] Fanon's black skin literally keeps him from spilling his guts, his blood, the trauma to his innermost self, for the child's words cut him to the quick, like a knife.

One final point on how Freud's notion of fetishism throws light on racial markings on the body: In Freud's text, the fetish is a substitution for the lost phallus of the mother; the fetish itself is a permanent memorial to the fetishist's horror of castration. The process of scotomization—the blind spot on the retina—occludes the mother's bodily difference through the substitution of the fetish. This substitution allows for two contrary beliefs to flourish—that women have penises and that they don't. Thus, the fetish functions in two ways: it keeps the fetishist's castration fear while simultaneously soothing it. The fetish object sutures over the castration anxieties, latent homosexuality, as well as visual materiality. Here the mechanics of fetishism—the substitution, the flourishing of two contrary beliefs—functions within the context of skin marking as well. Indeed, the process of scotomization, which is particular to the fetishist's interpretation of the fetish, throws light on the way black embodiment, skin, is culturally interpreted and regarded. I suggest that just as the fetish is a fictional substitution for the maternal phallus, so is skin a fictional synecdoche for physical and cultural differences. Just as the fetish wards off castration anxieties, the master signifier of skin wards off anxieties of the sense of incompletion of the dominant subject, and permits a repression of one's own Otherness that is an internal condition of all subjects within modernity. Just as the fetish prevents the disclosure of the fetishist's latent homosexuality, so does skin allow the bypassing of the anxiety of abjection.

To bring this section to a conclusion, I have suggested that the skin carries the status of signifier for the immutable body, which, in turn, is the dense materiality upon which theoretical, philosophical, and other cultural discourses are predicated. In this formula, however, even though the body is read as interiority, containing the core essence of the individual, the skin is perceived as a surface entity. Such a comprehension of the skin then suggests its flaying from the solid materiality of the body and subjects it to the fictions of difference, especially within the context of race. Thus, skin has a double contrary function: it endorses the sense of the natural and, therefore, the truth of the reading, while it also functions as a synecdoche, a metaphor for and therefore the subject of interpretation.

Kipling Sahib and Ruddy Baba

It is with the evoking of the double nature of skin that I begin my reading of Rudyard Kipling's *Kim,* whose early double life underscored Kipling's own sense of doubleness, his ambivalence over skin. Kipling, who was born in India in 1865 and raised by Indian servants, spent his early years speaking both Hindi and English. Salman Rushdie points out, "When the child Rudyard was admitted to his parents' presence, the servants would have to remind him to 'speak English now to Mama and Papa.'"[35] Sent to school in England when he was six, Rudyard returned to India in 1882 when he was seventeen. He remained in India until 1889.

Published in 1901, the story of *Kim* is well known as it was Kipling's most successful work. Kim is a young vagrant boy in undivided British India of the late 1880s. Racially ambivalent, Kim lives like an Indian, though his birth certificate and other papers contained in an amulet around his neck attest him to be the son of an Irish sergeant, Kimball O'Hara, and his wife, Annie Shott, an Irish woman. Becoming the disciple of a Tibetan monk, Kim goes on the road in search of a river that will cleanse all sins. Kim also has an Afghan friend, Mahbub Ali, a horse dealer who doubles as a secret agent for the British. The boy is drafted into the Great Game, the machinations of the British secret service in the Northwest Frontier. In addition, when Kim is discovered to be white, he is taught to behave white, thus underscoring race as a construction and a miming. Notwithstanding his education and his whiteness, Kim prefers to follow the monk while simultaneously participating in the Great Game. In the final scene, the monk gives up his claim on Kim's future, though Kim himself is unsure of where his destiny lies: as an Indian or as a European in India.

In his magisterial *Culture and Imperialism,* Edward Said assesses Rudyard Kipling's *Kim:* "Its author was writing not just from the dominating viewpoint of a white man in a colonial possession but from the perspective of a massive colonial system whose economy, functioning and history had acquired the status of a virtual fact of nature. Kipling assumes basically an uncontested empire."[36] For Said, Kipling's text is marked by the nineteenth-century European notion of "the inferiority of non-white races, the necessity that they be ruled by a superior race, and their absolute unchanging essence."[37] Locating Kipling alongside Joseph Conrad, Rider Haggard, and G. A. Henty, Said insists that *Kim,* though worthy of serious aesthetic and critical attention, nevertheless squarely belongs to the genre of adventure imperialism. Furthermore, Said does not engage with Kim's Irish heritage, and as a result there is a conflation of Irishness with Britishness that ignores the status of the Irish as colonized Other within British imperial discourses on Ireland. Said's occlusion is inexplicable, especially within the problematic history of the racialization of the Irish since the Enlightenment. Are the Irish British? Are they white or are all colonized people black? How do politics and history mark a body within race? Is whiteness a marker of evolution? Does the bourgeoisification of the body make it white? Is poverty a racialized sign? Can a body be marked as both black and white? Is this indeterminate body rich or poor? How does the miscegenated body signify? How does the text tolerate the limits of ambiguity and indeterminacy?

I examine the process of the unlinking of whiteness from power that Kim embodies through the trope of Irishness. As a trope, it dislodges black and white identities, both of which are entangled within fixed and primordial binarities. Further, in gesturing beyond race and power, *Kim* also lays bare the functions between and interactions among whiteness and class. How does this break of the bodies from their racialized significations resituate the discourse on the dense materiality of the body itself? The dissonance and dissidence that the Irish body brings to racially and culturally fixed bodies is suggestive, in that it scripts an aesthetics of the postwhite body, which draws on the local, the material, and the particular and calls out to a structure of feeling that goes beyond an allegiance to race, class, and caste. Three different aspects of Kim's embodiment bestow an indeterminacy to the text. First, I will examine the material density of some historical signifiers to see what light they throw on the ambiguously positioned Irish body. Second, I will examine what the disguises and the different clothing that abound in the text function as metaphors for. Third, I will examine the conclusion, which for Said suggests Kim's allegiance with his whiteness but which is nevertheless indeterminate in that it provides no answer to Kim's urgent question about who he is. I suggest that in these particular moments, all of which involve the body's relationships to identity, certain fissures become visible in the text of whiteness. These fissures, which all cohere around the comprehension of Irishness, provide alternative readings to the text, taking it beyond a simple novel that belongs to the genre of adventure imperialism with its emphasis on racialized imperial relationships.

THE VAGRANT BODY

As feminist scholars, among others, have established, historical formations shape and underpin theoretical and cultural comprehensions of the
body. It is commonly posited that the materiality of the bodies themselves is wrought not only by the social and cultural, but also by the
historical. If the white or the black body is a sign of irreducibility, then
markers of class and the significations of the body from the Enlightenment onward complicate any simple or straightforward comprehensions of race. I locate Kim's body within its historical specificity to suggest that such an excavation makes visible not only his Irishness, a term
often conflated with Englishness in the text, but also his poverty, both of
which function to render his body racially ambivalent in the text.

There are only two dates mentioned in *Kim*, 1857 and 1879, both of
which firmly locate the text within high colonialism and imperialism in
the mid- to late Victorian period. Oddly, the scarcity of any further
historical references also creates a sense of a dislocation from the material density of history and contributes to the various erasures, making
this novel to be overtly only about adventure imperialism. If the density
of history were reinscribed, how would it shift the way we read *Kim*?
The reference to the 1857 mutiny is indicated through a loyal Indian
soldier, an "old, withered man, who had served the government in the
days of the Mutiny as a native officer."[38] Accompanying Kim and the
Buddhist monk for a brief leg of their travels on the Grand Trunk
Road, he claims to have participated in no fewer than nineteen battles
and forty-six skirmishes of horse and countless other minor skirmishes,
and had borne nine wounds in the year of the mutiny.[39] The old soldier proceeds to refer to the mutiny itself as "a madness that ate into
all the army and they turned against their officers."[40] Thus, the Sepoy
Mutiny and the causes that led to it—the racist policies of the East India
Company's armies, the onset of British colonialism, the fear of losing
one's religion, the relentless modernization since the beginning of the
nineteenth century, the vast disparity in income between the European
officers and the native soldiers—get reduced to the signifier "madness"
that made the rebellious soldiers behave illogically. Said astutely asks
why any reference to the mutiny, an overdetermined moment within
Indian colonialism, has to be signaled by a loyal Indian soldier? He asks,
where are the representations of his nationalist counterpart?[41] The mutiny, which lasted for more than a year, with forty thousand European

soldiers outnumbered eightfold by close to three hundred thousand native soldiers, almost marked the decimation of the British population in India. Indeed, Kipling's description skews traditional descriptions of the mutiny, done either from the British or Indian perspectives. I want to emphasize, instead, that the citation of a precarious moment in British colonialism reveals its vulnerability as much as the representation of its superiority. The reference to the 1857 mutiny is a gesture to the text of white anxiety, the text of ambivalence.

I briefly examine the signifier 1879 as well before I do any further analysis of the references to vulnerability. In *Kim,* Kimball O'Hara (the father) had served in the second Afghan war[42] in the Irish regiment the Mavericks. The aim of the second Afghan war, fought between November 20, 1878, and September 1, 1880, was to forestall Russian influence over Afghanistan. Historically, Afghanistan had been the gateway between the West and the East in the Silk Road, an extremely lucrative trade passage that linked Europe, the Middle East, and Asia. By the nineteenth century, the Silk Road overland had been superseded by sea routes, but Afghanistan continued to have a strategic value in that it was a buffer zone between the Russian Empire, Persia, and British India. Politically, Russia's growing influence in Central Asia was problematic to Imperial Britain. The war between the British and the Afghanis to gain control over the politics in Afghanistan was long drawn out because of the hostile environment and harsh climate and the stiff resistance. The conclusion of the war was not decisive for the British who stopped Russian advances for the moment, but made no gains either.

If British imperial masculinity was predicated on the possession of the idealized body—invulnerable, non-orific, youthful, white—then events such as the Crimean War, the Sepoy Mutiny, the Morant Bay Rebellion, and the suffering of white bodies, their flimsiness and vulnerability revealed during the Afghan wars, belied its powers and laid bare the fictional origins of this myth. In "Concerning Violence" Frantz Fanon insists on the mimetic quality of violence done to the body.[43] In this text, the disorder and violence of the colonized functions as a referent for the originary violence of colonization. Thus, originary colonial violence can only be ever read retroactively. It also binds the colonized into a coherent unitary whole and lies at the core of their subjectivity within the emergent nation-state. Thus, the double subject is formed, both subject and object, an outsider to his own heritage while practicing it, constructed by colonialism while being a product of indigenous specificities. Fanon's reading of pain done unto the body and its resultant violence as being central to the construction of subjectivity is in line with psychoanalytic thinking as exemplified by Freud. In "The Ego and the Id," the ego is hailed into being through pain. Freud suggests that "pain seems to play a part in . . . the way we gain new knowledge of our organs during painful illnesses and is perhaps a model of the way in which in general we arrive at the idea of our own body."[44] If violence and pain engender a subjectivity and an awareness of the body, so are they fundamental in the very construction of imperial whiteness. I want to suggest that in contouring the white body, not only is racial difference essential but it also has a vulnerability, especially within the context of colonial rule. Whiteness can be forged only as being always under siege. The references to violent moments of its history reveal the anxiety and fear that underpin colonial, imperial constructions of embodiment and disembodiment.

I make one more reference to the overdetermined signifier 1879. In *Kim,* Kimball O'Hara belongs to the regiment the Mavericks, indicating a continued Irish presence in the Indian subcontinent. Between 1825 to 1850, the early years of Victoria's reign, Irishmen almost equaled the British among enlisted soldiers in the Bengal army.[45] Since the military service was considered one of very few employment opportunities for the Irish, who were also colonized by the British, there was an overrepresentation of them in the Indian army. In fact, it was only after the Mutiny of 1857 that the proportion of the Irish declined in India because a large number of them immigrated instead to Britain or to the United States, especially after the famine.[46] In Kipling's text, Kimball O'Hara is described as a "young colour-sergeant" of the Mavericks, who eventually took a post on the Sind, Punjab, and Delhi railway. The text indicates that eventually his regiment left without him while he himself became addicted to drinking and drugs. Some excavating of these details, the social fabric of enlisted Irishmen's life in India, needs to be done to avoid interpreting them as white men gone astray because of excess contact with native women or as an essentialized image of the drunken Irish.

If colonialism consisted of the exploitation of native resources and labor, did it exploit poor working-class whites? While in 1829 enlistments were for life, by 1870 the concept of a short service of twelve years was introduced in the military. The notion of the short service suggested that enlisted men could spend three to eight years under colors, or in active service, with the remainder to be served in the reserves. A number of the men in reserves took employment with the Indian Railways, just as Kimball O'Hara does. Railway constructions began in India in the 1850s, and since Indians were perceived as not being skilled enough to work as engine drivers, pointsmen, fitters, and so on, the railway companies, in order to maintain cost-effective labor, hired British men, particularly from the military already in India who were acclimatized and looking for alternative employment.[47] When the railways perceived it was cheaper to hire and train Indians, they did so, leading to the unemployment of the working-class white men in India. Further, sick and injured railway men were often dismissed without a pension or compensation by the railway companies. Kim is born within this nexus of social relations of Irish poverty, working-class vagrant white, and colonized status, an alcoholic father whose alcoholism is engendered by and ignored within life in the military, whose employment status is at risk because of the profit margin required by railway companies. Kim's orphan status and vagrancy were not unique to him but depressingly rather common. The orphanages and schools available for young boys and girls like him were hierarchized depending on what access to money these children had. In fact, discussions were held by the lama, Father Victor, and Reverend Bennett about where Kim was to be sent, now that he was rescued from his vagrancy: for instance, the regiment would pay for Kim to go to the military orphanage or he could go on the Punjab Masonic Orphanage list; the best education could be had at St. Xavier's at a cost of 300 rupees.[48] David Arnold points out, "The years at an orphanage were like the recycling of industrial waste: the orphans of one generation of soldiers, railwaymen and their wives were recast as the soldiers, railwaymen and wives of the next."[49] Such an end is predicted for Kim as well. The staff at St. Xavier's knew that the early maturing of the country-born Europeans such as Kim, caused by sun and surroundings, would also result in their rapid decline from the age of twenty-two or twenty-three.[50] All the discourse of anxiety and degeneration is written on Kim's ambiguous poor, vagrant, orphaned body. Indeed, I would suggest that there is an investment in the text of whiteness to avoid and make scarce references to historical specificity, because if the dense, material meanings of historical signifiers are unpacked, the anxiety of whiteness, its demand for the bourgeoisification of the body, its paranoia, and its occlusion of the problematic and oxymoronic poor white body becomes visible.

CLOTHING AND DISGUISES

My next point focuses on the significance of clothing and of disguises, both of which contribute to the text of indeterminacy and ambiguity in *Kim*. Clothing has a political edge, as it signifies racial, ethnic, or national pride or a subcultural style. The genealogy of Western male clothing is tightly imbricated within nationalism, race, and class and a particular reading of masculinity, despite its normalization. Anne Hollander suggests that the evolution of the suit in the West from the Enlightenment on was predicated on classic Greek nudes that provided the model for the idealized masculine figure. At the end of the eighteenth century, the masculine ideal shifted from courtly refinement to natural simplicity.[51] Sobriety, prudence, detachment, and restraint were conveyed through the suit. Western European male clothing thus interweaves aesthetics with politics, class, nation, and sexuality.

In *Kim*, a number of men wear disguises and dress as the other. For instance, Kim can transform himself into a Hindu or a Muslim through a change of clothing.[52] His Hindu kit can signify his low caste vagrancy as much as the outfit that Mahbub Ali buys him (a gold-embroidered Peshawur turban cap, rising to a cone, and a big turban cloth ending in a broad fringe of gold . . . a Delhi-embroidered waistcoat to slip over a milky white shirt . . . green pajamas with twisted silk waist string, Russia leather slippers, smelling divinely, with arrogantly curled tips)[53] converts him into a well-born Afghan. Again, by wearing English clothes, Kim transmutes into a European. When he accompanies the lama, his attire locates him as a Buddhist. Other characters who are involved in the Great Game also wear disguises to deceive the onlooker: Lurgan Sahib, Hurree Babu, and the Indian spy on the train, yet with some differences. Wearing disguises in this text can thus be seen to be a part of the fictional necessity of the plot of adventure imperialism. Yet the fact that racial cross-dressing is possible only for Kim and Lurgan Sahib, and not Hurree Babu, suggests that while European bodies can mime an Indian, the reverse is not possible. In fact, Hurree Babu's dark skin prevents him from even attempting to disguise himself as a white. Here we can see that skin works as a fetish, in that it contains the body, an identity, the well-being, and a value. Skin functions as boundary object within the context of disguises and becomes a sign of the subject's interiority. Father Victor peels off Kim's outer garment from his body and reveals his white skin underneath. Truth is thus revealed; notwithstanding his being burned black, or speaking Urdu as his first language, Kim is proven to be nothing else but white. Gail Low comments: "The lesson is that while on the one level visible difference constitutes racial difference, on another level, the difference must be disavowed. Kim is white on the inside; colour, clothes, dirt are merely empty signifiers."[54]

Yet the dense materiality of dirt, color, and clothes that lie in layers on Kim's body are not empty significations. If the text draws binary oppositions between white and black and the clothing each one must wear, the narrative is ambivalent in its regard to Kim's whiteness. Though the amulet and the skin covered by clothing bespeak his superior white status, the text also underscores his ambiguous marks: he has brown hands, sleeps like an Oriental, and feels most comfortable in Indian clothing even after spending time at St. Xavier's and learning to be white. Further, his Irish difference is constantly reiterated, in his parentage, his superstitious ways. When the lama is attacked by the Russian at the end of the text, it wakes "every unknown Irish devil in the boy's blood." The narrative acknowledges Kim's hybrid condition, "the Irish and the Oriental."[55] Here the two terms are at an equivalence, the Irish a metaphor for the Oriental.

Indeed, tracing Irish embodiment historically suggests that any arguments for the naturalized comprehensions of the body, the innate, prior power and superiority of whiteness, fall apart in the consideration of the nature of Irish whiteness. While the early Anglo-Norman conquest of Ireland did not racialize the Irish, the discourse of racism became significant during the Reformation in Britain.[56] It is indeed the accretive racializing and colonizing of Celtic Ireland that suggests that significations of blackness are directly linked to the political and economic policies of imperial powers. The blackening of the Irish is a retroactive construct as well in that they were racially located as being closer to blacks in John Beddoe's 1862 work, wherein he categorized the Celts, especially the Irish, as "Africoid." Focusing on the jawline in his "Index of Negrescence," Beddoe suggested that the Celts were prognathous (with prominent jaws), a negroid trait, whereas the Anglo-Saxons were orthognathous, with less prominent jaws.[57] For Beddoe, all geniuses also had less prominent jaws, further attesting to the lower hierarchical status of the Celts. Theodore Allen too makes a compelling case for the analogical relationship between the Irish, the Native American, and the African American via the nexus of the tropes of colonialism and slavery.[58] Just as the term "Negro" generally indicated a slave in eighteenth- and nineteenth-century America, the Latin term for an Irishman, "hibernicus," was also the legal term for unfree. If Native Americans were legally like immigrants and therefore not citizens, according to a U.S. Supreme Court decision in 1884, so were the Irish designated as foreigners for four centuries, according to English law. In 1652, the English House of Commons empowered the issuing of licenses to take cargoes of Irish men, women, and children as bond laborers; in the mid-seventeenth century, the Irish, like the enslaved Africans, were forcibly transported to Anglo-America for bond servitude.[59] Commenting on the Irish slave trade, Abbott E. Smith states that there followed a period of "licensed kidnapping on a large scale with the magistrates and officers of the law actively conniving at it under some pretence of statutory sanction."[60] Again Noel Ignatiev points out that Irish immigrants in America were often referred to as "niggers turned inside out." Alternatively, nineteenth-century African Americans were referred to as "smoked Irish."[61] In Britain, Carlyle referred to the Irish as "the white Negroes." Even Karl Marx insisted on this analogy: "The ordinary English worker hates the Irish worker . . . [and] he feels himself the member of the ruling nation. . . . His attitude is much the same as the 'poor whites' to the 'niggers.'"[62]

The multiple marking of the Irish as both black and white, its overlaying of ambivalence on white embodiment, suggests that racial demarcations, notwithstanding their naturalized effects, are themselves a process. It is easy enough to see that the repetitive references to the similarity between Negroes and the Irish accrete to render the latter black as well. Here the metaphoric principle is at work in that, notwithstanding the differences, it is the sameness that is validated, made visible, and insisted upon.

If we were to read the ambivalence of whiteness written on the specificity of the Irish body, how could we read Kim's chameleon shifts in the text? The text underscores the changes to his body from his time in St. Xavier's to walking on the foothills of the Himalayas with the lama: "The hills sweated the ghi and the sugar suet off his bones; the dry air taken sobbingly at the head of cruel passes, firmed and built out his upper ribs; and the tilted levels put new hard muscles into calf and thighs."[63] If Kim's body is essentialized, it is its reshaping from its geographical surroundings, its autochthony, that the text emphasizes. Thus, Kim rapidly shifts from being white (having the horror of the white person for snakes) to being Indian (having an Oriental's indifference to mere noise) to being a junior lama, an indecision as to who he is, white or Indian, spy or a follower of the lama, nomad or occupying a fixed racialized position in India.

Postscript: Postwhite

Finally, I examine the conclusion of *Kim,* primarily because it is so inconclusive. For Said, "as the novel ends, Kim returns to the Great Game and in effect enters the British colonial service full time."[64] But such a reading is problematic when Kim's Irishness and the materiality of its history are restored to his figure. Kim wonders at the end: "I am Kim; I am Kim; and what is Kim?"[65] It is at this moment that meaning slides into "proper portion" for him: "Roads were meant to be walked upon, houses to be lived in, cattle to be driven, fields to be tilled, and men and women to be talked to. They were all real and true . . . solidly planted upon the feet . . . clay of his clay, neither more nor less."[66] I suggest that Kim's finding of himself is underpinned by a materiality not mediated by social structures but by the impressions and sensations on the skin. His chameleonlike skin becomes an interface between the inside, its affections and emotions, and the outside world of the social. St. Xavier's might have taught him European skills, but his body remembers the joy of being on the road and the physical pleasures of his childhood. If the skin is the interface between the psyche and the body, self, and the Others, then Kim's skin, now white, now black, mediates between the two spaces and races that he inhabits. The surface of his skin becomes crucial in ascertaining and distinguishing his discrete self. He embodies and materializes some sort of racial transgression on his zebralike body. He declares to the lama, "I am not a sahib, I am thy chela [disciple],"[67] and thus refuses the command of the social and the cultural, of his racial superiority. He opts, instead, for embodied certainties and the confidence of the material body and its experience of its sensations.

Kim's Irish body is a postwhite body, beyond race and class (though definitely not beyond gender). It instead embodies through its skin memories the quite detailed specificities of life's histories. The inscription of the postwhite body is located within the politics of movement, of transformation. In the construction of embodiment in *Kim,* race and class function as mobile categories. (Set within the nineteenth century, there is a deafening silence around the politics of gender hierarchy, however.) All the different meanings of skin converge into a fine point in *Kim*—the history of the naturalization of racial marks as well as skin as a sensory gatepost, the gateway to perceiving pleasure, or pain, on the body. Just as there can be no body prior to discourse, as a number of poststructural feminist scholars have insisted, can there even be a body outside of its sensations? Can sensations dislocate the body, and skin, outside of the politics of race, class, and gender, and place it within an economy of emotions? How can one begin to perceive discourses of subjectivity alternative to the Cartesian split? I pencil in the concept of postwhiteness and trace the contours of the skin within the economy of emotions. Thus, between his skin, his body, and his memories, Kim's figure mimes the forms of authority at the precise moment it de-authorizes those forms, but not as subversion, as Homi Bhabha would have it, but as an inhabitant of a space beyond race. Indeed, if the Irish because of their white bodies function as copies and mimics, Kim's up-bringing, his black bits, also make him a copy of blackness, its mimic. As Kim declares at the end, echoing the lama, "There is neither black nor white."[68] The structure of feeling joy and experiencing the body not as hindrance but as facilitating movement challenges the order and orderliness of racial hierarchy, Britishness, and the nation-state. But Kim and his movements in the Grand Trunk Road, in the Kulu Valley, in Lucknow, in Lahore, emphasize a disruption of colonial power struc-tures. The shared conversations, histories, the emphasis on nonhierar-chical spaces such as the Grand Trunk Road, the memories, and the attachments of feelings that his movement produces also rematerialize his body and give it a new meaning and shape. The notion of race and Britishness cannot engage Kim's loyalty when his feeling for the lama and the latter's feelings for him are factored into his embodiment. Race and class function as disjunct registers of affiliation that run counter to the economy of emotions that his body is engaged in.

The multiple significations of skin include not only Kim's chame-leon skin, but also function as a gateway to reading Kim through a phe-nomenological approach, his selfhood as being inseparable from mate-rial being-in-the-world. If the normative subject is marked by the closed skin boundaries of the body, Kim's indeterminate skin is porous to its own histories; skin signifies the histories of racism, violence, and indif-ference. It seduces as a metaphor: colonialism can be seen as the process of laying a foreign skin upon the land, making its indigenous inhabi-tants wear their own skins uneasily, be ashamed of them. Under the skin of colonialism lie stories of how whites try to make the land their own. If skin signifies hierarchies, it also is a pointer to sensations of the body, its sense of comfort, well-being, the affections and bodily ties that one has to people and places. If migrancy, hybridity, and transculturation of culture are all markers of globalization, Kim and his Irishness in India is already a part of it. The Silk Road leads not only to globalization, but also to the gradual whitening and the bourgeoisification of all bodies. Therein lies the alternate future of Kipling's *Kim*.

Epilogue:
Europe as an Other

The trouble with the English is that their history happened overseas,
so they didn't know what it means.

Salman Rushdie, Satanic Verses

In the shadow of Europe attempting to consolidate itself as a sovereign, homogeneous body under the aegis of the European Union; in the shadow of Europe touting a single currency, a European passport, and a European economy; in the shadow of Europe reinserting each European citizen as representing the whole continent, I write this book. I write this book to examine the *process of consolidation of sovereignty,* the process through which homogenization takes place, to restore the hybridity to its nineteenth-century manifestation. In *A Critique of Postcolonial Reason,* Gayatri Chakravorty Spivak insists, "Feminist historiography excavates."[1] Armed with this charge, I have used the methodological training of one discipline to read and excavate the archives of another. The process can, in equal parts, create anxiety and provide exhilaration, and provides an alternative look into the familiar, the accepted, the received, the known. Reading history through the sensibility of the literary critic or the cultural critic renders the archives to be over-determined. Freud's notion of this term implies that you cannot hold a simple theory of text or expression, or read it only for its manifest content with a fully self-present deliberative consciousness of the subject. The overdetermined archive is that which is saturated, dense with meaning. The advantage of being from one discipline, foraying into another, is that your ignorance sanctions you into reading all sorts of texts to form your archive, to impute meanings differently in ways in which the historian would hesitate to do. And it is this density, this materiality, that I wished to explore in this work: the density and materiality of the body, history, the historical underpinnings of the body, the bodily underpinnings of standard history.

In her influential *Bodies That Matter,* a work I have repeatedly reread over the years, Judith Butler asks why we valorize materiality so much. She asks, "Is materiality a site or surface that is excluded from the process of construction, as that through which and on which construction works? Is this perhaps an enabling or constitutive condition, one without which construction cannot operate? What occupies the site of unconstructed materiality?"[2] Butler suggests that materiality functions as the site of the halting of analysis. Its physicality, its tangibility, its palpability makes it the site from which meaning itself is generated, even though it might itself be dislocated from the ambit of that meaning. Butler insists that the material is always cultural, a construction, yet

> the body posited as prior to sign, is always *posited* or *signified* as *prior.*
> This signification produces as an effect of its own procedure the very
> body that it nevertheless and simultaneously claims to discover as that
> which *precedes* its own action. If the body signified as prior to significa-
> tion is an effect of signification, then the mimetic or representational
> status of language, which claims that signs follow bodies as their neces-
> sary mirrors, is not mimetic at all. On the contrary, its productive, con-
> stitutive, one might even argue *performative,* inasmuch as this signifying
> act delimits and contours the body that it then claims to find prior to
> any and all signification.[3]

Butler's thesis on embodiment has over the years shaped my thinking and informs the premises of this work: that the meanings imputed to the body are always already constructed. Curiously, however, her evoking of Plato and Aristotle seems to render the meaning of the body as having remained unchanged in the last twenty-five hundred years: in short, almost an essentialized evoking of the body. Her agenda in this work, to expose the logic and rationale of patriarchal thinking, necessitates that she transmute the fleshy materiality of the body into a concept. But bodies and matter are more than concepts: there is a dense physicality to them that cannot be easily explained away in day-to-day living. Foucault himself senses and points to the density of the body in that magnificently horrible opening scene of the punishment of the man accused of regicide in *Discipline and Punish:* drawn and quartered and burned, his body stubbornly refuses to be reduced to ashes for hours and hours afterward.[4]

It is the tense interplay between the body as im-material, a concept, and the body as material, fleshy, that I have tried to negotiate and focus on by excavating its history. In the present, notwithstanding the promise of beaming technology and the dissolution of the body, if you are poor or black (or woman) you are out of the loop of its promise. If the dematerialized body is ironically also the idealized body and deemed hierarchically superior, there is still an urgent political need to comprehend why it is so. Weighing down the dematerialized body through the density of history, I have tried to contour and rematerialize British whiteness of the nineteenth century. My political aim in heterogenizing whiteness was not so much to ethnicize and destabilize it, but rather to track its unevenness and the tensions inherent within it, and, most important, to comprehend its power through the lens of history. And what history promises us is that the times they are (always) a-changin'. Only this promise and the knowledge of the how and when and why whiteness works also provides some solace to those of us who are not, and gives us some basis, some understanding, from which we can negotiate some agency.

In sum, what I have suggested is that the force of whiteness is contemporary with the Enlightenment, liberal democracy, and capitalism as well as mass slavery and colonialism. They are all imbricated. Nineteeth-century British masculinity was a masculinized form, constructed in his relationship to slave labor and his colonies and being bourgeois. Nineteenth-century British women are precariously and ambiguously positioned with regard to whiteness. They are not white unto themselves; it is in their heterosexual relationships with white men that they have whiteness conferred upon them. White embodiment is linked to the development and theorizing of anatomical and racial sciences. The discourse of heterosexuality is a racialized form of sexuality; it is white. Whiteness travels like plants and seeds, a Caucasian tsunami in the nineteenth century. In fact, it is the traveling, the contact with colonized, racial Others that greatly conferred a whiteness to British bodies of the Victorian Age. It defines itself through hygiene and the availability and use of plentiful water. Whiteness is also a melancholic formation; the white subject cannibalistically and mournfully consumes the Other. And most of all, it is relentlessly racist toward the less fortunate, colonized subject of its own color, across the Irish Sea.

Notes

INTRODUCTION

1. Toni Morrison, *Beloved* (New York: Knopf, 1987).

2. bell hooks, *Yearning: Race, Gender, and Cultural Politics* (Boston: South End Press, 1990).

3. Toni Morrison, *Playing in the Dark: Whiteness in the Literary Imagination* (Cambridge, Mass.: Harvard University Press, 1992).

4. Kalpana Seshadri-Crooks, *Desiring Whiteness: A Lacanian Analysis of Race* (London and New York: Routledge, 2000).

5. Sara Ahmed, "Declarations of Whiteness: The Non-Performativity of Anti-Racism," *Borderlands ejournal* 3, no. 2 (2004): 1.

6. Robyn Wiegman, "Whiteness Studies and the Paradox of Particularity," *boundary 2* 26, no. 3 (1999): 138.

7. David R. Roediger, *The Wages of Whiteness: Race and the Making of the American Working Class* (London: Verso, 1999); Noel Ignatiev, *How the Irish Became White* (New York and London: Routledge, 1995); and Theodore Allen, *The Invention of the White Race*, 2 vols. (London: Verso, 1994–1997).

8. Wiegman, "Whiteness Studies," 137.

9. Mike Hill and Damien W. Riggs, "Interview: Whiteness Redux," *Borderlands ejournal* 3, no. 2 (2004): 4.

10. See Gayatri Chakravorty Spivak and Sneja Gunew, "Questions of Multiculturalism," in *The Postcolonial Critic: Interviews, Strategies, Dialogues,* ed. Sarah Harasym (New York: Routledge, 1990), 62.

11. Ibid., 30.

12. See Vron Ware, *Beyond the Pale: White Women, Racism, and History*

(London: Verso, 1992), and Vron Ware with Les Back, *Out of Whiteness: Color, Politics, and Culture* (Chicago: University of Chicago Press, 2002).

13. Catherine Hall, *Civilising Subjects: Metropole and Colony in the English Imagination, 1830–1867* (Cambridge, UK: Polity, 2002).

14. Homi K. Bhabha, "The White Stuff," *Artforum* (May 1998): 21.

15. Paul Gilroy's *The Black Atlantic: Modernity and Double Consciousness* (London: Verso, 1993). Also see Simon Gikandi's *Maps of Englishness: Writing Identity in the Culture of Colonialism* (New York: Columbia University Press, 1996), in which he reads Carlyle, Trollope, Kingsley, and others, in their invention of "Europe" in its relationship to the colonies. One other work that influenced my thinking of the first part of this work is Robert Young's important *Colonial Desire: Hybridity in Theory, Race, and Culture* (London: Routledge, 1995), which is particularly useful in its explication of sexuality and gender within the context of the dialectical relationship between white and black.

16. Alfred Crosby, *Ecological Imperialism: The Biological Expansion of Europe, 900–1900* (Cambridge: Cambridge University Press, 1986), 5.

17. Sander Gilman, *Freud, Race, and Gender* (Princeton, N.J.: Princeton University Press, 1993).

1. White Masculinity

1. See Joseph Bristow, *Empire Boys: Adventures in a Man's World* (London: HarperCollins Academic, 1991), 53.

2. The murder and rape of British women and the slaughter of children obscured the part played by Britain in instigating the mutiny and shifted the focus onto the demonic tendencies and the treacherous nature of Indians. For instance, the *Times,* September 17, 1857, stated: "The history of the world affords no parallel to the terrible massacres which during the last few months have desolated the land. Neither age, sex nor condition has been spared. Children have been compelled to eat the quivering flesh of their murdered parents, after which they were literally *torn asunder* by the laughing fiends who surrounded them. Men in many instances have been mutilated and, being absolutely killed, have had to gaze upon the last dishonour of their wives and daughters previous to being put to death." The vengeance wreaked on the mutinous sepoys, which matched the worst atrocities committed by the mutineers themselves, was met with approval in Britain. The news of the forty soldiers in Peshawar who were executed by being blown from the mouths of cannons caused satisfaction. Thomas Macaulay commented, "The account of that dreadful military execution at Peshawar . . . was read with delight by people who three weeks ago were against all capital punishment." Martin Tupper, the poet, wrote poems demanding the razing of Delhi and the erection of "groves of gibbets." Writers such as Charles Dickens and Flora Annie Steel wanted to avenge the loss of British lives.

3. See Jeffrey Weeks, *Sex, Politics, and Society: The Regulation of Sexuality since 1800* (London: Longman, 1981), 40.

4. As cited in *Manliness and Morality: Middle-Class Masculinity in Britain and America, 1800–1940,* ed. J. A. Mangan and James Walvin (Manchester, UK: Manchester University Press, 1987), 1.

5. See Herbert Sussman, *Victorian Masculinities: Manhood and Masculine Poetics in Early Victorian Literature and Art* (Cambridge: Cambridge University Press, 1995), 1; Norman Vance, *The Sinews of the Spirit* (Cambridge: Cambridge University Press, 1985), 2.

6. See Jeffrey Weeks's work. Eric Hobsbawm's monumental study, *The Age of Capital: 1848–1875* (London: Weidenfeld and Nicolson, 1975), tends to read bourgeois life within the context of capital alone. Hobsbawm draws a continuum in European, white bourgeois life and situates it within the context of revolution and the spirit of nationalism that swept through Europe. He does not read the significance of the colonies in the construction of the European bourgeoisie until his next work, *The Age of Empire, 1875–1914* (New York: Pantheon Books, 1987). There is an arbitrary selection of 1875 as the onset of the age of imperialism, wherein the age of colonization is seen as separate from that of imperialism. Yet it is obvious to any student of postcolonial discourse that the two ages are in continuum; the age of imperialism could not have come into being without colonization. Catherine Hall's works, which have greatly influenced my reading of British masculinity, are the exception to the other works cited. Read her works *White, Male, and Middle-Class: Explorations in Feminism and History* (Cambridge, UK: Polity Press, 1992) and *Civilising Subjects: Metropole and Colony in the English Imagination, 1830–1867* (Cambridge, UK: Polity, 2002).

7. See Harry Magdoff, *Imperialism: From the Colonial Age to the Present* (New York: Monthly Press, 1978).

8. See A. J. Hammerton, *Emigrant Gentlewomen: Genteel Poverty and Female Emigration, 1830–1914* (Canberra: Australian National University Press, 1979).

9. See Thomas R. Metcalf, *New Cambridge History of India,* part III, vol. 4, *Ideologies of the Raj* (Cambridge: Cambridge University Press, 1994), 48.

10. See Percival Spear, *A History of India* (New Delhi: Penguin Books, 1978), 2: 140.

11. See Christopher Hibbert, *The Great Mutiny: India 1857* (Harmondsworth, UK: Penguin, 1978).

12. Charles Ball, *The History of the Indian Mutiny* (London: London Printing and Publishing Company, 1859), 1: 34, Ball's emphasis.

13. See Jenny Sharpe, *Allegories of Empire: The Figure of Woman in the Colonial Text* (Minneapolis: University of Minnesota Press, 1993), 60.

14. For instance, see R. C. Majumdar, *History of the Freedom Movement in India,* vol. 1 (Calcutta: Firma K. L. Mukhopadhyay, 1963).

15. See Earl de Schweinitz Jr., *The Rise and Fall of British India: Imperialism as Inequality* (London: Methuen, 1983), 111–13.

16. See R. C. Majumdar, *History,* and Earl de Schweinitz Jr., *The Rise and Fall,* for a full discussion of these points.

17. See T. R. E. Holmes, *A History of the Indian Mutiny and the Disturbances Which Accompanied It among the Civil Population,* as cited in R. C. Majumdar, *History,* 113.

18. See chapter 5 in R. C. Majumdar, *History.*

19. See Thomas Metcalf, *The Aftermath of Revolt: India, 1857–1870* (Princeton, N.J.: Princeton University Press, 1964).

20. My thanks to Simon Burrows for giving me a quick tour of nineteenth-century British history.

21. See "The Era of Reform," in Metcalf, *The Aftermath of Revolt.*

22. Metcalf, *The Aftermath of Revolt,* 29.

23. See T. B. Macaulay, "Minutes on Education," in *Sources of Indian Tradition,* ed. W. Theodore de Bary (New York: Columbia University Press, 1958), 2: 49.

24. As quoted in Metcalf, *The Aftermath of Revolt,* 12.

25. See Max Black, *Models and Metaphors: Studies in Language and Philosophy* (Ithaca, N.Y.: Cornell University Press, 1962), 31.

26. See David Lloyd, "Race under Representation," *Oxford Literary Review* 13 (1991): 71.

27. See John Stuart Mill, "Of the Government of Dependencies by a Free State" in *Considerations on Representative Government* (New York: Harper and Brothers, 1892). Accessed from Project Gutenberg e-text/5669 on March 26, 2007.

28. Bhabha invokes the Freudian trope of the fetish object to explain the metonymical principle of the mimic. In Freud, the young boy invokes a fetish object to ward off castration anxiety at the presence of his mother's already castrated body because he realizes it could be his lot as well. The boy's replacement of her lost penis with that of a fetish substitute reinvokes a time before his knowledge of sexual difference when his mother's body was complete and unmutilated. Bhabha suggests that, within colonial discourse, "the fetish mimes the form of authority at the point at which it deauthorizes them. Similarly rearticulates presence in terms of its 'otherness,' that which it disavows" (91). Bhabha, *The Location of Culture* (New York: Routledge, 1994), 96, 90.

29. See Homi Bhabha, "Signs Taken for Wonders: Questions of Ambivalence and Authority under a Tree outside Delhi, May 1817," in *The Location of Culture,* 114.

30. See *Race and the Enlightenment: A Reader,* ed. Emmanuel Chukwudi Eze (London: Blackwell Publishers, 1997).

31. See Graham Dawson, *Soldier Heroes: British Adventure, Empire, and the Imagining of Masculinities* (London: Routledge, 1994).

32. See Thomas Hughes, *Tom Brown's School Days* (London: Collins Clear Type Press, 1904).

33. See "Mapping Adventures," in Richard Phillips, *Mapping Men and Empire: A Geography of Adventure* (London: Routledge, 1997).

34. See D. Vincent, *Literacy and Popular Culture in England, 1750–1914* (Cambridge: Cambridge University Press, 1989).

35. D. Vincent, *Literacy and Popular Culture,* 11–12.

36. See Robert Dixon, *Writing the Colonial Adventure: Race, Gender, and Nation in Anglo-Australian Popular Fiction, 1875–1914* (Cambridge: Cambridge University Press, 1995), 4.

37. See J. A. Mangan, *Athleticism in the Victorian and Edwardian Public School* (Cambridge: Cambridge University Press, 1981), 13–17.

38. See "The Industrial Revolution," in E. J. Hobsbawm's *The Age of Revolution, 1789–1848* (London: Weidenfeld and Nicolson, 1962).

39. J. A. Mangan, *Athleticism,* 15.

40. Hughes, *Tom Brown's School Days,* 256.

41. As cited in Jeffrey Richards, "Passing the Love of Woman: Manly Love and Victorian Society," in *Manliness and Morality: Middle-Class Masculinity in Britain and America, 1800–1940,* ed. J. A. Mangan and James Walvin (Manchester: Manchester University Press, 1987), 103.

42. Thomas Hughes, *Tom Brown at Oxford* (London: Collins Clear Type Press, 1889), 99.

43. See Mangan, *Athleticism.*

44. As quoted in Mangan, *Athleticism,* 106.

45. See especially the chapter on "Images of Boyhood," in Bruce Haley, *The Healthy Body and Victorian Culture* (Cambridge, Mass.: Harvard University Press, 1978), 155.

46. See especially the chapter on "Victorian Health," in Haley, *The Healthy Body.*

47. Haley, *The Healthy Body,* 9.

48. Ibid., 20–21.

49. See Edward Said, *Culture and Imperialism* (London: Chatto and Windus, 1993), 78.

50. I refer to Foucault's term in *The History of Sexuality,* vol. 1, *An Introduction,* trans. Robert Hurley (New York: Vintage, 1980).

51. See Francis Barker, *The Tremulous Private Body: Essays on Subjections* (London: Methuen, 1984), 53–65.

52. See Peter Stallybrass and Allon White, *The Politics and Poetics of Transgression* (London: Methuen, 1986), 22.

53. Ibid., 192.

54. See Thomas Laqueur, *Making Sex: Body and Gender from the Greeks to Freud* (Cambridge, Mass.: Harvard University Press, 1990). This premise had led to the development of gynecology. Yet as Ornella Moscucci notes, "The growth of gynaecology was paralleled by the evolution of a complementary 'science of masculinity' or 'andrology.'" Also see Ornella Moscucci, *The Science*

of Woman: Gynaecology and Gender in England, 1800–1929 (Cambridge: Cambridge University Press, 1990), 2.

55. George L. Mosse, *Nationalism and Sexuality: Respectability and Abnormal Sexuality in Modern Europe* (New York: Howard Fertig, 1985), 21.

56. See Jeffrey Richards, "'Passing the Love of Women,'" in *Manliness and Morality.*

57. Mosse, *Nationalism and Sexuality,* 113.

58. See Collette Guillamin, "Race and Nature: The System of Marks, the Idea of a Natural Group and Social Relations," *Feminist Issues* 8, no. 2 (Fall 1988): 32.

59. Ibid., emphasis in the original, 32.

60. See, for instance, the work of Ivan Hannaford, *Race: The History of an Idea in the West* (Washington, D.C.: Woodrow Wilson Press, 1996). Also see Nancy Leys Stepan, *The Idea of Race in Science: Great Britain, 1800–1960* (London: MacMillan Press, 1982).

61. Foucault, *History of Sexuality,* vol. 1, 17.

62. See Judith Butler, *Gender Trouble* (New York: Routledge, 1990). Also see her *Bodies That Matter* (New York: Routledge, 1995). For works on the performative, see Dorinne Kondo, *About Face: Performing Race in Fashion and Gender* (New York: Routledge, 1997); *Performing Feminisms: Feminist Critical Theory and Theatre,* ed. Sue-Ellen Case (Baltimore, Md.: Johns Hopkins Press, 1990); *Cruising the Performative: Interventions into the Representation of Ethnicity, Nationality, and Sexuality,* ed. Sue-Ellen Case, Philip Brett, and Susan Leigh Foster (Bloomington: Indiana University Press, 1995). See Louis Althusser, "Ideology and Ideological State Apparatuses (Notes Towards an Investigation)," in *Lenin and Philosophy and Other Essays,* trans. Ben Brewster (London: New Left Books, 1971).

63. See Butler, *Bodies That Matter,* 121.

64. See "Britannia's Daughters: Race, Place, and the Antipodean Home," in my work, *Black Body: Women, Colonialism, and Space* (Minneapolis: University of Minnesota Press, 1999), for an expansion on the relationship between imperialism and Victorian femininity. The term "Angel in the House" was coined by Coventry Patmore to represent the bourgeois, self-sacrificing woman. See Coventry Patmore's poem "The Angel in the House," in *Poems* (London: George Bell and Sons, 1906), 1–145.

2. The Whiteness of Women

1. See A. James Hammerton, *Emigrant Gentlewomen: Genteel Poverty and Female Emigration, 1830–1914* (Canberra: Australian National University Press, 1979), 28–30.

2. See Jose Harris, *Private Lives, Public Spirit: A Social History of Britain, 1870–1914* (Oxford: Oxford University Press, 1993), 43–45.

3. See Jeffrey Weeks, *Sex, Politics, and Society: The Regulation of Sexuality since 1800* (London: Longman Group, 1981), 65.

4. Harris, *Private Lives, Public Spirit*, 43.

5. See "Britannia's Daughters: Race, Place, and the Antipodean Home" and "Woman-Body-Nation-Space" in my work *Black Body: Women, Colonialism, and Space* (Minneapolis: University of Minnesota Press, 1999). Examining the liminal position occupied by women in the nation-state, one sees that they enumerate some of woman's biological functions within the politico-cultural framework of the state. Among others, women function as biological reproducers of members of ethnic collectivities; as reproducers of boundaries of ethnic/national groups; as central participants in the ideological representation of the collectivity and as transmitters of culture; and as signifiers of ethnic/national differences. See Floya Anthias and Nira Yuval-Davis, eds., *Woman-Nation-State*, ed. (London: Macmillan, 1989). Also see M. Jacqui Alexander, "Erotic Autonomy as a Politics of Decolonization: An Anatomy of Feminist and State Practice in the Bahamas Tourist Economy," in *Feminist Genealogies, Colonial Legacies, Democratic Futures*, ed. M. Jacqui Alexander and Chandra Talpade Mohanty (London: Routledge, 1997), 63–100.

6. Harris, *Private Lives, Public Spirit*, 44.

7. See Thomas Laqueur, "Orgasm, Generation, and the Politics of Reproductive Biology," in *The Making of the Modern Body: Sexuality and Society in the Nineteenth Century*, ed. Catherine Gallagher and Thomas Laqueur (Berkeley: University of California Press, 1987), 1–41.

8. Laqueur, "Orgasm," 18.

9. Jeffrey Weeks, *Sex, Politics, and Society: The Regulation of Sexuality since 1800;* Catherine Hall, *White, Male, and Middle Class: Explorations in Feminism and History* (Cambridge, UK: Polity Press, 1992); Ann Stoler, *Race and the Education of Desire: Foucault's History of Sexuality and the Colonial Order of Things* (Durham, N.C.: Duke University Press, 1995).

10. See Nancy Leys Stepan, "Race, Gender, Science and Citizenship," *Gender and History* 10, no. 1 (April 1998): 26–52.

11. Richard Dyer, *White* (London: Routledge, 1997), 122–42.

12. See Hall, *White, Male, and Middle Class.*

13. See Hall, "The History of the Housewife," in *White, Male, and Middle Class.*

14. Jean Louis Flandren, *Families in Former Times: Kinship, Household, and Sexuality* (Cambridge: Cambridge University Press, 1979), 9.

15. See Lawrence Stone, *The Family, Sex, and Marriage in England, 1500–1800* (London: Weidenfeld and Nicolson, 1977); also see Randolph Trumbach, "Europe and Its Families: A Review Essay of Lawrence Stone," *Journal of Social History* 13, no. 1 (Fall 1979).

16. Weeks, *Sex, Politics, and Society*, 26.

17. See Coventry Patmore's poem "The Angel in the House," in *Poems* (London: George Bell and Sons, 1906), 1–145.

18. John Ruskin, "Of Queens and Gardens," in *Sesame and Lilies: The Two Paths and the King of the Golden River* (London: J. M. Dent and Sons, 1907), 60.

19. Eric Hobsbawm, *The Age of Capital, 1848–1875* (New York: Scribner, 1975), 244, emphasis added.

20. See chapter 1 of A. J. Hammerton, *Emigrant Gentlewomen*.

21. Pierre Bourdieu, *Distinctions: A Social Critique of the Judgement of Taste*, trans. Richard Nice (Cambridge, Mass.: Harvard University Press, 1984), 466.

22. Bourdieu, *Distinctions*, 466.

23. Michel Foucault, *The Order of Things* (New York: Pantheon, 1970), 136.

24. Harriet Ritvo, *The Animal Estate: The English and Other Creatures in the Victorian Age* (Cambridge, Mass.: Harvard University Press, 1987), 3.

25. Ritvo, *The Animal Estate*, 4.

26. My debt to Jacques Derrida's thinking is very visible here. See Derrida, "The Parergon," *October* 9 (1979): 3–40; also see "Living On: Border Lines," in Bloom et al., *Deconstruction and Criticism* (New York: Seabury, 1979), 75–175.

27. Carole Pateman, *The Disorder of Women: Democracy, Feminism, and Political Theory* (Cambridge, UK: Polity Press, 1989), 121.

28. Homi Bhabha, *The Location of Culture* (New York: Routledge, 1994), 9.

29. Judith Walkowitz, *Prostitution and Victorian Society: Women, Class, and the State* (Cambridge: Cambridge University Press, 1980), 49.

30. Ronald Hyam, *Empire and Sexuality: The British Experience* (Manchester: Manchester University Press), 126.

31. Walkowitz, *Prostitution and Victorian Society*, 49.

32. William Acton, as cited in Walkowitz, *Prostitution and Victorian Society*, 59.

33. Flexner as quoted in Walkowitz, *Prostitution and Victorian Society*, 15.

34. See Walkowitz, *Prostitution and Victorian Society*. Also see E. M. Sigworth and T. J. Wyke, "A Study of Victorian Prostitution and Venereal Disease," in *Suffer and Be Still: Women in the Victorian Age*, ed. Martha Vicinus (Bloomington: Indiana University Press, 1972), 77–99.

35. Sigworth and Wyke, "A Study of Victorian Prostitution," 79.

36. Weeks, *Sex, Politics, and Society*, 85.

37. Hyam, *Empire and Sexuality*, 123–24.

38. George L. Mosse, *Nationalism and Sexuality: Respectability and Abnormal Sexuality in Modern Europe* (New York: Howard Fertig, 1985), 5.

39. See Peter Gaskell, *Artisans and Machinery: The Moral and Physical Condition of the Manufacturing Population* (London: John W. Parker, 1836), 89.

40. Weeks, *Sex, Politics, and Society*, 58.

41. See Michel Foucault, *The History of Sexuality*, vol. 1, *An Introduction*, trans. Robert Hurley (New York: Vintage, 1978).

42. Françoise Barret-Ducrocq, *Love in the Time of Victoria*, trans. John Howe (London: Verso, 1991), 41.

43. Such a discursive effect of the opposition between the public and private can be likened to Michel Foucault's notion of the Panopticon, whose major effect, he states, is "to induce in the inmate a state of conscious and permanent visibility that assures the automatic functioning of power." At another instance, Foucault points out that the object of surveillance is seen, "but he does not see; he is the object of information, never a subject in communication." See Michel Foucault, *Discipline and Punish: The Birth of the Prison*, trans. Alan Sheridan (New York: Vintage, 1979), 200–201.

44. William Acton, *Prostitution Considered in Its Moral, Social, and Sanitary Aspects* (London: Cass, 1972), 52.

45. Hyam, *Empire and Sexuality*, 128–33.

46. Nancy Leys Stepan, *The Idea of Race in Science: Great Britain, 1800–1960* (Houndsmill, Bassingstoke: Macmillan's, 1982), 5.

47. See "The Search for Historical and Biological Origins, 1815–1870," in Ivan Hannaford, *Race: The History of an Idea in the West* (Washington D.C.: Woodrow Wilson Center Press, 1996).

48. See Stepan, *The Idea of Race;* and Stepan, "Biology and Degeneration: Races and Proper Places," in *Degeneration: The Dark Side of Progress*, ed. J. Edward Chamberlin and Sander L. Gilman (New York: Columbia University Press, 1985), 97–120.

49. Stepan, "Biology and Degeneration."

50. Stepan, *The Idea of Race*, 21.

51. Paul Topinard as referred to in Stepan, "Race and Gender," 43.

52. See Nancy Armstrong, "The Occidental Alice," *differences* 2, no. 2 (1990): 3–40.

53. Victorian social scientists correlated a woman's moral condition with her facial features or her genitals. Certain facial characteristics were common to white prostitutes and Asian and African women. See Sander Gilman, *Difference and Pathology*, and Daniel Pick, *Degeneration.*

54. As quoted in Sander Gilman's "Black Bodies, White Bodies: Toward an Iconography of Female Sexuality in Late Nineteenth-Century Art, Medicine, and Literature," in *"Race," Writing, and Difference*, ed. Henry Louis Gates Jr. (Chicago: University of Chicago Press, 1986), 245.

55. Gilman, "Black Bodies, White Bodies," 256.

56. Stepan, "Race, Gender, Science and Citizenship" 48.

57. See Hayden White, *Tropics of Discourse* (Baltimore, Md.: Johns Hopkins University Press, 1978), 2.

58. See Theodore W. Allen, *The Invention of the White Race* (London: Verso, 1996), 2: 244.

59. Elaine Showalter, *The Female Malady: Women, Madness, and English Culture, 1830–1980* (New York: Pantheon, 1985), 107.

60. See Freud's introduction to *New Introductory Lectures on Psychoanalysis*, trans. and ed. James Strachey (New York: W. W. Norton, 1965), 5.

61. See *The Complete Letters of Sigmund Freud to Wilhelm Fliess*, trans. and

ed. Jeffrey Moussaeiff Masson (Cambridge, Mass.: Belnap Press of Harvard University, 1985), 272; emphasis added.

62. See "The Riddle's Repression," in Teresa Brennan's *The Interpretation of the Flesh: Freud and Femininity* (New York: Routledge, 1992), for a summary and bibliography of the debates over the essay by Freud.

63. I quote Diana Fuss's classic definitions of essence from *Essentially Speaking: Feminism, Nature, Difference* (London: Routledge, 1989), 3.

64. Gilman, "Black Bodies, White Bodies," 204.

65. Martin Bernal, *Black Athena: The Afroasiatic Roots of Classical Civilization*, vol. 1, *The Fabrication of Ancient Greece, 1785–1985* (London: Free Association Press, 1987).

66. Ibid., 209.

67. Richard Jenkyns, *The Victorians and Ancient Greece* (Oxford, UK: Basil Blackwell, 1980), 41.

68. George Mosse, *Nationalism and Sexuality*, 14.

69. As quoted in Mosse, *Nationalism and Sexuality*, 14.

70. See Jenkyns, "The Origins of Hellenism," in *The Victorians and Ancient Greece.*

71. Mosse, *Nationalism and Sexuality*, 16.

72. As quoted in Jenkyns, *The Victorians and Ancient Greece*, 87–88.

73. As referred to in ibid., 99.

74. Mosse, *Nationalism and Sexuality*, 98.

75. See ibid. Also see Foucault, *The History of Sexuality.*

76. Sander Gilman, *Freud, Race, and Gender* (Princeton, N.J.: Princeton University Press, 1993).

77. Thomas Laqueur, *Making Sex: Body and Gender from the Greeks to Freud* (Cambridge, Mass.: Harvard University Press, 1990), 4.

78. Ibid., 57.

79. Ibid., 58.

80. See, for instance, Daniel Pick, *Faces of Degeneration: A European Disorder, c. 1848–1918* (Cambridge: Cambridge University Press, 1989); Max Nordau, *Degeneration* (London: William Heinemann, 1895); Chamberlin and Gilman, eds., *Degeneration: The Dark Side of Progress.*

3. Victoria's Secret

1. See the chapter "White Power, White Desire," in Robert J. C. Young, *Colonial Desire: Hybridity in Theory, Culture, and Race* (New York and London: 1995).

2. See William Acton, *Prostitution, Considered in Its Moral, Social, and Sanitary Aspects in London and Other Large Cities and Garrison Towns with Proposals for Control and Prevention of Its Attendant Evils* (London: Cass, 1972); A. J. B. Parent-Duchatelet, *De la Prostitution dans la Ville de Paris* (Brussels:

Société Encyclographiques des Sciences Médicales, 1838); Charles Darwin, *The Origin of Species: By Means of Natural Selection,* 6th ed. (London: John Murray, 1885), and also his *Descent of Man: and Selection in Relation to Sex* (London: J. Murray, 1971); Alfred Kinsey, *Sexual Behaviour in the Human Male* (London: Saunders, 1948), and also his *Sexual Behaviour in the Human Female* (London: Saunders, 1953).

3. Jeffrey Weeks, *Sexuality* (London: Routledge, 1989). Also his *Sex, Politics, and Society: The Regulation of Sexuality since 1800* (London: Longman, 1981) and his *Making Sexual History* (Cambridge, UK: Polity, 2000). Weeks reads *The History of Sexuality* more widely than does Foucault. In *Sexuality,* Weeks posits three key moments in the evolution of Western sexuality within the last two thousand years and locates the first epistemological break in sexual discourse with the spread of Christianity, its demand for austerity, and its need for sex to be contained purely within reproduction. The second significant moment within this history, according to Weeks, occurred in the twelfth and thirteenth centuries, wherein the significance of the social practice of marriage was emphasized in the control and containment of sexuality. The third break in the late eighteenth and nineteenth centuries inaugurated the era in which we now live with its emphasis on the definitions of the norm against that of deviance in sexual behavior. Also see Mary Mackintosh, "The Homosexual Role," *Social Problems* 16 (Fall 1968): 182–92; Arnold Davidson, "Sex and the Emergence of Sexuality," *Critical Inquiry* 14 (Autumn 1987): 16–48.

4. Michel Foucault, *The History of Sexuality,* vol. 1, *An Introduction,* trans. Robert Hurley (New York: Vintage, 1980).

5. Foucault, *History of Sexuality,* 125.

6. See Ann Laura Stoler, *Race and the Education of Desire: Foucault's History of Sexuality and the Colonial Order of Things* (Durham, N.C.: Duke University Press, 1995), 97, 7.

7. See George L. Mosse, *Nationalism and Sexuality: Middle-Class Morality and Sexual Norms in Modern Europe* (Madison: University of Wisconsin Press, 1985).

8. See *Nationalisms and Sexualities,* ed. Andrew Parker, Mary Russo, Doris Sommer, and Patricia Yeager (New York and London: Routledge, 1992).

9. Sander L. Gilman, *Difference and Pathology: Stereotypes of Sexuality, Race, and Madness* (Ithaca, N.Y.: Cornell University Press, 1985). See in particular the chapter "The Hottentot and the Prostitute: The Iconography of Female Sexuality."

10. Anne McClintock, *Imperial Leather: Race, Gender, and Sexuality in the Colonial Contest* (New York: Routledge, 1995).

11. See Roy Porter, "History of the Body," in *New Perspectives in Historical Writing,* ed. Peter Burke (University Park: Penn State University Press, 1991), 215.

12. See Weeks, *Sexuality,* 37.

13. See, for instance, "That Damned Morality," in Weeks, *Sex, Politics, and Society.*

14. See Weeks, *Sexuality,* 39.

15. See "An Interview with Jeffrey Weeks," *Journal of Homosexuality* 25, no. 4 (1993), 126.

16. Thomas Laqueur, *Making Sex: Body and Gender from the Greeks to Freud* (Cambridge, Mass.: Harvard University Press, 1990), 149.

17. Laqueur, *Making Sex,* 134–35.

18. See Ornella Moscucci, *The Science of Woman: Gynaecology and Gender in England, 1800–1929* (Cambridge: Cambridge University Press, 1990).

19. See Carole Pateman, *The Disorder of Women: Democracy, Feminism, and Political Theory* (Cambridge, UK: Polity Press, 1989). Also see her *The Social Contract* (Cambridge, UK: Polity Press, 1988).

20. Pateman, *The Disorder of Women,* 4.

21. See, in particular, "The Public/Private Dichotomy," in *The Disorder of Women.* Such an argument for the valorization of civil society over the sphere of the family suggests that women are located in the private, are an atavistic form, and therefore neither part of modernity nor of the public arena.

22. Moscucci, *The Science of Woman,* 2.

23. See Linda Schiebinger, "Skeletons in the Closet: The First Illustrations of the Female Skeleton in Eighteenth Century Anatomy," in *The Making of the Modern Body,* ed. Catherine Gallagher and Thomas Laqueur (Berkeley: University of California Press, 1987), 42–82.

24. See "More than Skin Deep: The Scientific Search for Sexual Difference," in Linda Schiebinger, *The Mind Has No Sex: Women in the Origins of Modern Science* (Cambridge, Mass.: Harvard University Press, 1989).

25. See, for instance, Sherry Ortner's classic work, "Is Female to Male as Nature to Culture?" in *Woman, Culture, and Society,* ed. Michelle Zimbalist Rosaldo and Louise Lamphere (Stanford, Calif.: Stanford University Press, 1974), 67–87; also see Donna Haraway, *Simians, Cyborgs, and Women: The Reinvention of Nature* (London: Free Association, 1991). I find a lack of awareness of historical changes in the meanings of nature and culture in Ortner's work and recommend that it be read alongside Ludmilla Jordonova, "Natural Facts: A Historical Perspective on Science and Sexuality," in *Nature, Culture, and Gender,* ed. Carol MacCormack and Marilyn Strathern (Cambridge: Cambridge University Press, 1980), 42–69; and Maurice Bloch and Jean H. Bloch, "Women and the Dialectics of Nature in Eighteenth Century French Thought," also in *Nature, Culture, and Gender,* 25–41. Both articles emphasize the shifts in the meaning of nature in the eighteenth and nineteenth centuries.

26. To this I must add, so were the "primitive peoples," who were perceived as having a close relationship to and harmonious coexistence with the external world of plants, animals, and the countryside.

27. Collette Guillamin, "Race and Nature: The System of Marks. The Idea

of a Natural Group and Social Relations," *Feminist Issues* 8, no. 2 (Fall 1988): 32; emphasis in the original.

28. Guillamin, "Race and Nature," 34; emphasis in the original.

29. See, for instance, Ivan Hannaford, *Race: The History of an Idea in the West* (Washington, D.C.: Woodrow Wilson Center Press, 1996), 207–8.

30. See, for instance, Phillip R. Sloan, "The Idea of Racial Degeneracy in Buffon's Histoire Naturelle," in *Racism in the Eighteenth Century*, vol. 3, *Studies in Eighteenth Century Culture*, ed. Harold E. Pagliaro (Cleveland, Ohio: Case Western Reserve University Press, 1973), 293–321; Tzvetan Todorov, *On Human Diversity: Nationalism, Racism, and Exoticism in French Thought*, trans. Catherine Porter (Cambridge, Mass.: Harvard University Press, 1993); Nicholas Hudson, "From Nation to Race: The Origin of Racial Classification in Eighteenth Century Thought," *Eighteenth-Century Studies* 29, no. 3 (1996): 247–64.

31. Hudson, "From Nation to Race," 254.

32. As cited in Schiebinger, *The Mind Has No Sex*, 189.

33. See Arthur Lovejoy, *The Great Chain of Being: A Study of the History of an Idea* (Cambridge, Mass.: Harvard University Press, 1936).

34. See Luce Irigaray, "Cosi Fan Tutti," in *This Sex Which Is Not One*, trans. Catherine Porter with Carolyn Burke (Ithaca, N.Y.: Cornell University Press, 1985), 86. Also see Irigaray's magnificent "The Blind Spot of an Old Dream of Symmetry," in which she coins the term "sexual indifference" in *Speculum of the Other Woman*, trans. Gillian C. Gill (Ithaca, N.Y.: Cornell University Press, 1985).

35. Teresa de Lauretis, "Sexual Indifference and Lesbian Representation," in *Lesbian and Gay Studies Reader*, ed. Henry Abelove, Michele Aina Barale, and David Halperin (New York: Routledge, 1993), 141–58.

36. Gayatri Chakravorty Spivak, "Woman in Difference: Mahasweta Devi's 'Doulati the Bountiful,'" *Cultural Critique* (Winter 1989–90): 105–28.

37. As quoted in Peter Markie, p. 142. See Peter Markie, "The Cogito and Its Importance," in *The Cambridge Companion to Descartes*, ed. John Cottingham (Cambridge: Cambridge University Press, 1992), 140–73.

38. In the "Analytic of the Sublime," Kant posits: "By the name *sensus communis* is to be understood the idea of a *public* sense, i.e. a critical faculty which in its reflexive act takes account *(a priori)* of the mode of representation of everyone else, in order, *as it were,* to weigh its judgement with the collective reason of mankind, and thereby avoid the illusion arising from subjective and personal conditions which could readily be taken for objective, an illusion that would exert a prejudicial influence upon its judgement, not so much with actual, as rather with the merely possible, judgements of others, and by putting ourselves in the position of everyone else, as the result of a mere abstraction from the limitations which contingently affect our own estimate." See Immanuel Kant, *The Critique of Judgement*, trans. James Creed Meredith. (Oxford: Oxford University Press, 1952), 151.

39. See David Lloyd, "Race under Representation," *Oxford Literary Review*

13 (1991): 62–94. This article is rich with suggestions, some of which I explore in this chapter. Lloyd connects the work of Schiller and Kant: "The Subject without properties is the philosophical figure for what becomes, with increasing literalness through the nineteenth century, the global ubiquity of the white European. His domination is virtually self-legitimating since the capacity to be everywhere becomes the historical manifestation of the white man's gradual approximation to the universality he everywhere represents" (70).

40. See "The Embodiment of Blackness," in Radhika Mohanram, *Black Body: Women, Colonialism, and Space* (Minneapolis: University of Minnesota Press, 1999), for a detailed explanation of this point.

41. Ferdinand de Saussure, *Course in General Linguistics* (London: Peter Owen, 1960), 120.

42. Jacques Derrida, *Positions* (Chicago: University of Chicago Press, 1981), 26.

43. Beyond liberal humanism, within poststructuralist thought, marking problematizes the status and meaning of bodies. For instance, following Foucault's lessons, in *Gender Trouble* Judith Butler suggests gender and the body must be comprehended as "fabrications manufactured and sustained through corporeal signs and other discursive means." In short, the true gender of the body emerges in a retroactive loop in that it internalizes and incorporates cultural constructions of masculinity and femininity and rematerializes it on the body as natural. Thus, the body itself is a manifestation of political regulation. Similarly, ambivalence is at the core of Homi Bhabha's description of bodily difference. For Bhabha, as for Butler, the body is simultaneously and conflictually inscribed in both, the economy of pleasure and desire as well as the economy of dominance and power. Thus, for Bhabha there is a political agency to be gained by underscoring this lack of fixity of the body and the deconstruction of the marked body's structural function.

It suffices for both theorists that the unfixed marked body destabilizes hierarchies as well as terms like masculine and white that set these hierarchies in motion. Their insistence on the lack of fixity of marked bodies functions to heterogenize the body so no one set of stereotype terms can adequately signify it. But what of the white, male heterosexual body, that which is hinted at and used as the norm in both Bhabha and Butler? The emphasis on marked bodies ultimately reinstates liberal humanism's framework of identity and difference where difference can only signify negatively. In short, poststructuralist embodiment reproduces a difference or a marked body that is always outside of the ambit of power. In so doing, the heterogenized marked body merely gets assimilated by the norm, leaving the difference behind as a residue, always to function as an Other. Judith Butler, *Gender Trouble: Feminism and the Subversion of Identity* (London: Routledge, 1990); Homi K. Bhabha, *The Location of Culture* (London: Routledge, 1994).

44. See "Body/Power," in Michel Foucault, *Power/Knowledge: Selected In-*

terviews and Other Writings, 1972–1977, ed. Colin Gordon (Basingstoke: Harvester Press, 1980), 55–62.

45. Foucault, *The History of Sexuality,* 1: 93.

46. Ibid., 57.

47. Ibid., 124.

48. See Daniel Pick, *Faces of Degeneration: A European Disorder, c. 1838–1918* (Cambridge: Cambridge University Press, 1989).

49. Gareth Stedman Jones, *Outcast London* (New York: Pantheon, 1971), 11.

50. See Anne McClintock's *Imperial Leather: Race, Gender, and Sexuality in the Colonial Contest* (London: Routledge, 1995).

51. See *Sir Charles Lyell's Scientific Journals on the Species Question,* ed. Leonard Wilson (New Haven, Conn.: Yale University Press, 1970), 347.

52. See William Ripley, *The Races of Europe: A Sociological Study* (New York: Appleton 1899), 561–64; also see Nancy Leys Stepan, "Biological Degeneration: Races and Proper Places,"in *Degeneration: The Dark Side of Progress,* ed. J. Edward Chamberlin and Sander L. Gilman (New York: Columbia University Press, 1985), 97–120.

53. Hyam's emphasis. See Ronald Hyam, *Empire and Sexuality: The British Experience* (Manchester: Manchester University Press, 1990), 89–90.

54. See Young, *Colonial Desire,* 175.

55. As quoted in Gilman. See Sander Gilman, "Sexology, Psychoanalysis, and Degeneration: From a Theory of Race to a Race to Theory," in *Degeneration: The Dark Side of Progress,* 76.

56. Foucault, *The History of Sexuality,* 1: 123.

57. Stoler, *Race and the Education of Desire,* 136, 209.

58. See Gayatri Chakravorty Spivak, "Can the Subaltern Speak?" in *Marxism and the Interpretation of Culture,* ed. Cary Nelson and Lawrence Grossberg (London: Macmillan Education, 1988), 280.

59. See Kenneth Ballhatchet, *Race, Sex, and Class under the Raj : Imperial Attitudes and Policies and Their Critics, 1793–1905* (London: Weidenfeld and Nicolson, 1980), as well as Hyam, *Empire and Sexuality,* 121.

60. As quoted in Ballhatchet, *Race, Sex, and Class under the Raj,* 146.

61. The Crewe Circular, as reproduced on pages 182–84 in Ronald Hyam, "Concubinage and the Colonial Service: The Crewe Circular (1909)," *Journal of Imperial and Commonwealth History* 14, no. 3 (May 1986): 170–86.

62. Judith Walkowitz, *Prostitution and Victorian Society: Women, Class, and the State* (Cambridge: Cambridge University Press, 1980), 70.

63. See Frank Mort, *Dangerous Sexualities: Medico-moral Politics in England since 1830,* 2nd ed. (London: Routledge, 2000).

64. See "Literature," in Gayatri Chakravorty Spivak, *A Critique of Postcolonial Reason: the Vanishing Present* (Cambridge, Mass.: Harvard University Press, 2000).

65. See Ronald Hyam, *Empire and Sexuality,* 123.

66. See Philip Howell, p. 325 n14, in "Prostitution and Racialised Sexuality: The Regulation of Prostitution in Britain and the British Empire before the Contagious Diseases Acts," *Society and Space* 18 (2000): 321–39.

67. See Sean Quinlan, "Colonial Bodies"; also Alfred Crosby, *Ecological Imperialism* and *Germs, Seeds, and Animal Studies in Ecological History.*

68. Philippa Levine, "Venereal Disease, Prostitution, and the Politics of Empire: The Case of British India," *Journal of History of Sexuality* 4, no. 4 (1994): 590.

69. As quoted in Nancy Armstrong, "The Occidental Alice," *differences: A Journal of Feminist Cultural Studies* 2, no. 2 (1990): 6.

70. See "The British Home Base" in Hyam, *Empire and Sexuality.*

71. Jeffrey Weeks, "An Interview with Jeffrey Weeks," *Journal of Homosexuality* 25, no. 4 (1993): 127.

72. See Anna Davin, "Imperialism and Motherhood," *History Workshop Journal* 5 (Spring 1978).

4. WHITE WATER

My gratitude to Liz Deloughrey, Pacific and Caribbean scholar extraordinaire, and to Luisa Pèrcopo, for sharing their knowledge, books, resources, and scholarship with me.

1. As cited in Tom Ryan, "Le President des Terres Australes: Charles de Brosses and the French Enlightenment Beginnings of Ocean Anthropology," *Journal of Pacific History* 37, no. 2 (2002): 157–86.

2. Edward Said, *Orientalism* (New York: Vintage, 1979), 116–17.

3. See *Earth* in the *Guardian* (with Action Aid), August 2002, 6.

4. As quoted in Gaston Bachelard, *Water and Dreams: An Essay in the Imagination of Matter,* trans. Edith R. Farrell (Dallas, Tx.: Pegasus Foundation, 1983), 118.

5. Bachelard, *Water and Dreams,* 120–21.

6. Ibid., 125.

7. Ibid., 8.

8. See, for instance, Sherry Ortner's classic work "Is Female to Male as Nature to Culture?" in *Woman, Culture, and Society,* ed. Michelle Zimbalist Rosaldo and Louise Lamphere (Stanford, Calif.: Stanford University Press, 1974), 67–87; also see Donna Haraway, *Simians, Cyborgs, and Women: The Reinvention of Nature* (London: Free Association, 1991); and Maurice Bloch and Jean H. Bloch, "Women and the Dialectics of Nature in Eighteenth Century French Thought," in *Nature, Culture, and Gender,* ed. Carol MacCormack and Marilyn Strathern (Cambridge: Cambridge University Press, 1980), 25–41, who emphasize the shifts in the meaning of nature in the eighteenth and nineteenth centuries.

9. Maurice Bloch and Jean Bloch, "Women and the Dialectics of Nature," 27–31.

10. See, for instance, Gwendolyn Wright, *Moralism and the Model Home: Domestic Architecture and Cultural Conflict in Chicago, 1873–1913* (Chicago: University of Chicago Press, 1980). Wright states: "The most important private space in the home, the bathroom, was just coming to be accepted in middle-class American families during the last decades of the nineteenth century, although the acceptance was by no means universal. Still, it did become more common to unite in a single room the various pieces of equipment formerly found in separate niches or in individual bedrooms: a tub, a sink or wash-bowl, certainly the water closet, earth closet or chamber pot. The special room for these sanitary functions did not look too different from other rooms in terms of surface materials, size or lighting; but it was luxuriously private" (40).

11. See Margaret Morgan, "The Plumbing of Modern Life," *Postcolonial Studies* 5, no. 2 (2002): 172.

12. See Alain Corbin as cited in Charles Bernheimer, *Figures of Ill-Repute* (Cambridge, Mass.: Harvard University Press, 1981), 16.

13. See "Place in My Place," in *Black Body: Women, Colonialism, and Space.*

14. See Charles Creighton, *A History of Epidemics in Britain,* 2 vols. (Cambridge: Cambridge University Press, 1891, 1894), 2: 206, 208, 391.

15. See Bruce Haley, *The Healthy Body and Victorian Culture* (Cambridge, Mass.: Harvard University Press, 1978), 9.

16. Ibid., 16.

17. See Laura Brown, *Fables of Modernity: Literature and Culture in the English Eighteenth Century* (Ithaca, N.Y.: Cornell University Press, 2001), 25.

18. See Ivan Illich, *H2O and the Waters of Forgetfulness* (London: Marion Boyars, 1986), 57.

19. See Anna Davin, *Growing Up Poor: Home, School, and Street in London, 1870–1914* (London: Rivers Oram Press, 1996), 51.

20. See Andrew Mearns, *The Bitter Cry of Outcast London: An Inquiry into the Condition of the Abject Poor (1883)* (London: Frank Cass, 1970).

21. Charles Booth as cited in Gareth Stedman Jones, *Outcast London: A Study in the Relationship between Classes in Victorian Society* (Oxford, UK: Clarendon Press, 1971), 132.

22. Octavia Hill, *Homes of the London Poor (1875)* (London: Frank Cass), 1970, 51.

23. J. Rawlinson, "Sanitary Engineering: Sanitation," in *A History of Technology,* ed. Charles Singer (Oxford: Oxford University Press, 1958), 4: 511.

24. Ibid., 518.

25. See Sigmund Freud, *Civilisation and Its Discontents,* trans. James Strachey (New York: W. W. Norton, 1961), 46n, 53n.

26. Condillac as cited in Dominique Laporte, *The History of Shit,* trans. Nadia Benabid and Rodolphe el-Khoury (Cambridge, Mass.: Harvard University Press, 2000).

27. Kant, *The Critique of Judgement,* 55–56.

28. See Laporte, *The History of Shit,* 80.

29. See Mary Douglas, *Purity and Danger: An Analysis of the Concepts of Pollution and Taboo* (London: ARK Paperbacks, 1966), 35.

30. Ibid., 35.

31. See Alfred W. Crosby, *Germs, Seeds, and Animals: Studies in Ecological History* (Armonk, N.Y.: M. E. Sharpe, 1994), 59. Also see his *Ecological Imperialism: The Biological Expansion of Europe, 900–1900* (Cambridge: Cambridge University Press, 1986).

32. Crosby, *Germs, Seeds, and Animals*, 57.

33. See Sean Quinlan, "Colonial Encounters: Colonial Bodies, Hygiene, and Abolitionist Politics in Eighteenth-Century France," *History Workshop Journal* 42 (1996): 107–25. Also see William Coleman, "Health and Hygiene and the Encyclopédie: A Medical Doctrine of the Bourgeoisie," *Journal of the History of Medicine* 29 (1974): 399–421.

34. See Quinlan, "Colonial Encounters," 108.

35. For further discussion see ibid., 112–13.

36. Laporte, *The History of Shit*, 83–84.

37. See David Lindsey and Geoffrey Bamber, *Soapmaking: Past and Present, 1876–1976* (Nottingham, UK: Gerard Brothers, 1965); also see "Soft Soaping Empire," in Ann McClintock, *Imperial Leather* (London: Routledge, 1995).

38. T. B. Macaulay, "Government of India," in *Macaulay Prose and Poetry*, ed. G. M. Young (London: Rupert, 1952).

39. McClintock, *Imperial Leather*, 211.

40. See Michel Foucault, *The History of Sexuality, Part I*, trans. Robert Hurley (New York: Vintage, 1978), 123.

41. Ibid., 125.

42. See Julia Kristeva, *Powers of Horror: An Essay on Abjection*, trans. Leon S. Roudiez (New York: Columbia University Press, 1982).

43. See Janet Abu-Lughod, "On the Remaking of History: How to Reinvent the Past," in *Remaking History*, ed. Barbara Kruger and Phil Mariani (Seattle: Bay Press, 1989), 111–30.

44. As referred to in James Anthony Froude, *Oceana, or England and Her Colonies* (London: Longman's Green and Company, 1886), 1.

45. Ibid., 11, 10.

46. Ibid., 14.

47. Ibid., 18.

48. See the fabulous article by Christopher L. Connery, "The Oceanic Feeling and the Regional Imaginary," in *Global/Local: Cultural Production and the Transnational Imaginary*, ed. Rob Wilson and Wimal Dissanayake (Durham, N.C.: Duke University Press, 1996): 284–311.

49. Ibid., 297.

50. Herman Melville as quoted in Charles Olson, *Call me Ishmael* (San Francisco: City Lights Books, 1947), 117.

51. See Ralph Davis, *The Rise of the English Shipping Industry in the Seventeenth and Eighteenth Centuries* (London: Macmillan, 1962), 388–85.

52. See B. K. Drake, "The Liverpool-African Voyage c 1790–1807," in *Commercial Problems in Liverpool: The African Slave Trade and Abolition,* ed. Roger Anstey and P. E. H. Hair (Widnes: Historic Society of Lancashire and Cheshire, Occasional Series, 1976), 2: 137.

53. See James Walvin, "Sugar and the Shaping of Western Culture," in *White and Deadly: Sugar and Colonialism,* ed. Pal Ahluwalia, Bill Ashcroft, and Roger Knight (Commack, N.Y.: Nova Science Publishers, 1999), 21–32.

54. Hugh Tinker, *A New System of Slavery: The Export of Indian Labour Overseas, 1830–1920* (London: Institute of Race Relations, Oxford University Press, 1974), 17.

55. Ibid., 114–15.

56. As referred to in J. H. L. Cumpston, *The Inland Sea and the Great River: The Story of Australian Exploration* (London: Angus and Robertson, 1965), 61.

57. Matthew Flinders, *Journal on the Investigator* 2: 17, Project Gutenberg e-book.

58. As referred to in Cumpston, *The Inland Sea,* 64.

59. *Two Expeditions into the Interior of Southern Australia,* Project Gutenberg e-book vols. 1 and 2 by Charles Sturt, *Two Expeditions,* 62.

60. Ibid., 62.

61. Gayatri Chakravorty Spivak, "The Rani of Sirmur," in *Europe and Its Others,* ed. Francis Barker, Peter Hulme, Margeret Iverson, and Diana Loxley (Colchester: University of Essex Press, 1985), 1: 133.

62. See "Maps and Their Cultural Constructedness," in Simon Ryan, *The Cartographic Eye: How Explorers Saw Australia* (Cambridge: Cambridge University Press, 1996).

63. Sturt, *Two Expeditions,* 21.

64. *Journals of Two Expeditions into the Interior of New South Wales,* by John Oxley, 21, Project Gutenberg e-book.

65. *Journals of Expeditions of Discovery into Central Australia,* by Edward John Eyre, Project Gutenberg e-book.

66. See "Plotting" in Paul Carter, *Living in a New Country: History, Travelling, and Language* (London: Faber and Faber, 1992), 12–13. Also see the previous groundbreaking work by Paul Carter, *The Road to Botany Bay* (London: Faber and Faber, 1987).

67. Mary Louise Pratt, *Imperial Eyes: Travel Writing and Transculturation* (London: Routledge, 1992), 29–31.

68. Eyre, *Journals of Expeditions,* 17.

69. Chandra Mukherjee, "Visual Language in Science and the Exercise of Power: The Case of Cartography in Early Modern Europe," *Studies in Visual Communications* 10, no. 3 (1984): 31. Also see Simon Ryan, *The Cartographic Eye;* Graham Huggan, *Territorial Disputes: Maps and Mapping Strategies in Contemporary Canadian and Australian Fiction* (Toronto: University of Toronto Press, 1994); *The Iconography of Landscape: Essays on the Symbolic*

Representation, Design and Use of Past Environments, ed. Denis Cosgrove and Stephen Daniels (Cambridge: Cambridge University Press, 1988).

70. Eyre, *Journals of Expeditions,* 48.

71. Ibid., 48.

72. Ibid., 107.

73. Ibid., 70.

74. Sturt, *Two Expeditions,* 58.

5. Mourning and Melancholia

1. Pakeha is the Maori nomenclature for immigrants of white British origin (and their descendants) in New Zealand.

2. See *Reminiscences of Sarah Selwyn,* ed. Harry Bioletti (Auckland, New Zealand: privately printed, 2002).

3. *Mission and Moko: Aspects of the Work of the Church Missionary Society in New Zealand, 1814–1882,* ed. Robert Glen (Christchurch: Latimer Fellowship of New Zealand, 1992).

4. Mary Martin, *Our Maoris* (London: Society for Promoting Christian Knowledge, 1884).

5. Ibid., 3–4.

6. Ibid., 143.

7. For instance, see Richard Dyer, *White* (London: Routledge, 1997); *Whiteness: A Critical Reader,* ed. Mike Hill (New York: New York University Press, 1997); *Critical White Studies: Looking behind the Mirror,* ed. Richard Delgado and Jean Stefancic (Philadelphia: Temple University Press, 1997).

8. See James Belich, *Making Peoples: A History of the New Zealanders,* vol. 1 (Auckland: Penguin, 1996).

9. Sigmund Freud, "Mourning and Melancholia," in vol. 14 of *Standard Edition of the Complete Psychological Works of Sigmund Freud,* ed. James Strachey, 24 vols. (London: Hogarth Press).

10. Sigmund Freud, "The Ego and the Id," in *SE,* 19: 30.

11. See Paul de Man, *Allegories of Reading: Figural Language in Rousseau, Nietzsche, Rilke, and Proust* (New Haven, Conn.: Yale University Press, 1979), 296. As Eric Santner suggests, "In Demanian discourse the speaking subject is perpetually, constitutionally, in mourning: for the referent, for beauty, for meaning, for home, for stable terms of orientation, because these losses are always already there as soon as one uses language. As de Man has said, 'Death is a displaced name for a linguistic predicament.' The speaking subject is, as it were, always 'celebrating some funeral.'" Eric L. Santner, *Stranded Objects: Mourning, Memory, and Film in Postwar Germany* (Ithaca, N.Y.: Cornell University Press, 1990), 15.

12. Santner, *Stranded Objects,* 29.

13. Ibid., 29.

14. See Greg Forter, "Against Melancholia: Contemporary Mourning Theory, Fitzgerald's *The Great Gatsby,* and the Politics of Unfinished Grief," *differences: A Journal of Feminist Cultural Studies* 14, no. 2 (Summer 2003): 137.

15. Julia Kristeva, *Black Sun: Depression and Melancholia,* trans. Leon S. Roudiez (New York: Columbia University Press, 2000), 3.

16. Kristeva's reading of the maternal and the Symbolic has been consistent since her early texts, "Motherhood according to Giovanni Bellini" and "Place Names" in *Desire in Language: A Semiotic Approach to Literature and Art,* trans. Thomas Gora, Alice Jardine, and Leon S. Roudiez (New York: Columbia University Press, 1981). Also see Kaja Silverman's feminist critique of Kristeva in *The Acoustic Mirror: The Female Voice in Psychoanalysis and Cinema* (Bloomington: Indiana University Press, 1988). See especially chapter 4.

17. For instance, see Philip Novak, "Circles and Circles of Sorrow: In the Wake of Morrison's *Sula,*" *PMLA* 114 (1999): 184–93, who, within his analysis of African American subjectivities, suggests that, far from being a pathological condition, melancholia becomes a necessary response for African Americans to hold on to their specific culture. Also see Michael Moon, "Memorial Rags," *Professions of Desire: Lesbian and Gay Studies in Literature,* ed. George E. Haggerty and Bonnie Zimmerman (New York: Modern Language Association, 1995), 233–40, for whom melancholia becomes the way gay men might extend their attachments to the dead.

18. See Anne Anlin Cheng, *The Melancholy of Race* (Oxford: Oxford University Press, 2001), 10.

19. David Lloyd, "Race under Representation," *Oxford Literary Review* 13 (1991): 71.

20. Maggie Kilgour, "The Function of Cannibalism at the Present Time," in *Cannibalism and the Colonial World,* ed. Francis Barker, Peter Hulme, and Margaret Iversen (Cambridge: Cambridge University Press, 1998), 246–47.

21. See William Arens, *The Man-Eating Myth: Anthropology and Anthropophagy* (Oxford: Oxford University Press, 1979).

22. Peter Hulme, *Colonial Encounters: Europe and the Native Caribbean, 1492–1797* (London: Methuen, 1986), 66.

23. H. L. Malchow, *Gothic Images of Race in Nineteenth-Century Britain* (Stanford, Calif.: Stanford University Press, 1996). See chapter 2, "Cannibalism and Popular Culture," for its fascinating account of cannibalism among the whites and the anxieties that it signaled.

24. As quoted in Malchow, *Gothic Images of Race,* 158.

25. Ibid., 71.

26. See Crystal Parikh, "Blue Hawaii: Asian Hawaiian Cultural Production and Racial Melancholia," *JAAS* (October 2002): 199–216. Parikh suggests "The melancholic object made neither dead nor fully alive, must experience its own subjectivity as suspension, as excess and denigration—and in this way, replicate the melancholic subject" (205). Also see Juliana Chang, "'I Cannot

Find Her': The Oriental Feminine, Racial Melancholia, and Kimiko Hahn's 'The Unbearable Heart,'" *Meridians: Feminism, Race, Transnationalism* 4, no. 2 (2004): 239–60.

27. Cheng, *The Melancholy of Race,* 11.

28. Alexander and Margerete Mitscherlich, *The Inability to Mourn: The Principles of Collective Behavior,* trans. Beverley R. Placzek (New York: Grove Press, 1975), 16.

29. Freud, "The Ego and the Id," 37.

30. It is this same sense of melancholy that Paul Gilroy levels on postwar Britain as well. In Gilroy's assessment, though the end of the Second World War coincided with the end of Empire, Britain had privileged the first event to occlude its own brutality in the acquisition of Empire. Thus, contemporary Britishness is founded in its hard-fought victory over Germany. See Paul Gilroy, *After Empire: Melancholia or Convivial Culture* (New York and London: Routledge, 2004).

31. The emancipation of Britain's slaves was prompted by rebellions in Demerera in 1823 and Jamaica in 1831. See Alan Lester, *Imperial Networks: Creating Identities in Nineteenth-Century South Africa and Britain* (London: Routledge, 2001), 29.

32. Lester, *Imperial Networks,* 29.

33. See chapters 2 and 5 in Lester, *Imperial Networks.* Also see his article "Obtaining the 'Due Observance of Justice': The Geographies of Colonial Humanitarianism," *Environment and Planning: Society and Space* 20 (2002): 277–93.

34. *British Parliamentary Papers: Report from the Select Committee on Aboriginal British Settlements* (Shannon: Irish University Press, 1968), 5.

35. Thomas Haskell, "Capitalism and the Origins of Humanitarian Sensibility," part I, *American Historical Review* 90, no. 2 (April 1985): 339–61; "Capitalism and the Origins of Humanitarian Sensibility," part II, *American Historical Review* 90, no. 3 (June 1985): 547–66.

36. Haskell, "Capitalism and the Origins of Humanitarian Sensibility," part II, 548.

37. Thomas Laqueur, "Bodies, Details, and the Humanitarian Narrative," in *The New Cultural History,* ed. Lynn Hunt (Berkeley: University of California Press, 1989), 176–204.

38. *British Parliamentary Papers: Report from the Select Committee,* 249.

39. As quoted in Lester, *Imperial Networks,* 116.

40. While Claudia Orange gives an estimate of Maori at the time of the treaty to be around 200,000, James Belich insists that the number was closer to 70,000. See Belich, *Making Peoples,* 148, and Claudia Orange, *The Treaty of Waitangi* (Wellington, New Zealand: Allen and Unwin, 1987), 6–7.

41. See especially chapter 5 in James Belich, *Making Peoples.*

42. Margaret Steven, *Trade, Tactics, and Territory: Britain in the Pacific, 1783–1823* (Melbourne: Melbourne University Press, 1983), 68.

43. As quoted in Orange, *The Treaty of Waitangi*, 10.

44. Ibid., 274 n 78.

45. See Belich, *Making Peoples*, 249–50.

46. Ibid., 283.

47. Michel de Certeau, *The Writing of History*, trans. Tom Conley (New York: Columbia University Press, 1988), 3.

48. See Homi K. Bhabha, "Introduction: Narrating the Nation," in *Nation and Narration* (London: Routledge, 1990), 1.

49. See Bill Ashcroft, Gareth Griffiths, and Helen Tiffin, *Key Concepts in Post-Colonial Studies* (London: Routledge, 1998), 212.

50. de Certeau, *The Writing of History*, 3.

51. Selwyn, *Reminiscences of Sarah Selwyn*, 61.

52. Ibid., 21.

53. Ibid., 33.

54. Ibid., 33.

55. Ibid., 64.

56. Ibid., 65.

57. Ibid., 69.

58. Gayatri Chakravorty Spivak, "The Rani of Sirmur," in *Europe and Its Others*, ed. Francis Barker, Peter Hulme, Margaret Iversen, and Diana Loxley (Colchester: University of Essex, 1985), 1: 133.

59. Selwyn, *Reminiscences of Sarah Selwyn*, viii.

60. Ibid., 55.

61. Martin, *Our Maoris*, 182.

62. As compiled in *My Hand Will Write What My Heart Dictates*, 114. Despite Richmond's perception of women's roles vis-à-vis politics, Sarah Selwyn too had strong opinions on the role of Pakeha. Sharply aware of the violation of the treaty (in the subsequent treatment meted out to Maori) and the political implications to Maori as well as the racializing of Pakeha, she exclaimed: "Oh! We are sinking so low in the eyes of the Maories *[sic]*. Where is our good faith? Where are our assurances that the Queen would never do them wrong? It is a foul shame to mix up her name and lower the respect they were quite ready to pay to her, with this miserable degrading land jobbing. . . . It goes to the heart to see a noble race of people stigmatised as rebels and drawn to desperation by the misrule of those who are at the same time lowering their own people in their eyes." See *Extracts of Letters from New Zealand on the War Question*, printed for private circulation, London 1861, as quoted in *My Hand Will Write What My Heart Dictates*, 122. *My Hand Will Write What My Heart Dictates: The Unsettled Lives of Women in Nineteenth-Century New Zealand as Revealed to Sisters, Family, and Friends*, ed. Frances Porter and Charlotte Macdonald with Tui MacDonald (New Zealand: Auckland University Press, Bridget Williams Books, 1996).

63. *Mission and Moko*, 137.

64. Francis Hall to the Church Missionary Society on August 4, 1823, as

quoted in Frances Porter, "All That the Heart Does Bear: A Reflection on the Domestic Life of Missionary Wives," in *Mission and Moko*, 135.

65. As quoted in ibid.

66. See Belich, *Making Peoples*, 217–18.

67. As quoted in *My Hand Will Write What My Heart Dictates*, 118.

68. Martin, *Our Maoris*, 174.

69. Ibid., 161–62.

6. Dermographia

1. Michel Foucault, *Discipline and Punish*, trans. Alan Sheridan (New York: Vintage Books, 1979); E. P. Thompson, "Time, Work-Discipline, and Industrial Capitalism," *Past and Present* 38 (1967): 56–97.

2. See "Docile Bodies," in Foucault, *Discipline and Punish*.

3. E. P. Thompson, "Time, Work-Discipline, and Industrial Capitalism," 91.

4. See Donna Haraway, "A Manifesto for Cyborgs: Science, Technology, and Socialist Feminism in the 1980s," in *Feminism/Postmodernism*, ed. Linda J. Nicholson (London and New York: Routledge, 1990), 191.

5. David Lloyd, *Ireland after History* (Cork: Cork University Press, 1999), 104.

6. See Noel Ignatiev, *How the Irish Became White* (New York: Routledge, 1995); Theodore W. Allen, *The Invention of the White Race*, 2 vols. (London: Verso, 1994–1997); David Roediger, *The Wages of Whiteness: Race and the Making of the American Working Class* (London: Verso, 1991).

7. Didier Anzieu, *Skin Ego: A Psychoanalytic Approach to the Self*, trans. Chris Turner (New Haven, Conn.: Yale University Press, 1989), 14.

8. See Julia Kristeva, *Powers of Horror: An Essay on Abjection*, trans. Leon S. Roudiez (New York: Columbia University Press, 1982).

9. See Sander Gilman, *Inscribing the Other* (Lincoln: University of Nebraska Press, 1991), 37.

10. Ibid., 33.

11. Freud, *Three Essays on the Theory of Sexuality*, trans. and revised by James Strachey (New York: Basic Books, 1962), 57.

12. Ibid., 58.

13. Kant as cited in Gilman, *Inscribing the Other*, 37.

14. See W. Von Leyden, *Seventeenth-Century Metaphysics* (London: Duckworth, 1968).

15. Johann Gottfried von Herder as referred to in Ivan Hannaford, *Race: The History of an Idea in the West* (Washington, D.C.: Woodrow Wilson Center Press, 1996).

16. See, for instance, Dante A. Puzzo, "Racism and the Western Tradition," *Journal of the History of Ideas* 25 (1964): 579–86; G. V. Scammel, "On the Discovery of the Americas and the Spread of Intolerance, Absolutism, and Rac-

ism in Early Modern Europe, *International History Review* 13 (1991): 502–21; Richard Popkin, "The Philosophical Basis of Eighteenth Century Racism," in *Racism in the Eighteenth Century,* ed. Harold E. Pagliaro (Cleveland: University of Cincinnati Press, 1975), 245–62; Ivan Hannaford, *Race: The History of an Idea in the West.*

17. See Nancy Leys Stepan, *The Idea of Race in Science: Great Britain, 1800–1960* (Hamden, Conn.: Archon Books, 1982), xiii.

18. Collette Guillamin, "Race and Nature: The System of Marks: The Idea of a Natural Group and Social Relations," *Feminist Issues* 8, no. 2 (Fall 1988): 32.

19. See David Brion Davis, *The Problem of Slavery in Western Culture* (Ithaca, N.Y.: Cornell University Press, 1966).

20. Stepan, *The Idea of Race in Science,* 2. Compare, for instance, the genealogy of polygenism and monogenism in Stepan with that by Siep Stuurman, "Francoise Bernier and the Invention of Racial Classification," *History Workshop Journal* 50 (Autumn 2000): 1–21.

21. Linnaeus, "The System of Nature," as excerpted in *Race and the Enlightenment,* ed. Emmanuel Chukwudi Eze (Cambridge, Mass.: Blackwell, 1997), 13.

22. Ibid.

23. See John Dupré, *The Disorder of Things: Metaphysical Foundations of the Disunity of Science* (Cambridge, Mass.: Harvard University Press, 1993), 27.

24. Donna Haraway, "The Promises of Monsters: A Regenerative Politics for Inappropriate/d Others," in *Cultural Studies,* ed. Lawrence Grossberg, Cary Nelson, and Paula A. Treichler (London: Routledge, 1992), 297.

25. For instance, Derridean deconstruction, which deals with meanings that emerge within the structure of binary oppositions, would deem the location of nature outside the orbit of culture and the text as problematic. In his framework, Foucault's division between the natural and the unnatural (or the perverse) reveals them to be effects of discourse and classification.

26. See Kate Soper, *What Is Nature: Culture, Politics, and the Non-Human* (Oxford, UK: Blackwell, 1995); *Global Nature, Global Culture: Gender, Race, and Life Itself,* ed. Sarah Franklin, Jackie Stacey, and Celia Lurie (London: Sage, 2000).

27. John Locke, *Two Treatises of Government,* vol. 2, ed. P. Laslett, 2nd ed. (Cambridge, UK: Cambridge University Press, 1967), Sec 11.

28. Carole Pateman, *The Sexual Contract* (Stanford, Calif.: Stanford University Press, 1989), 52.

29. See "Contract, the Individual, and the Slave," in Pateman, *The Sexual Contract.*

30. See Diana Fuss, *Essentially Speaking: Feminism, Nature, and Difference* (London: Routledge, 1989), xii.

31. Sigmund Freud, "The Ego and the Id," in *The Standard Edition of the Complete Psychological Works of Sigmund Freud,* trans. James Strachey (London:

W. W. Norton, 1960); "A Note on the Mystic Writing Pad," in ibid., 19: 227–32. Also see the fabulous article by Jay Prosser, "Skin Memories," in *Thinking through the Skin,* ed. Sarah Ahmed and Jackie Stacey (New York: Routledge, 2001), 52–68.

32. Freud, "The Ego and the Id," 26, 25.

33. Anzieu, *Skin Ego,* 32–33.

34. See Frantz Fanon, *Black Skin, White Masks,* trans. Charles Lamm Markmann (New York: Grove Weidenfeld, 1967), 112.

35. Salman Rushdie, *Imaginary Homelands: Essays in Criticism, 1981–1991* (London: Granta Books, 1991), 74.

36. See Edward Said, *Culture and Imperialism* (New York: Vintage, 1993), 162.

37. Ibid., 182.

38. Kipling, *Kim,* 44.

39. Ibid., 50.

40. Ibid., 49.

41. Said, *Culture and Imperialism,* 178–79.

42. Kipling, *Kim,* 101.

43. See Frantz Fanon, *The Wretched of the Earth,* trans. Constance Farrington (London: Penguin, 1990).

44. Freud, "The Ego and the Id," 25–26.

45. See the comprehensive Web site http://www.britishempire.co.uk. (accessed on June 15, 2004).

46. See, for instance, Kevin Kenny, "Diaspora and Comparison: The Global Irish as a Case Study," *Journal of American History* 92, no. 3 (June 2003): 134–62.

47. See, for instance, David Arnold, "White Colonisation and Labour in Nineteenth Century India," *Journal of Imperial and Commonwealth History* 11, no. 2 (January 1983): 133–58. Arnold adds that the argument for having European drivers became weaker when situated against the costs involved in having only European workers. While the salary of a European engine driver was 200 rupees, an Indian trained to do the same would be paid only 50 rupees. Arnold points out: "By 1879, when the number of its Indian drivers had reached 208, the East India Railway claimed it was saving £30,000 a year by using drivers it had recruited and trained locally. The very considerable economies that could be made in this way was one of the main arguments behind the Government of India's recommendation in February 1880 that there should be 'a large infusion of natives into the ranks of engine drivers.'"

48. See Kipling, *Kim,* 88.

49. David Arnold, "European Orphans and Vagrants in India," *Journal of Imperial and Commonwealth History* 7, no. 2 (1979): 113.

50. Kipling, *Kim,* 117.

51. Anne Hollander, *Seeing through Clothes* (Berkeley: University of California Press, 1993).

52. Kipling, *Kim*, 5.

53. Ibid., 160.

54. Gail Ching-Liang Low, *White Skin/Black Masks: Representation and Colonialism* (London: Routledge, 1996), 215.

55. Kipling, *Kim*, 231.

56. See Theodore W. Allen's monumental work, *The Invention of the White Race*, vol. 1, *Racial Oppression and Social Control* (London: Verso, 1994), 48.

57. My thanks to Bill Ashcroft for drawing my attention to this work. See John Beddoe, *The Races of Britain: A Contribution to the Anthropology of Western Europe* (Bristol, UK: J. W. Arrowsmith, 1885).

58. Allen, *The Invention of the White Race*, 1: 46.

59. Ibid., 174.

60. See Abbott E. Smith, *Colonists in Bondage: White Servitude and Convict Labor in America, 1607–1776* (Chapel Hill: University of North Carolina Press, 1947), 167.

61. Ignatiev, *How the Irish Became White*, 41.

62. Karl Marx, *Karl Marx and Friederich Engels on Britain* (London: Foreign Languages Publishing House, 1953), 551–52.

63. Kipling, *Kim*, 216.

64. Said, *Culture and Imperialism*, 165.

65. Kipling, *Kim*, 262.

66. Ibid.

67. Ibid., 251.

68. Ibid.

Epilogue

1. See the chapter on history in Gayatri Chakravorty Spivak, *A Critique of Postcolonial Reason: A History of the Vanishing Present* (Cambridge, Mass.: Harvard University Press, 2000).

2. Judith Butler, *Bodies That Matter: On the Discursive Limits of "Sex"* (London: Routledge, 1993), 28.

3. Butler, *Bodies That Matter*, 30; emphasis in the original.

4. Michel Foucault, *Discipline and Punish*, trans. Alan Sheridan (New York: Vintage, 1979).

Index

Radhika Mohanram teaches in the School of English, Communication, and Philosophy and at the Center for Critical and Cultural Theory at Cardiff University, Wales. She is the author of *Black Body: Women, Colonialism, and Space* (Minnesota, 1999).